WEEKEND WARRIOR

This book is dedicated to British, American and other coalition forces who fought in Operation Telic and Operation Iraqi Freedom. And to those who bravely gave their lives and paid the ultimate price for the sake of freedom, which we all take for granted.

Freedom should be for those who
have served and fought,
for those who inherit should earn.

Kevin J. Mervin

WEEKEND WARRIOR

A TERRITORIAL SOLDIER'S
WAR IN IRAQ

MAINSTREAM
PUBLISHING

EDINBURGH AND LONDON

First published in Great Britain in 2005 by
MAINSTREAM PUBLISHING COMPANY
(EDINBURGH) LTD
7 Albany Street
Edinburgh EH1 3UG

ISBN 1 84018 974 6

The author has used pseudonyms to protect the
identities of those appearing in the book

A catalogue record for this book is available
from the British Library

Typeset in Galliard

Printed in Great Britain by
Cox & Wyman Ltd

ACKNOWLEDGEMENTS

Thank you to the officers and staff from all TA units who were available 24/7 throughout the campaign, answering questions and organising weekend activities for the wives and families, giving them the chance to meet others in the same boat. Also, a thank you to the families who gave great support to loved ones in the conflict, sending blueys (letters) and parcels which were a great boost to our morale. I must also give thanks to all the staff at 34 Field Hospital, which was based on Shaibah Airfield, Iraq. I was made as comfortable as possible during my four-day stay, given the extreme conditions we had to endure, including the pet scorpion that lived in the window covers.

This book is not only dedicated to the TA soldiers of the British Army but to all part-time soldiers, including American and other coalition reservists. The majority of us faced a real enemy with real bullets, enduring sights, sounds and smells which we will never want to experience ever again. As a whole, our entire outlook on life has changed; we now think and act differently to those who haven't had to deal with the emotions roused by the atrocities of war.

CONTENTS

BRITAIN NEEDS YOU

When we hear stories of daring patrols, covert operations and dangerous high-risk missions, the SAS immediately comes to the forefront of our minds. It is a regiment that is wrapped in secrecy and mystery, which naturally generates a great deal of curiosity and a thirst for any inside information; hence the many books on the subject. But there is another highly trained source the British Army can tap into. One that is just as professional, just as skilled and just as eager to participate in operations around the world, yet about which little is known. In many ways, it is more secret than the SAS and, in its own way, just as elite.

The men and women who make up this force undergo the same training, the same discipline and abide by the same rules as the regular army. This extra-special force was formed in 1908 and has since been called upon to fight alongside its regular counterpart in most conflicts around the world – the First and Second world wars, the Suez Crisis of 1956, the Falklands conflict of 1982 and the Gulf War of 1991, to name but a few. However, the courageous and fearless acts carried out by its members are often overshadowed by the regular units they fight alongside.

When the conflict is over, the men and women of this force disappear and blend back into society, carrying with them their secret, unnoticed by the public and the media. The government relies on this force, which makes up a quarter of the strength of the regular army, not only to fight wars, but also to quash civil unrest, maintain homeland defence and assist the emergency services with national and international disasters. This organisation is, of course, the Territorial Army (TA).

Since the 1991 Gulf War, the TA has been called upon to assist in many other operations, including those carried out in the Balkans and Afghanistan, and yet its activities have generally gone unnoticed. In February 2003, this was about to change.

Not since the Suez Crisis has such a large number of TA soldiers been mobilised to fight alongside its regular counterpart in a single conflict. After 47 years, they were once again in the public eye. Television, radio and the world's press followed them as they assisted the regular coalition forces in the search for weapons of mass destruction (WMD), and fought to liberate Iraq from the notorious regime of Saddam Hussein.

Over 6,000 TA personnel were informed of their duty, of which 2,351 were actually mobilised to join a British task-force of approximately 45,000 on Operation Telic, the name used for UK military operations in Iraq. Over half of them, a total of 26,000, served with 1 (UK) Armoured Division and 16 Air Assault Brigade. Of those TA soldiers, 216 came from my battalion, of whom 114 were deployed to the Gulf. They included VMs (vehicle mechanics), cooks, supply specialists, and signals and recovery mechanics (recy mechs). From the lowest rank of craftsman/private to officer, via sergeant and WO (warrant officer), they contributed to the 40 per cent of all REME (Royal Electrical & Mechanical Engineers) soldiers on Operation Telic.

Over the weeks that followed, all TA and reserve forces called to arms went first through the RTMC (Reserves Training and Mobilisation Centre) at Chilwell in Nottingham for selection. Then it was on to Grantham and Beckingham in Lincolnshire for further pre-deployment training. Within two weeks, we were in Kuwait, 3,000 miles from home, facing a war, something none of us had ever experienced before. We were about to embark on the worst time of our lives. At first, it seemed like a huge exercise, but when the Scud missiles started to pound our location, carrying the threat of chemical warheads, and the enemy fired live bullets, we realised the so-called exercise was for real.

By the time war broke out on 20 March 2003, I'd been in the TA for over eight years. I never really expected to be called out for actual fighting, but I was. I had joined a REME V (volunteers) unit in 1995 where I trained as a recy mech to recover battlefield-damaged heavy- and light-armoured vehicles, under fire if necessary. In Iraq this turned out to be the case more often than not. Just think of your training and you'll be OK, I was told, as I set off on my first real battlefield-recovery task; what I wasn't told about were the emotions I'd experience when I witnessed innocent children being mowed down by machine-gun fire, or how I'd react to my first fire-fight using live rounds.

Within minutes of crossing the border into Iraq with my battle group, I'd had my first taste of war and experienced someone shooting at me for real. Over the weeks that followed, I felt I had no choice but to face the reality of the war – the shock waves we felt from dropped bombs, snipers picking us off one by one (most injuries were non-life threatening, thank God), the cracking of rounds above our heads and the constant pounding of tank and artillery fire. I realised I had to grow hard towards the atrocities that I came across daily, which seemed part of life in Iraq during my tour, otherwise I'd have fallen to pieces and ended up a nervous wreck. Often, I felt completely helpless – which hurt, and still hurts today.

This book is an account of my experiences, a 'part-time' soldier's view of the war, based on the diary I kept during my time in Iraq. My aim is to highlight the important role played by the TA and other 'weekend warrior' soldiers in the twenty-first century and illustrate how we coped with the horrors of a modern war. It spans the period from the day I was called out to the day I was casevac'd (casualty evacuated) out of theatre due to an injury. What follows is a diary extract from my last evening in Kuwait, just before my battle group moved into Iraq:

THURSDAY, 20 MARCH 2003
No turning back, this is it. My heart is pounding like a racehorse after running the Grand National and my stomach is tying itself in knots, for the war has started. And to make matters worse, a huge sandstorm has hit our location. The Iraqi Army have taken advantage of this and launched a major attack on our position, using a large number of T72 tanks to bombard us. Twelve Challenger 2 MBTs [main battle tanks] thunder past, heading for the T72s' position to take 'em out.

I can't believe what I'm witnessing. Is this for real? Are we really going to war? Am I going to die? Am I going to live? It'll be our turn soon to go across the border and into a war, and for what? Freedom, fucking freedom? This better be worth it, that's all I can say. They better appreciate it, the Iraqis, and the people back home, moaning about the war. Do they actually realise what we're going through? Have they been told?

Nah, they won't listen anyway; they couldn't give a shit.

MAP OF IRAQ

1

CAN IT BE TRUE?

Sunday, 2 February 2003 is a day which will be imprinted on my mind forever. None of us really thought it possible that the TA would be called out for Op Telic in such great numbers and with such a variation of trade requirements, but it was. Now we had to face the fact our unit was on its way to war.

***

The weekend of 1–2 February was supposed to be nothing more than a normal maintenance weekend, involving the repair of vehicles and equipment. However, because of Op Fresco, the operational name for military cover given during the fire brigade's national strike, the majority of our recovery kit had been diverted to our local headquarters. This allowed the regular army's Green Goddess fire-tenders to operate from our units, as well as others around the country. With the build-up of military kit for Op Telic – which meant our precious Fodens, the 6x6 recovery vehicles, were summoned for service elsewhere – recovery training and maintenance of vehicles and equipment was difficult to achieve.

The firefighters had been on strike over pay for a good three months, and we were getting used to seeing these regular army guys taking over our units. Some of these soldiers were dragged in from various REME units, whilst others belonged to the RA (Royal Artillery).

Before they'd ventured into our humble abodes, they didn't really know what the TA was about or indeed what we actually did for the regular army. After seeing their ugly mushes over a period of time, we introduced them to TA life, inviting them on various piss-ups which arose from time to time. Of course, they accepted and accompanied us to our local drinking pits. We would often ask them about their fire-fighting experience and, likewise, they would quiz us about our civvy employment and TA training. It wasn't long before a trust was forged between us, allowing both sides to benefit from a better understanding of one another.

Saturday, 1 February 1600hrs We packed away kit and finished jobs we'd started through the day, because it was now time to shut up shop and get ready for the evening's activities: mainly consuming vast amounts of alcohol. After the traditional after-work cup of tea and a cigarette, there was a mad dash for the showers. The usual arguments would soon echo around the workshop hangar, mainly over which pubs we would hit first, before we spilt into a nightclub. This would go on for about an hour whilst we downed a few cans from our bar. After two or three of them, we'd finally decide and head out to town.

That night, Cpl (corporal) Simon Wright decided on the plan of action. Simon was one of our regular, diehard TA soldiers. A truck mechanic by trade in his civvy life and a

VM in the army, he was in his mid-30s with blond hair receding sharply from the front and top; his regulation number two haircut made him look as if he was going bald. Mind you, I'm the same age as Simon and although I haven't started to go bald yet, I certainly have the odd grey hair. For me, trying to disguise it with a number two didn't really work because the grey contrasted too much with my dark brown hair. Being 6 ft tall, however, does have its advantages. At the time, I was 192 lbs and could disguise my slight beer belly with my height. Simon, the short-arse, couldn't.

Sgt (sergeant) Gary Hedges, a recy mech who'd recently been promoted, agreed with the plan. He was also blond and in his mid-30s, about my height, but slightly heavier. 'No plan-zeds!' he shouted, wearing a cheeky grin across his face. 'Plan-zeds' is the call sign for the ugliest women on the planet.

The idea is to put money into a kitty, usually enough to buy a round of drinks, then off we go to chat up the ugliest women we can find. We then try and persuade them to buy the drinks throughout the night, which are usually doubles of whatever, and the person who manages, wins the kitty. Gary was the undisputed champion and, as usual, as the night drew deeper into alcohol-induced bullshit, Gary pulled a prize-winning plan-zed. The rest of us fell about laughing in a drunken stupor. Eventually, we ended up back at the TA centre, collapsed in a heap, and slept where we fell, only to be greeted by a mighty hangover a few hours later when we dragged ourselves up for work.

Sunday, 2 February 1030hrs As we nursed our pounding heads, we decided a tea break was called for. We sent a few of the crafties (craftsmen – the lowest rank in the REME) to make the tea and fetch some pick-me-ups from the local garage. By this stage, we'd been up for two and a half hours and, bearing in mind we'd been out until 4.30 a.m., it was inevitable we'd be feeling a little fragile. The crafties made the tea and wheeled it from the kitchen into the hangar on our hostess trolley.

The hangar/workshop was nothing more than a long warehouse area, about 100 metres in length and 20 metres across. Six steel roller-shutter doors, roughly five metres in diameter and separated by brick pillars, gave just enough room to reverse a four-metre-high vehicle inside. The steel rafters, with fluorescent strip lighting attached to the entire length of the ceiling, had the odd tube blown out, casting deep shadows across the floor. Inside the hangar, there were 2 D6 bulldozers, 24-tonne tracked monsters used for recovery purposes. There was also a 20-tonne (maximum load) Tasker trailer which we used to ferry casualty vehicles. The only recovery vehicles remaining, due to Op Telic and Op Fresco, were the two ageing Leyland Scammell EKAs – 6x4 recovery vehicles which started life some thirty or so years ago and should have been in a museum.

The Foden 6x6 is the monster B (wheeled) vehicle of the British Army. It's a 27-tonne off-road brute capable of recovering mechanical casualties weighing up to 50 tonnes. Steel alloy bins, where the recovery kit is stowed, surround the chassis. The main recovery winch sits on top, in the centre of the chassis. Above the main winch sits a jib. The cab is made of a GRP, a plastic fibreglass construction favoured by the Foden truck company. The driver and crew sit about two and a half metres above the ground.

Simon, Gary and I grabbed a brew from the trolley and added our milk and sugar. The rest of the lads soon followed as they appeared from dark corners of the hangar. L/Cpl (lance corporal) Mike Callolm appeared from behind one of the D6s and walked towards the trolley. He was another recy mech. A thickset lad and in his mid-30s, at first appearance he looked like a right bruiser, but in fact he was a real softie at heart. His shaven head was sweating profusely due to whatever he had been doing with his D6 and his eyes seemed heavy and red in colour. He was obviously suffering from the night before. He grabbed a cup and added his milk and sugar. As he took his first sip, he sighed with relief, enjoying the instant pick-me-up sensation the tea had given him for his hangover.

Cpl Sean Houghton, a VM, looked up from his cup as he stirred his tea and gave a half smile. Sean was a whippersnapper of a lad in his late 20s and a potential PTI (physical training instructor). I didn't really know much about him except that he was definitely one of the lads and liked a good laugh.

Gary searched for his cigarettes, hidden somewhere in his green cuvvies (coveralls). When he found them, he passed a few around to those who smoked, eventually giving one to me. We finished our smokes then drank our tea whilst standing round the trolley, taking the piss out of Gary and his predictable plan-zed performance the previous night. Straight away, he went into defensive mode, trying to explain why he'd won, yet again. His first and obvious excuse – 'I was pissed' – which he thought would suffice every time, was just as predictable.

Sgt Dave Foster then ran across the garage. We presumed he'd come for a brew before it had all gone, so I grabbed a spare cup and poured him some stewed tea from the old rusty teapot as he reached the trolley, somewhat out of breath. He grabbed his cup and took a couple of sips of lukewarm tea.

'What's up?' asked Sean. 'You look as if you've had some bad news.'

Dave eventually caught his breath and downed the rest

of his tea in a few gulps. He was in his mid-30s, and also a dual trader (a VM and a recy mech – the best of both worlds, I suppose). Still puffing and panting, he told us the important news. 'You are not going to believe this, but I think we're about to be called up for Op Telic.'

Gary gave his usual reply to any outrageous comments: 'Bollocks!'

'No, honest. I've just finished speaking to Frammy on the phone.'

Captain Frampton, or Frammy as we called him out of earshot, was the CO (commanding officer) of our platoon. He'd flown up the ranks to captain after what had seemed like a career of 200 years with the TA. A recy mech/VM in the TA and a company director on civvy street, he unfortunately couldn't get an extension on his commission, which meant he had no alternative but to retire. This was a shame because, once again, we were losing one of the decent officers who knew all the ropes. The 'been there, done that, got the T-shirt' type.

'Nah!' added Simon, 'I can't see the government using the TA for Op Telic. Maybe for the fire strike but not the Gulf. Maybe that's it, we're to be used for the fire strike to relieve the regulars.'

I had to agree. I couldn't see the army using us. The intelligence services, medics and even the signals from the TA maybe, but not us recy mechs. Our role was for the impending invasion of the Russians, which had been a redundant concept since the fall of the Berlin Wall and the collapse of Communism in the former USSR.

Dave held up his hands, submitting his comments. 'Look, I don't know the whole story but I can tell you that Frammy is on his way here from a meeting in London and we can't go home until he's seen us.'

'This must be serious shit,' commented Gary. 'Maybe

we are being called up. Did he say when he'll be here?'

'About three or four o'clock this aft. So we've until then to straighten this place up,' Dave replied.

We set about finishing our jobs and cleaning the place ready for the boss later that day. When he did arrive, none of us realised he was there, as we were too busy preparing for his supposed inspection. Dave mustered us together and we reported to the office, which was located above the stores. A couple of desks were pushed together in the middle of the 5x8-metre floor space and we all sat in the chairs spread around the desks. Some of the lads rolled cigarettes, using the desks to catch bits of tobacco escaping from the papers. I took out my tailor-mades and shared them around as Captain Frampton entered the room.

'Carry on, lads, light up if you wish. I'll be with you in a second,' he said as he searched through bits of paper he had folded in one of his pockets. I couldn't be certain, but I'm pretty sure he had tears in his eyes. Some of the other lads also noticed and Simon mimicked a crying child by rubbing his eyes and pulling a face. I acknowledged his exaggerated acting by nodding to him, agreeing with his observation.

Frammy, wearing a white sweatshirt and blue jeans, stood in front of us with his head bowed, looking into the bits of paper he held in his trembling hands. He looked up and stared at each of us with his tearful eyes, taking in every individual face as if it would be the last time he would ever see us alive. He started his speech, which was obviously unrehearsed. 'I've just arrived from a meeting in London where [I learnt that] certain individuals from our battalion will be required for the forthcoming Operation Telic.' He paused for a while, expecting some kind of reaction, but he didn't get one. All he got was a bunch of motionless, silent, dumbfounded squaddies looking at each other, wondering if what he had just said was for real. The silence was deafening; you could even hear lads nearby drawing in smoke from their cigarettes.

He continued his speech. 'Our company has put forward 22 names made up of recovery mechanics and vehicle mechanics. The rank structure will be craftsman to no higher than sergeant, and the trade qualification will be no less than a B2. Our platoon has seven names put forward for the following regiments. L/Cpl Mervin . . .' Oh, shit, he had to call out my name first! '. . . SDG [Scots Dragoon Guards], the Challenger 2 tanks.' He quickly looked at me. 'You're off to the front, mate. Sgt Hedges, RRF [Royal Regiment of Fusiliers], L/Cpl Callolm, SDG.' He looked at me once again. 'At least you'll know someone, Kev. Sgt Foster, 23 Pioneers . . .'

He continued with his list but I didn't pay much attention, my mind was elsewhere. Without realising it, I'd smoked three cigarettes in a row and, judging by the amount of smoke in the office, the other lads had done likewise.

Frammy eventually reached the end of his list. 'So, there you have it. I'm sorry I won't be with you guys but unfortunately they don't want any officers, especially old ones like me. Any questions?'

I had one. 'Just one, Sir. Well, more like a passing comment rather than a question. I think you've found a cure for a hangover, cos mine has just disappeared.' The others sniggered at my comment, but I was being serious.

After a few minutes to allow the news to sink in, questions were fired left, right and centre. Unfortunately, Frammy couldn't answer them all, because he had been given limited information on a need-to-know basis, I suppose.

Then Sean shouted out a brilliant idea. 'I'm going to open the bar, care to join me, anyone?' We didn't need asking twice as we stumbled out of the office and made our way there. Sean opened the hatch and leant over the counter. 'What does everyone want, the usuals?' He stood bottles of lager and cans of beer on the counter.

'What the fuck will the missus say?' Gary asked, with a nervous quiver. We all shook our heads at the thought of telling our wives and girlfriends. Then I suddenly realised, 'Shit! What about our jobs?'

Frammy quickly answered my question. 'They're safe. You can't be fired because you've been officially called out. Serving your country and all that.'

I sighed with relief. 'Thank fuck for that, cos I've just started a new one.' Little did I know that would cause major problems in the future.

Risking only the one can or bottle, we all decided to call it a day and go home to tell our families the delightful news. The details Frammy gave us on the impending call-out were strictly confidential, so we shouldn't have known any of this information until officially notified by our call-out papers, which would take a further two weeks to arrive. Then, and only then, could we start organising our lives, but then it never worked out like that. Some of us ended up with notices a week before the departure date but couldn't organise anything beforehand because they didn't know anything officially. Frustrating? Yep.

The drive home was only 15 kilometres but it seemed to take for ever. I thought about my granddad, my mother's father, and how he must have felt when he was called out during the Second World War, and what his reaction must have been when he was told he was going to Burma. He was lucky – he came back. I then started to think about my great-uncles on my father's side of the family: one died in the First World War, at Thiepval in northern France in 1916; one was killed in Ireland by the

IRA in 1920; and one was shot down in 1942 during the Second World War as he patrolled the coastline over the North Sea in his Catalina. A shiver ran down my spine and I thought to myself, I hope I take after my mother's side of the family.

I soon came round to thinking how I was going to tell the wife. I could either just come straight out with it or bring it up gradually in conversation – or not mention it at all, because we hadn't been told officially. Frammy did say we could tell our families but did he mean immediate family or the whole bloody lot? One thing he did say, and was certain about, was that the tour would be for nine months. That would mean until mid-December. Well, at least we'd be home for Christmas, I thought. But then I quickly remembered that same comment had been made by lads called out in the First World War and look what happened to them. I felt another shiver run down my spine.

I pulled up in front of the house, moaning under my breath because my wife had nicked the parking space on the driveway again. I locked the car, walked towards the door and placed my hand on the handle. Then I paused, sorting out in my mind how I would break the news. Right, here goes. I opened the door and without hesitation blurted out, 'I've been called up!' and threw my keys on the pine table standing to my right. As I walked down the hall into the kitchen, I stopped burbling. Damn, she'd gone out. I walked through the kitchen and into the utility room at the back of the house to take off my boots. As I started to undo the laces, the front door slammed with a bang and a three-year-old monster named Rachel came running into the utility room, crash-landing into my legs.

'Daddy, you're home!' She may have only been three

years old but she was very loud. My wife, Helen, then walked into the kitchen carrying a handful of shopping bags.

'Hi, you're home, then. My mum just dropped me off. We've been shopping. How was your weekend?' she asked as she placed the shopping bags on the kitchen floor. I had finished taking off my boots and left them for Helen to clean and polish later.

'Er, well, you're not going to believe this but . . .' I hesitated.

'What is it, luv?'

I drew up the courage yet again. 'I've been called up for the Gulf.'

'Yeah, yeah. Are you hungry? I'll cook you something quick, if you like.'

I was always winding her up about being called out for operations. The last time it was Bosnia, then Kosovo and now a few times over this Iraq crisis, so she had become thick-skinned about my jibes. Talk about the boy who cried wolf. I walked up to her and grabbed both her arms as she reached down to put away the shopping. This time I sounded solemn and subdued. 'I mean it this time, I've been called up. We've all been called up, the bloody lot of us.'

Helen looked up and stared right into my eyes, to see that I wasn't joking. 'You're serious, aren't you?'

'Yes, bloody serious, but you don't know this yet, not officially anyway.'

She shook her head. 'What? Well, have you been called up or not?' she snapped, sounding confused and annoyed with my reply.

I gripped her arms tighter to give an indication I was most definitely serious. 'Yes, we have, but we don't get the official paperwork for a couple of weeks. So don't tell anyone, apart from the immediate family.'

'What about my mum and dad, can I tell them?' she asked, dropping a bag of shopping on the floor and breaking the odd jar and bottle.

'Yes, that's fine, but no one outside the immediate family; not yet anyway.'

Helen quickly diverted her attention to the broken jars, giving me the perfect excuse to make a sharp exit into the front room, only to be greeted by my daughter asking awkward questions.

'What's a call-up, Daddy?' she asked, whilst colouring in a picture in her book. She never missed a thing. I ignored her, aggravating her even more. She asked me again but this time with a more assertive tone. 'What's a call-up, Daddy?'

'Oh, it's to do with the army, nothing to worry about, kidda.' Rachel seemed to take on board what I said but I could tell she wasn't happy with the answer. At that precise moment, though, it was more important to find an orange crayon which was desperately needed to colour in a picture of an elephant.

Helen came storming into the front room, holding a bag of frozen oven-ready chips. 'So . . .' she paused, thinking how to put her question across, 'you'll be going to Iraq. Does that mean you'll be gone for a few weeks, a month or what?'

That was one question I could answer. 'The tour –'

Helen interrupted. 'Ha! The tour, you make it sound like a TA camp.'

I frowned at her comment but continued to answer. 'The tour will be for nine months, which means I should be home for Christmas.' Shit! As soon as I said it, I realised I shouldn't have. She most probably had some sort of date in her head before she asked the question. At worst, she would have thought a one-month tour.

'*Nine months!* You can't go for nine months, how will I cope?' She threw the bag of chips on the carpet in a fit of temper. It split instantly on impact causing a 'bomb burst' of frozen potato chips. Boy, was she upset.

I tried to reassure her with pathetic promises and bullshit. Helen listened for a while as she picked up the chip shrapnel, then spurted out her own bullshit.

'Well, you're not going.'

'Helen, I don't have a choice.'

'You must have a choice, they can't just call you up. Besides, it's that President Bush's war, not ours.' I was surprised she took an interest, let alone knew who the President of the United States was. 'They'll never find any weapons of mass-thingy cos that Saddam bloke would have hidden them too well.' She looked at me, waiting for some sarcastic comment, but she didn't get one. I was still gobsmacked she could name the US president. 'I do take some interest, you know. I'm not a complete idiot.' She then disappeared back into the kitchen.

'I know you're not an idiot,' I replied, following her like an obedient puppy, 'I just didn't know you took any interest.'

'So, you're going to the Gulf. When?' she asked sternly.

'Sometime towards the end of this month.' She gave me one of her 'I'm not too sure if I should believe you' looks. 'You still don't believe me, do you?'

'No, yes, well, I'm not sure. You've wound me up so much in the past, I don't know whether to believe you or not.'

She had a point, I couldn't deny that. I leant against the work surface and watched Helen pottering around the kitchen. I was just about to try and convince her I was serious when the front door opened, followed by two knocks. Oh God, I thought. That's all I needed, a visit from the bloody in-laws.

'Only us,' a voice shouted from behind Helen's dad; it was her mother. She'd obviously dropped Helen off, picked up my father-in-law and returned to the house immediately. It was as if she knew there was some news breaking and had to be a part of it.

'Kevin reckons he's been called up for the Gulf, Mum.'

My father-in-law looked at me, frowning, wondering whether to believe me or not. He knew how much I wound his daughter up. 'Have you, Kev?'

I answered him by nodding my head.

'Called up to go to Iraq?'

I nodded again.

'You won't go; they don't need the TA,' Liz, Helen's mum, said, butting into the conversation as per usual. I didn't know whether to take that as an insult or a compliment. 'Besides, you're married with a family, and you're a part-time soldier, not a proper one.' I certainly took that as an insult.

Greg intervened. 'That doesn't bloody matter, the government doesn't care about things like that.'

'Of course they do!' replied Liz, which was followed by a full-blown argument in the middle of the hallway. I slowly shook my head and let them get on with it, disappearing into the utility room to smoke a cigarette.

A few minutes later, I heard Liz shouting through to the kitchen, 'We're off now, Kev, see you later.'

'Yeah, see you later,' I replied, hoping I wouldn't.

Helen's dad walked into the utility room wearing a worried look. 'See you later, lad, and keep us posted, won't you?'

At first I didn't acknowledge what he said and shook my head as if I was in a trance. 'Yeah, as soon as I hear anything, I'll let you know.' Happy with my reply, he winked and obediently caught up with his wife.

I finished my cigarette and went back into the kitchen in the hope of convincing Helen I was telling the truth and that it wasn't a squaddie wind-up. Eventually, she believed me, but I don't think she ever realised the seriousness of the call-out until the day I left for pre-deployment training. During the weeks before I left, we had decided to try and live as normal as possible, even to the point of not mentioning a single word about the growing tension in Iraq. Of course, this was difficult because of newspapers and television ramming it down our throats 24/7.

It was a further three days before the company meeting at our HQ, where the guys who had been told they were being called out, including myself, would get a clearer picture as to what was happening. And although Helen didn't want to hear any more about it – in a way, I think she was sticking her head in the sand – I naturally wanted to learn as much as possible. I wanted to know all I could about Iraq, Saddam's regime, his armed forces – everything. And the only way I could do this was to watch the 24-hour news channels, after Helen went to bed.

2

PACK UP YOUR OL' KITBAG

We attended a big meeting at HQ, where the entire company strength gathered for a question-and-answer evening, but left none the wiser. The only new information we were given was the total number of soldiers called out from the company and those from the battalion. So we had a further mini-meeting with just the 22 on the call-out list, firing even more questions at the PSAO (permanent staff army officer).

We learnt about the benefits of being part of the regular army in theatre, including the overseas and separation allowances. Overall, they bumped up my basic pay by a further couple of thousand pounds, spread over the entire nine-month tour. I quickly added up in my head the difference between my civilian employment pay and the wages I would receive from the army. I was actually £3,500 better off. Some of the other guys appeared worse off, but this wasn't a disaster because of the pledge from the government. If we fell short of our civvy pay, the army would make up the difference, within reason, since there were certain ceilings the government couldn't go beyond.

On the whole, it worked out OK – on paper anyway. So we all left the meeting reasonably happy.

My brown envelope arrived at last on 18 February. I could finally and officially tell my family and employer I'd been called out to serve on Op Telic. Ah, my employer. I decided to use all my holiday entitlement in one go, with about six days' leave left to take. I'd explained to my boss I'd been called out and was waiting for official notification. I also mentioned that I'd be using all my holidays and that if my papers came during my leave, I would not be coming back until the end of my tour. My boss didn't really care and reacted by saying he'd be on holiday himself that week, so he'd see me in December. OK, so far so good, I thought.

The day my papers arrived I separated the details for my employer and sent them to them, for the attention of the personnel department. As far as I was concerned, that would be the end of it. The rest of the A4 sheets of bumf were details of what to do next, what kit I required and how long I'd be on tour. And, yes, printed in black and white, the tour would be for nine months, ending 17 December 2003. I quickly telephoned the other call-upees to see if they had their paperwork. Amazingly, a few hadn't, including Dave and Gary, and a few others from our sister platoons.

I was to report at Chilwell, Nottinghamshire, by 1400hrs on 28 February 2003. That left just six working days to sort out my life. I travelled to my local army surplus store, owned by an ex-squaddie, who boasted he could get anything I wanted. I settled for purchasing a pair of desert boots (because I had heard they were a bit scarce), a field wallet and notebook holder, spare socks and a new KFS (knife, fork, spoon) kit. The store gave a 10 per cent discount to service personnel with proof of identity, but that wasn't really necessary – he could sniff out a squaddie at 100 paces simply by the way we used army terminology.

He asked if there was anything else I might need, then went on to try and sell me a solar-heated portable shower kit (a plastic bag which heated the water from the sun's rays). I declined the offer, but he did warn me I'd regret not buying one. He even threw in a glossy brochure to show the lads in the Gulf and said he could send kit out to us. I thanked him and made my way back to my car.

On the way home, and for no apparent reason, it suddenly dawned on me I was actually going to war. I knew the tree-hugging, paint your arse blue and howl at the moon brigade were praying for some unrealistic peace agreement, but we all knew it was inevitable war would begin, and soon. It also occurred to me that it was possible I might not make it back.

As soon as I got home, I grabbed the phone to call Gary. We just waffled on about any crap. In fact, that's all we kept doing for the week or so that followed. When the rest of the lads received their call-out papers, we just called each other for a chinwag, probably for comfort, but it seemed to help us cope. We were pretty good friends before all the call-out business but we definitely became a lot closer during those first few weeks leading up to our departure. The phone bill for February that year, I discovered at a later date, was £134 and, for a change, I couldn't blame the wife.

The next day, I thought I'd better telephone Mother and tell her the good news. This will be fun, I thought. Before I could say anything, she bellowed down the phone, 'You've got your call-up papers, haven't you?'

'How did you know?'

'Mother's intuition. Now listen . . .' Here we go, lecture time.

After she'd finished rabbiting on for about ten minutes, she asked how was I going to get to Chilwell. 'I'm glad you brought that up, Mother. I was hoping you would take me.'

'I'll be pleased to take you. 28th, isn't it? What time?'

I thought about this one, remembering my actual time of arrival was 1400hrs. 'I've to be there by midday.' A little white lie, but Mother being Mother and a woman, if you know what I mean.

She continued talking for a further ten minutes, mainly stuff about staying safe, keeping my head down, that sort of thing. I suddenly realised I'd have to go through all this again when I phoned my dad, who lived in Manchester. I decided to get it over with and called him. It was nice to hear his voice again. We didn't talk enough as it was and I certainly didn't see him as often as I would have liked to. I promised I'd see him before I left but, of course, never did. I regretted this at the time, just in case something did happen to me, and he received a phone call from the MoD saying his son was dead.

Before I knew it, 28 February had come around. I'd spent the whole of the day before packing my kit, then I'd repacked the whole bloody lot, adding and taking out excess kit. I now had to wrestle with my standard-issue bergen and webbing, dragging it from the garage through the kitchen and into the hallway, then returning for my day bergen (a smaller, ten-litre rucksack). This was a Dutch bergen I had bought for about a tenner, which was great for my coveralls, maps and recy-mech paperwork. I checked and rechecked the brown A4 envelope, making sure all my documents were intact, and placed it securely into my day bergen. At that point, the doorbell sprang to life and in walked Mother.

'Only me, are ya ready?'

'Just these,' I answered.

'Bloody 'ell, what's this lot? You'll never carry that across the desert.'

All my clothing, spare boots and other bits of kit were in my bergen, with my roll mat secured to the bottom, my sleeping system, or 'doss bag', strapped on the top and my Kevlar helmet strapped to that. Zipped on either side were my day sacks. One had my NBC (nuclear, biological, chemical), or 'noddy', suit inside and the other had my poncho, waterproofs (as if I'd need them), and a wash and shave kit. The total weight, including my webbing, was roughly 30 kg.

I let out a snigger. 'Mum, I'm a recy mech. I certainly won't be carrying this lot, my Foden will. Leave all that tabbing shit to the infantry.'

'Oh, isn't that what you do then?'

I just smiled at her. I must have told her a thousand times what I actually did in the TA, and this time I couldn't be bothered to explain all over again. I loaded up the back of her V40 Volvo estate with all my kit and slammed the tailgate shut. As I walked back into the house, Mother was sorting out some old photos on the kitchen work surface.

'What you got there?'

'Some photos to take with you. Most of 'em are of your gramps and nan.'

My gramps was my granddad on my mother's side, the one who'd gone to Burma during the Second World War. He'd told me many funny stories of the trouble he had got himself into. He was definitely my hero. Unfortunately, he died of pneumonia in November 2001 at the ripe old age of 80. I took my wallet from my jeans pocket and opened it to reveal a picture I already had of my gramps, which I always carried with me: an old photograph from the Second World War, with him wearing his jungle uniform and smoking a cigarette. On the back, it said, 'Calcutta 1945', where he'd ended up after the war, prior to coming home.

'Where did you get that?'

'I've had this for years, Mum, bloody years. I take it everywhere with me.'

'Well, here's a few more.' She passed me the photos, which I had to trim first before placing them in my wallet. Whilst I was doing this, Mother realised the house was quiet and empty of the three-year-old monster, and my wife. 'Where's Helen and Rachel?'

'Er, they're not coming with us. Helen went to work and Rachel is at nursery.' I waited for the fireworks.

'*Why not?*'

'Look, just hear me out, Mum. Helen wanted it to be just another day for Rachel, so she thinks Daddy is going away with the TA. She knows Daddy spends days away but this time it'll be nine months. We all said our goodbyes last night, anyway.'

She thought for a moment: 'Yeah, I suppose you're right,' then checked the time on her watch in an attempt to change the subject. 'C'mon, we'd better get going.'

'No rush, we don't have to be there until two o'clock.' As soon as I said it, I realised I should have kept my gob shut.

'But you said . . .'

I interrupted her. 'I know, I know. Fancy a cuppa before we go?'

We finished our tea and Mother carried on walking towards her car whilst I locked the front door. As I turned the key, I thought, this might be the last time I'll do this. I shook my head in a feeble attempt to get rid of the stupid thought but I couldn't. Immediately, other thoughts sprung into my mind: the last time I'll drive

Mother's car, the last time I'll lock up my house, the last time I'll see my silver birch in the corner of the front garden, the last time . . .

These thoughts soon turned into feelings of apprehension and fear. All of a sudden, I didn't want to go, not yet anyway. I felt I needed to achieve a few more things, see a few more places but it was too late; time to face reality. I'd had plenty of time to do all the things I wanted to do before my call-out date but I hadn't bothered because they seemed trivial, until now. I walked towards the car, taking in every footstep, listening to every sound – birds singing, a bus in the background and a child screaming blue murder in a pushchair as his mother pushed him along the pavement. These sounds became almost surreal and I wanted more, I didn't want them to end. I took one last look at the house and made a mental picture of it, then quickly jumped in the driver's seat, started the engine and drove off without looking back. Today was like any other day, I thought to myself. Bollocks, who was I kidding?

On the way, we chatted about anything but the impending war, or what I'd expect to see. One hour later, we were a few kilometres from Chilwell, so I pulled into a garden centre with a small café next to it which served all-day breakfasts. My mobile phone sprang to life. It was Mike. He had the same call-out date and time of arrival as me and was after directions. I told him how to get to the garden centre, just off the motorway, so we could meet and follow each other to the barracks after some food.

Mike eventually found us and only had a quick brew before we continued our journey, with me following Mike. As we reached the gatehouse, we were stopped by a civilian MoD (Ministry of Defence) security guard, who was no doubt an ex-squaddie, because they usually were for some reason. Mike flashed his MoD 90 (military ID card) at him. I quickly fished mine out of my wallet as the security guard checked Mike's and he drove into the camp.

I wound down my window so I could lean out a little. 'All right, mate?' I politely asked and flashed him my MoD 90. He gave me some vague directions, then walked to the car behind me. I drove past the open barrier and tried to catch up with Mike but he'd driven ahead and was nowhere in sight.

'Where's Mike gone?' Mother asked.

'I haven't a clue.' I was now lost. 'I've been to Chilwell a few times on TA weekends but never in this bit.' I drove around the block but couldn't find any sign of him. 'Sod him, I'll turn around and try that hangar back there.' Driving towards a long warehouse-type building, I picked up a sign saying 'RTMC RECEPTION' with an arrow pointing left towards the hangar. I followed the sign and parked in the car parking area opposite its entrance. I switched off the engine and looked at Mum. 'Well, this is it but I think I'll have a cigarette first.' I passed one to her and lit one myself, muttering, 'I can't get used to this.' The feeling I had was like that of a kid going to a new school but I couldn't understand why.

Mother frowned at me, straining to hear what I'd said. 'What was that?'

I looked at her. I knew she'd heard what I said but I didn't want to confirm it. 'Oh, nothing, just thinking aloud.'

Now she looked worried. 'You'll be OK, won't you?'

I finished the last few drags of my cigarette and flicked it out of the window. 'I'll be fine. C'mon, let's get into this bloody war.'

I got out of the car and opened the tailgate, debussing my kit from the back of the Volvo and leaving it in a heap on the ground. I noticed Cpl Jim Worcester from one of the other company platoons walking towards me. He was a big lad, over 6 ft tall and quite well-built. He wore a big grin across his weathered face, which definitely showed his age, mid- to late 30s. We greeted each other like long-lost brothers, maybe for that comfort thing more than anything else. I introduced my mother then asked him if he'd seen Mike. He hadn't but he'd seen some of the other lads from the company going through the booking-in process inside the hangar.

I said goodbye to Mum after she'd embarrassed me with a few kisses and hugs, which definitely made me feel like a schoolboy starting a new school. As Mother drove out of the car park, she gave me a little wave, just to add to my humiliation. 'Right then, Jim, let's get into this shit! But we'll have another cigarette first.'

3

YOU'RE IN THE ARMY NOW

Friday, 28 February 1350hrs We finished our cigarettes and walked through the entrance to the hangar. We were greeted by a Gurkha rifleman standing to our right, next to a row of blue, partitioned office areas. In front of us were rows of metal-framed plastic chairs, the type you might see in a school classroom. The Gurkha ushered us to some seats and told us to wait our turn to be booked in.

'Do we need anything, mate?' asked Jim. 'Our kit's outside in the car park.'

A young split-arse (female) corporal must have overheard Jim and approached us from behind the row of seats. 'All you need at the moment, lads, are the documents you were sent and your personal ID. You can throw your kit in those aisles over there.' She pointed to some temporary chain-link fence panels to our left, linked together and standing in concrete blocks to make aisles for our kit. Four of the six aisles were already crammed with bergens and civilian bags. We quickly fetched our kit from the car park and grabbed a couple of spaces in the aisles, then returned to our seats.

'Wait here and remain seated,' she added, 'until it's your turn to go in.' She gave us a 'Welcome to Chilwell' smile and went to attend to the next lost souls wandering into the hangar entrance.

We sat down amongst half a dozen or so other 'victims' waiting to be rushed into the system. 'I'm waiting for some loud-mouthed hairy-arsed RSM (regimental sergeant major) to give us some bollocking,' whispered Jim.

'Why? We're not recruits, you know, we did all that shit years ago.'

Jim looked at me, wearing an 'I know that, you prick' expression. 'But we've never been called out before, have we? Who knows what mill we'll be put through.'

He had a point. We prepared ourselves for the worst. Days before, we'd all received text messages from lads who'd already gone through this stage. They wrote of 10-kilometre CFTs (combat fitness tests), 6-kilometre runs before breakfast, PT (physical training) and reveille at 0500hrs. Just like recruit training, really. To make up for my lack of fitness, I'd been going to the gym and had been running about 15–20 kilometres a week for the couple of weeks prior to the call-out date, simply because we had expected the worst.

'*Next!*' a voice shouted from behind the partition wall beside us. 'C'mon, I haven't got all day!'

Jim and I looked at each other. 'Bloody 'ell, Jim, I think you're right – recruit training all over again.'

The next in line quickly jumped up and dropped his A4 envelope of documents all over the floor. He jumbled them together as he raced into the cubicle. In doing so, he ran into the partition and nearly knocked it over, shaking the whole construction with the impact.

'*Sort yourself out, laddie, get a grip!*' the same voice shouted.

The lad gingerly walked out of sight. All we could hear was a lot of mumbling and the sound of paperwork being shuffled about.

'This is going to be the longest nine months of our lives,' Jim said, as he folded his arms and sunk deeper into his chair.

At that point, I started to think how my gramps must have felt when he turned up at his recruit centre back in 1940. He must have shit himself. The big difference was that he didn't have any military training prior to his call-out.

'*Next!*' The same voice again. By now, Jim and I had got used to this arsehole shouting his head off.

'Here goes, wish me luck,' Jim said in a low voice, as he stood up to venture into the unknown.

'*Next!*'

Bloody 'ell, I thought. That was quick. I jumped out of my seat and caught up with Jim, and was greeted by a short-arse, overweight sergeant standing behind the first of many desks lined up in front of us. With a messy moustache, a balding head and the tail of his shirt hanging out of his combats, there sat a desk jockey. There was no way he was an RSM. He was most probably a TA soldier like me.

The desktops were covered in piles of A4 sheets of paper and the corporals manning the stations handed us one sheet from each pile as we worked our way down the line. We then reached a desk where a lance jack (lance corporal) asked stupid questions, like 'What's your name?' and 'What sex are you?', and eventually we made it to the last desk with our arms full of paperwork. Another lance jack stood at the end of the line and pointed at another area, full of scattered tables so we could complete our mountain of paperwork in some sort of comfort.

'Over 'ere, Kev,' a voice shouted from one of the tables, which were already full of reservists and TA soldiers dressed in civilian clothing, scratching their heads and biting pen tops as they completed the questionnaires.

I stood stretching my neck in the direction of the voice shouting my name. I noticed a table towards the back of the enclosed area with the lads from the other platoons sitting around it. Mike was there with L/Cpl Dave Harris, a recy mech of about 30, and next to him Cpl Paul Fletcher, a recy mech, who was a big lad of about 6 ft. At Paul's side was Cpl Frank Clipston, or 'Dad' as we called him – he was going grey and was a lot older than us, about 45 years old. He was another dual trader. The voice shouting my name came from Cfn (craftsman) Chris Webster, a recy mech, the last of the call-upees from our company and my partner in crime when I go skydiving. He was a bit of an action man, with his skiing and mountaineering exploits as well as his high-altitude pastimes. He was a stocky lad in his mid-30s, with a little grey showing through his thick, black cropped hair – it was just short enough for the army; he wasn't brave enough to go for the closer number two look like the rest of us.

I nudged Jim's shoulder as he took in the atmosphere. 'Over there, Jim, look,' I said, pointing towards Chris and the gang. Jim looked towards the table and acknowledged them with a single nod. We both made our way over, dodging and weaving in between the squaddies sitting around the other tables.

'You made it, then. Good trip?' Chris asked me.

'Yeah, not too bad, got here about 20 minutes ago.' I looked at Mike. 'And where the fuck did you get to?'

Mike looked up from his paperwork, sucking on his pen top. 'I thought you followed me, Kev. Besides, you're here, aren't you?' he snapped, looking a tad flustered. He returned to his questionnaire, shaking his head and muttering, 'This is bullshit.'

'What's up?' I asked, grabbing a couple of chairs from the table behind. Jim promptly sat on one of the chairs and started to arrange his paperwork on an already cluttered table.

'These bloody questions repeat themselves over and over again.' Mike replied, still wearing a confused expression.

Jim intervened, reaching across to have a look at the sheet Mike was having problems with. 'Give it 'ere and let me have a look.' He studied it and tutted a couple of times whilst slowly shaking his head. He looked at his paperwork and noticed a similar sheet on Dave's pile, which Mike had inadvertently completed. 'You twat, Mike, you've done this one twice. You've taken the same one off Dave's lot, completed it and now you're filling in your own.'

Dave looked up from what he was doing, interrupted by the sound of his name. 'Eh?'

He grasped the conversation and looked at Mike's pile. 'You twat! Go and get another one, numb nuts!'

Mike shuffled back to the cubicles to fetch some fresh questionnaires whilst the rest of us fell about laughing. Dave, however, didn't find it funny.

An hour passed as we completed our forms. At the front of the area, a row of three desks with three squaddies, again in uniform, waited for those who had finished. We sat in front of the two sergeants and corporal and had our paperwork scrutinised. It was then passed for processing. Afterwards, we returned to our table and wondered what to do next.

'Right, what else have these bastards got in store for us?' As soon as I asked the question, a split-arse QMS (quartermaster sergeant) stood behind me. The table went deadly silent. Dave looked at me, wide-eyed, waiting for the QMS to start shouting obscenities.

'What?' I asked, unaware of her presence.

Frank, sitting next to Chris, directed his eyes above me to indicate where the QMS was hovering. I looked around slowly and faced an overweight mid-section, dressed in CS95s (combat soldier 95 uniform). I turned back to face the front, cringing and waiting for her to explode but she didn't. She just told us in a very soft voice that we'd finished for the time being, and directed us to a waiting area. Whether she'd heard me or not, I don't know; we didn't hang around to find out. We left the table as if it was on fire and made our way to the adjoining waiting area with tea and coffee facilities and a large TV screen at the front with Sky News on. We quickly abused the tea and coffee, and sat around another table chatting about the impending war and what might happen to us when we reached Iraq.

'Where's Chris gone?' I asked, realising he was missing.

Jim pointed to the rear left corner of the area where Chris was studying a board showing details of each regiment going to the Gulf. I joined him and started to look up and down the list, searching for the Scots Dragoon Guards, which were part of 7 Armoured Brigade, the Desert Rats. Chris was to join up with 3 RHA (Royal Horse Artillery), which had the AS90 self-propelled field gun.

The others soon joined Chris and me as their curiosity got the better of them. Whilst we were talking about the kit on its way to the Gulf, some sergeant approached us and told us to sit down for a lecture, which turned out to be the first of many. The lecture went on for about 20 minutes, with some captain rabbiting on about safety drills. He explained about the smoking areas and the rest of the day's activities, which consisted of more lectures in the afternoon and even more forms to complete.

Eventually, he came to the subject of scoff, which immediately caught our otherwise dwindling attention – dinner would be served at 1800hrs and the evening was our own with no restrictions as such. The only thing we couldn't do was wander off the camp area but the NAAFI (Navy Army Air Force Institute) bar was all right to use. Accommodation would be in the newly built barrack blocks. Reveille was 0700hrs, and breakfast between 0730 and 0830hrs, to which we would report in our CS95 uniform. The first activity of the following day was the dreaded medical, commencing at 0930hrs. The captain then dismissed us and told us to make our way to the next area for our final questionnaires and lectures, before we could disappear for the evening.

Jim and I looked at each other in disbelief. 'There must be a catch,' I said.

Chris leant over the back of my chair. 'This is too easy; they must be giving us a false sense of security. No PT and reveille at 0700. This is a bloody holiday camp.'

We were all taken aback by how relaxed the timetable was. Although crammed full of lectures and never-ending visits to the medical centre, there didn't seem to be any rush to get us through the training. The day was full of tea breaks, smoke breaks and 'chill-out' breaks, whatever they were for.

'It's psychological torture,' Mike said.

Paul slowly shook his head and rolled his eyes. 'What?'

'Psychological torture; part of the course, to see if we break under the strain.'

Paul shook his head again. 'You've been watching too many Special Forces programmes.'

'No, honest, it's designed to see if you crack under the strain; to see if you're suited for war.'

'Bollocks!' came Paul's response.

'No, listen—' Mike tried to explain but Paul gave him a sharp slap across the back of his bald head, stopping him in mid-sentence.

Scoff time finally arrived, followed by a few hours in the NAAFI bar. Sod it, we thought, we'll take advantage of this kind but uneasy generosity whilst we can – and we did with a vengeance. If they sprung a CFT on us in the morning, we mused, we would just have to put up with it.

The following morning, we were greeted with a sample bottle from the medics, ready for the first piss of the day. We thought nothing of it until we realised what we'd drunk the night before. The contents of our urine could have been used for rocket fuel. The medical was thorough and reasonably painless, apart from the four injections I had to have. The polio drops tasted awful (no sugar cubes for grown-ups) and the dentist decided to give me a filling without any anaesthetic – apart from that, no dramas. The rest of the lads had similar experiences with four or five injections covering typhoid, cholera, hepatitis A and B, and tetanus. We were also issued with a course of malaria tablets: two of one sort to be taken first thing in the morning with food, and two of another type to be taken at the end of each week. The course, we were told, started immediately.

The afternoon consisted of a trip to the stores to collect even more kit and to complete even more paperwork. Whilst we queued outside the building, we chatted and smoked cigarettes as the line thinned out. Eventually, we made it inside the warm corridor. The QMS standing at the end of the long counter was pulling his hair out as his precious stores was ravaged of kit. Each of us was handed a brown or blue holdall for the extra kit issued, which consisted of four thirty-round magazines (heavy duty); a rifle-cleaning kit, plus rifle sling; an extra NBC suit, shrink-wrapped, complete with gloves and boots; a CBA (combat body armour) vest complete with two Kevlar chest plates; and an extra CS95 uniform.

It was then a trip to the armoury for our rifle, a 5.56 mm or an SA80 (small arms of the '80s) (A2) rifle. Supposedly, this new improved rifle didn't need any forward assist, which meant tapping forward the breach block when cocking the weapon to ensure it engaged, preventing a potential stoppage. We were also issued with our bayonet and scabbard. Some of us weren't issued with these if we were carrying the LSW (light support weapon), which is basically an SA80 with a longer barrel fitted with a bipod and SUSAT (sight unit small-arms Trilux) with x4 magnification. The Trilux is the chemical glow-in-the-dark spot on the sight, which assists targeting on night shoots. If issued with an LSW, like Chris, it meant carrying eight magazines. This was due to the extra rounds required to put down on an enemy position during an attack or when defending a position.

The last cubicle was by now within sight. This contained a desk with a staff sergeant sitting behind it swiping our barcode cards arranged on an A4 sheet of paper, which we carried around with us when we visited each cubicle or room. The details on the form were sectioned in boxes and a pass or fail was added to each box, depending how well we did. Each one represented an individual test on our form, consisting of preliminary health checks for teeth, eyesight, hearing and blood/urine tests. We also had a weapon-handling test – to make sure we knew how to handle our rifles. The information on the barcode strips was kept on a computer, giving a pass or fail rating. To fail meant you were RTU'd (returned to unit), which was usually for medical reasons or because your trade wasn't required. If you were surplus to requirements, your name was placed on a separate list for operational tours in the future. Luckily, all the lads from my company passed. After all the tests, the staff sergeant would cross out the names on his list, highlighting them with a green pen. The fails had a red mark through their names, and it was then I noticed there were more fails than passes.

It was then chill-out time and the rest of the evening was ours. Of course, this was spent in the NAAFI bar, where we unwound and japed about the day's events. Morale was high and the atmosphere was that of going on exercise rather than to war.

Reveille was once again at 0700hrs. After breakfast, we stood around in the hangar drinking tea and coffee, smoking cigarettes and chatting amongst ourselves for a few hours. Behind the scenes, staff were running around like headless chickens sorting out last-minute paperwork and organising transport for those unfortunates that hadn't made the grade. For the rest of us, it was a case of 'hurry up and wait', which was a blessed relief. The last thing we wanted to do was fill in more paperwork or attend further lectures – we'd had a gutful.

A corporal raised his voice over the background noise in the reception area. '*Listen in!*' The room fell silent. 'Collect your kit from the accommodation blocks, making sure there's no mess left behind. Bring it all into this hangar and leave it with your bergens. Check and double-check you haven't forgotten anything.' We all looked at each other, waiting for someone to make the first move. 'Well, go on then, fuck off!'

We wandered back to our accommodation blocks and stuffed our sleeping bags into the compression sacks, gathered any kit we had and made our way back to the reception area to place it with the rest of it, stacked in the aisles.

'*Listen in!*' another voice shouted as we checked our kit. The sergeant with the scruffy moustache, and still with his shirt-tail hanging out of his trousers, once again raised his ugly voice after first clearing his throat. 'Hmmhmm!' He paused as the reception area fell silent. 'Make your way to the armoury and collect your weapons by . . . [he checked his watch] . . . 1130hrs. This gives you one hour, after which the armoury will be closed. Return back here for further instructions. That is all!'

'It's started, then, the bullshit!' Jim said under his breath as he strapped his sleeping bag to the top of his bergen.

'C'mon, we'd better collect our weapons. Where are the others?' I asked.

Jim stopped fighting with the straps on his bergen for a second to point a finger towards the aisle on his right where the others were struggling to repack kit into their bergens. I caught Chris's attention and mimicked myself taking a drag of a cigarette, indicating we disappear for a quick smoke before starting to queue outside the armoury. He nodded in agreement and we went outside the hangar for a quick cigarette.

After queuing for about half an hour for our weapons, we made it back to the hangar for a brew. We sipped our tea as we watched a further 200 or so weary bodies going through the same process we'd had to endure only a few days before – all of them looking wide-eyed and unsure of what was ahead.

'*Listen in!*' Shirt-tail started again, pausing for silence. 'Grab all your kit and make your way to the hangar next door, where coaches are waiting to take you to Grantham and Beckingham.'

We all raced to grab our bergens from the aisles and carried them to the hangar next door. Luckily for our company, we'd all managed to get on one of the two coaches for Prince William Barracks at Grantham, Lincolnshire, which is now used by the RLC (Royal Logistic Corps). It was originally built for the RAF and used for training pilots.

Due to the hurry up and wait, the time was fast approaching 1730hrs. The coach trip from Chilwell to Grantham took an hour and by the time we reached the barracks, it was close to 1830hrs and almost dark. We disembarked from the coach and stood in groups trying to keep warm in the icy wind, something that ex-RAF bases seem to attract.

A corporal from the Royal Green Jackets greeted us with a surprisingly welcoming smile. 'Right, lads . . .' He scanned the crowd in front of him, then added, 'and lasses'. 'Listen for your names and group number, then make your way to the armoury and hand in your weapons; I'll tell you where to go in a minute. You may then make your way to the accommodation blocks.' He paused for a second, checking the paperwork on his clipboard. 'Evening meal is served until 1930hrs. Reveille is at 0700hrs and breakfast is 0730 to 0830hrs. Make sure you are at building No. 4 by 0930hrs.' He raised his clipboard in the air and pointed to a building on his A4-sized map, hoping we could all see it in the dimming light. After a few seconds, he pulled down his arm and continued his ready-made, rehearsed speech. 'You are not allowed off the camp but the NAAFI bar is open, which you are welcome to use. But don't go mad. The evenings are yours and I don't want to see your ugly faces until tomorrow morning, 0930hrs. Any questions?'

There was silence, apart from the shuffle of the soles of polished boots on damp tarmac. Someone plucked up enough courage to ask the question to which we all wanted to know the answer: 'What about parade?'

'Fuck all that!' the corporal answered quickly. We all sniggered, before he interrupted us. 'There's too much for you to do over the next five days, so all that bullshit is out of the window. You're all supposed to be switched-on soldiers, so you should be able to conduct yourselves in a proper manner.' He waited for some wisecrack from his audience but didn't receive one, so he continued with his speech. 'Don't go mad tonight, and just behave the way you should on camp. Now, listen for your names and group number, grab a timetable and map off me, then you can disappear!'

After our names were called out, we collected the paperwork, stuffed it in our jacket pockets and grabbed our rifles, leaving our kit in a pile to collect later. Luckily for our gang, Mike had done his recruit training at the barracks and knew exactly where to find all the key buildings. We followed him, taking a short cut to the armoury, then made our way to the accommodation blocks. We unpacked our kit, raced for the showers and did a quick change into civvy clothing before scoff. After wolfing down our evening meal, it was a race to the NAAFI bar, where we spent the rest of the evening laughing and joking about the day's events and talking about the impending war – again.

4

BACK TO BASICS

The next day, we were greeted by a typical early March morning – cold and wet with an icy wind that cut right through to the bone – but the atmosphere remained bright and cheery. The thought of no bullshit or some RSM shouting his head off at us made the forthcoming training seem a little more bearable.

As we waited outside building No. 4 for the instructors to arrive, it suddenly dawned on me that there was a huge age difference within the group, ranging from 18 to mid-40s. Most of the lads were TA, with a proportion made up of reservists (soldiers who had left the regular army but were immediately called out because of a clause which allows the government to recall them within five years of leaving the forces). Some of them had left five years ago, only to be welcomed by a brown envelope one morning. There was also an element of reservists who'd left the army only a few months before, who had organised a new civvy life with a job and mortgage, only to find they too were called out and soon back in uniform.

After 15 minutes or so, a corporal decided to make an

appearance and let us into the building. Inside was an auditorium used for lectures and film shows, with rows of seating raised one row slightly higher than the other. We talked amongst ourselves until a lieutenant, who couldn't have been much older than his mid-20s, addressed us from the raised platform stage at the front of the theatre, explaining the forthcoming events. It was then I noticed – or rather didn't notice – any PT or CFT training on our timetables.

Dave and Mike, who were sitting either side of me, must have noticed at the same time because we all looked at each other, wearing huge smug grins. I thought of those bastards from our unit who had already been through the process, telling us they'd been running every day and 'beasted' from pillar to post. A wind-up – which many others, including myself, fell for hook, line and sinker.

The lieutenant continued to explain the forthcoming lectures and lessons of the pre-deployment training, emphasising the importance of the first-aid and NBC aspects. These particular lessons each took a day to complete. First aid wasn't so bad but a full day of NBC training just didn't bear thinking about.

The whole five-day course involved: theatre background (what to expect from the enemy); environmental health (personal hygiene); mine awareness; conduct if captured; E&E (escape and evasion); PW (prisoners of war) handling; law of armed conflict; battle stress and how to recognise it; battlefield first aid (slightly different to general first aid); AFV (armoured fighting vehicle) recognition (friendly and enemy forces); weapon handling (which included a day at the ranges to test-adjust-group and zero our rifles); and finally, not forgetting NBC training. This was taken very seriously due to the chemical weapons we were expected to face in the desert. It was imperative that we understood the effects of nerve, blood, choking and blister agents such as mustard gas, sarin and anthrax which we knew the Iraqi forces had had at their disposal at one time. We were also told the life-expectancy of certain agents in a hostile environment should they be used.

Chemical weapons were not designed for hot, dusty desert conditions; instead they thrive in a more temperate climate such as that of western Europe. This means a chemical agent used in a desert environment, where temperatures exceed 30 degrees, could be useless and tactically ineffective against troops. The chemical agents Iraqi forces had would only have an atmospheric life of about 20 minutes, due to the extreme conditions. If used in western Europe, the colder climate would allow them a life-expectancy of many hours. The tactical effectiveness of an agent, however, wherever it's used, relies on wind direction and ensuring that it won't blow back on friendly positions. This is one of many reasons why the UK doesn't have any chemical weapons.

NBC training day wouldn't be complete without the 'gas chamber'. We took it in turns, groups of half a dozen or so, to venture into a brick-built shed the size of an average garage. A small window at the rear and one on either side let in enough light to see the person standing next to you. The S10 filter, screwed onto the left-hand side of our respirators, was supposed to be the most effective against an NBC attack and was supposed to allow us to breathe 30 per cent better air through the carbon-layered filter than the old S6 filter would have provided. Personally, I found it more restrictive.

We donned our respirators and ensured our Mk5 NBC suits (consisting of jacket, trousers, rubber over-boots and rubber gloves with cotton inner gloves) were sealed correctly before entering the building. The room was thick with CS gas, caused by the CS tablets which were smoking vigorously on a house brick in the middle of the floor. The instructor, standing in the middle of the room, encouraged us to stand in a circle and start jumping up and down. After a few minutes, he had us running in a tight circle, changing direction after only a few seconds. The idea was to get us sweating a bit and make us breathe more heavily. Being out of breath wearing a respirator was one of my biggest fears. My first instinct was to take it off because I simply couldn't breathe properly, but I knew I'd end up taking a lungful of gas in a CS environment, which was not a good idea.

After ten minutes of gentle exercise and a couple of eating and drinking drills, it was on to decontamination training using DKP1 pads, a perforated cotton wrap filled with fuller's earth (a chalky clay powder not unlike cat litter). We had to 'blot, bang, rub' the two-inch pad of DKP powder over our heads, respirators and gloves to soak up any chemical agent. We then used the DKP2 puffer bottle to decontaminate our Kevlar helmets, over-boots and the surrounding ground. Towards the end of the lesson, the instructor lined us up at the bottom of the chamber to let us out.

It was soon to be my turn. First, I had to close my eyes and hold my breath before taking off the respirator. I could then walk the few steps out of the chamber and into the fresh air; however, the instructor insisted on asking stupid questions, which I had to answer before I was let out, things like, 'What's your name?', 'How old are you?' and 'What's your dog's name?' He'd ask anything to make us take a gulp of CS. Without a breath left inside me, I immediately took a gasp of CS-enriched air which made me choke and caused my eyes to water. When I walked outside, I could feel my lips and throat burn from the gas residue left in my mouth.

The effects of the gas soon wore off but the experience would stay in my mind for ever, which was the idea of the exercise. If a chemical or biological agent contaminated us for real, we would have only minutes to live. During that time, we would experience a slow and agonising death. We would be issued with three 'combo pens' full of atropine to stabilise the effects of a chemical agent, along with NAPS (nerve agent pre-treatment set) and BATS (biological agent treatment set) tablets to take as a course, but these were not 100 per cent effective against an NBC attack. The idea behind these tablets was for the body to build up a tolerance to certain nerve and biological agents, which can invade the body through the respiratory system or be absorbed through the skin. The tablets, however, could not counteract all chemical and biological agents, or be effective against continuous contamination, hence the need for NBC suits and respirators. We would also have a course of anthrax injections which weren't foolproof. This was why it was important we could carry out our IA (immediate action) drills with ease. We had to ensure we could don a respirator within nine seconds (which is the estimated time before feeling the effects of a chemical attack) – not easy wearing gloves and having to extract a respirator that is stowed in a haversack strapped around your waist.

Other lessons included understanding and recognising the symptoms of a blood, blister, choking or nerve agent, and what to do when administering battlefield first aid in a chemical environment – under fire. The CSR (chemical safety rule), which is the routine for what to do if you have to don your respirator and NBC suit without being ordered to do so, was also drummed into our heads. This important rule should be enforced when experiencing a bombardment of any kind from hostile or unknown flying aircraft; if you notice any suspicious mist, smoke, droplets or splashes, or smell anything unusual; if you hear an alarm, such as someone shouting, 'Gas! Gas! Gas!' or a vehicle horn sounding one second on, one second off; if changing the respirator S10 canister when not ordered to do so, for example if it's damaged or blocked; if you have had three weeks' occasional exposure to a chemical environment or encountered six continuous chemical attacks, or four months' continuous wear. We were drilled on how to change full IPE (individual personal equipment) in a chemical environment and how to carry out the urination/defecation procedure, as well as what to do if our 'one colour' detector paper turned blue from a chemical attack. Throughout all this, we would still be expected to work and fight.

The battlefield first-aid lessons were as intense as the NBC lessons. The only difference was the video selection used as an aide-memoire: *Black Hawk Down* and *We Were Soldiers* were the preferred choices. Both of them were chosen for their casualty content and to illustrate how the soldiers tried their best to administer battlefield first aid. Again, we were expected to experience such casualty injuries. We were also given a battlefield casualty card, which was about the size of a sheet of A4, folded in a concertina fashion, which gave instructions on how to treat a casualty under battle conditions. It included injuries such as broken bones, severe bleeding, burns, phosphorous-grenade injuries and sucking chest wounds (which are the result of shrapnel piercing the lungs on entry and exit, thereby removing the vacuum in the lungs and causing them to collapse). Lessons were also given on how to treat these injuries and when to administer morphine, using the issued morphine pens. We were taught procedures for casevac'ing casualties after or even during a fire-fight.

Again, we were told to expect such scenarios. By this stage, our sense of humour had taken a considerable bashing and was in desperate need of first aid itself.

At last, the week was over and we were told which regiments we'd been posted to, as if we didn't know already, but being told officially confirmed it all. We packed our kit, collected our rifles from the armoury and waited for the coaches to take us to the seaport at Harwich. A civilian ferry transported us to the Hook of Holland, then a further coach took us to an army camp outside Rheindahlen in Germany. We stayed there for two days whilst our flight to the Gulf was organised and were soon repacking our kit and jumping on yet another coach bound for Hanover Airport. A chartered Boeing 747 was waiting for us away from public eyes – the paint your arse blue peace protestors didn't exactly agree with what we were doing and were keen to let us know about it.

We made it through a checkpoint, handed over our luggage to be screened just in case we were trying to smuggle dangerous weapons on board, believe it or not, and watched the bags being literally thrown into the aeroplane. The departure lounge was full of squaddies all waiting for the same flight, some in desert kit and some in the CS95 green uniform.

'Coming for a smoke?' asked Chris. I nodded and searched for my cigarettes in my deep jacket pockets as we walked over to the smoking area. 'How do you feel, Kev?'

'Not too bad, considering all of a sudden we're waiting in a departure lounge bound for Kuwait. It doesn't seem real, not yet anyway. How d'you feel?'

'Ask me the same question in a week's time, I'll let you know then,' he replied. I didn't really understand his answer but decided to let it go over my head.

The public-address system burst into life and a voice

announced our flight number and asked us to make our way to the reception desk for final instructions. Once we had received them, it was a mad dash across the tarmac towards our plane. We climbed the portable stairs at the front nearside of the plane and could hear the wings creaking above the sound of the jet engines ticking over. This was one trip I wasn't looking forward to.

As I approached the entrance to the plane, a civilian airline hostess greeted me. I was taken aback but it also cheered me up and took my mind off the flying rust-bucket I was boarding. It was a bizarre sight to see, hundreds of squaddies, all in mixed uniform, climbing into a civvy aeroplane to be flown into a potential war zone. We were dispensable but the civvy crew weren't. They were either brave or had been offered so much money they couldn't refuse. At a guess, I'd go for the latter.

We settled down in our seats as the captain spoke over the public-address system, asking us to stay seated during take-off, to fasten our seatbelts, not to smoke and all the other pre-flight bollocks. The air hostesses went into their routine of displaying the life-jacket procedure and showing us where the fire exits were. For a split second, I felt as if I was flying to Spain for a two-week holiday. I quickly snapped out of this fantasy when I glimpsed the CS95 uniforms around me. When we were airborne and had gained sufficient height, the plane settled into cruise control for the six-hour journey to Kuwait.

The sun was setting fast and all I could see out of the window were the well-lit cities of Europe. The air hostesses came round with trolleys of hot meals, which was a nice surprise as we thought this would be a military flight and expected bog all. The only courtesy we didn't get was the in-flight movie but I suppose we couldn't have everything.

Meals and drinks were soon finished and we thought it

a good idea to grab a few hours' kip before we landed at Kuwait City Airport. Trying to sleep on a 747 bound for a war zone, though, was easier said than done. I don't think I managed more than an hour because of the many thoughts whizzing around my head, like what to expect and if I was going to make it through the war. I imagined the other 299 passengers thought the same, but somehow Chris managed to snore through the entire journey. He was either oblivious to the expected shit we were about to endure or didn't give a toss. Or maybe he was concerned but didn't show it.

My confidence in the aeroplane's ability to fly grew just as we were landing. There also came an audible sigh of relief from the seats behind me, quickly followed by the typical British holidaymaker's reaction when a plane lands – cheers and applause for the pilot. He must have heard us, because he thanked us for flying with 'Air Squaddie' and wished us all luck. He parked the plane towards the rear of the airport and looking out of the window, I could see patrolling American soldiers tooled up and wearing their webbing and NBC haversacks, guarding crates of cargo scattered outside the sodium-lit hangars. This was serious stuff.

I had to violently wake Chris, almost to the point of stamping on him. A moan then a stretch of his arms was quickly followed with a passing question, 'Are we there yet?'

Monday, 10 March 0300hrs local (although time had taken a back seat with us at that moment) We arrived utterly jet-lagged – we'd gone from GMT to German time to Kuwaiti time, which is three hours ahead of GMT, and were then told to change back to 'zulu' time (GMT).

We disembarked and those who smoked, including me,

rushed to the side of the taxiway to light a well-deserved cigarette. Fork-lifts soon arrived and unloaded the cargo of bergens and weapons. They manoeuvred like a well-rehearsed ballet, placing the cargo pallets in pre-arranged positions alongside the end of the taxiway. Two clapped-out civvy articulated Mercedes trucks then arrived, ready for us to load the trailers with our kit.

At the edge of the taxiway next to the perimeter fence, an open drainage ditch became a temporary latrine. Hundreds of squaddies lined up to relieve themselves, filling the warm night air with a distinctive odour. As I stood in the row doing my bit, I had my first encounter with the local wildlife. I looked down to witness a large scorpion crawling over the top of my left boot, no doubt disturbed by the sudden rush of full bladders thundering over its territory. I let out a somewhat girlie scream and jumped back in horror. As I did, drips of urine went over my hands and down my CS95 trousers, much to the amusement of everyone else standing next to me. I continued to jump about whilst trying to re-zip my trousers. As I turned away from the ditch, I noticed the American soldiers laughing as well. This was a great start to my tour.

The cargo pallets were unloaded and it was the turn of the elected 'baggage party' members, me included, to load the kit onto the trailers. Chris perched himself on the back of one of them and grabbed the CEMO (complete equipment marching order) – bergens, day sacks and webbing – as we threw them at him. He then passed them down the chain to waiting squaddies towards the front of the trailer to be carefully stowed, army style. After half an hour, all the kit had been loaded. We collected our rifles, grabbed our day bergens and made our way towards the waiting coaches, which would take us to our next destination.

5

WELCOME TO THE
MIDDLE EAST

As I stood waiting for the rest of the group to gather in the coach parking area, I noticed one of the local drivers praying on a mat at the front of his coach. This was my first experience of the local Muslim culture and after looking at the state of the coaches, I was thinking of praying myself. Most of them had their wheel arches missing, whilst dents and gouges adorned the front and rear of the bodywork, making them look as if they'd already been in a war. All the windows were blacked out with dark-coloured curtains, either to stop locals peering in at the foreign troops or us shitting ourselves when some 'chogie' (a nickname given to members of the Iraqi militia) fired an RPG (rocket-propelled grenade) at the coach.

The warm night air, combined with the body heat of 30 or so squaddies crammed into each coach, soon had us sweating. The air conditioning in our crate wasn't working – surprise, surprise – so we had to put up with it. Jackets and shirts were soon ripped off and the need for a cold drink became urgent. After an hour's journey, the coach turned off the main tarmac dual carriageway and onto a dusty dirt track before reaching our destination, Camp Centurion.

We disembarked and stood around taking in the surroundings. Although it was dark (it was 0430hrs local time), the mobile lights around the camp subtly illuminated large white tents, about 8x20 metres and 6 metres high. Beyond the tents, it looked as though there was nothing but barren desert. A mixed bag of British and American squaddies soon congregated in small groups and we chatted amongst ourselves, but we could barely hear one another above the many generators scattered throughout the camp.

We were ushered into one of the tents, which had been turned into a booking-in centre to make sure we hadn't gone AWOL (absent without leave) and, of course, to provide us with yet more paperwork to fill in. Details such as the units we were posted with, a Gulf-region aide-memoire card, a 'what to do' list on the law of armed conflict, landmine encounter details and a theatre allowance card. This one was the most important card of them all because it allowed us to withdraw $100 per month (providing we had a chequebook handy). Various other welfare allowances were listed, along with a twenty-minute satlink (satellite) phone card, issued free every seven days.

By the time we had pushed through the reception tent, it was close to 0600hrs local. Once booked in, I stood outside the tent with my Saudi-supplied desalinised water and took a few gulps from the one-litre plastic bottle. The morning sun was beginning to light up the sky and I could see the desert landscape a little clearer. We were in the middle of nowhere, miles from civilisation. It was difficult to appreciate the size of the camp but the line of military vehicles and tents following the three-metre-high sand-berm boundary certainly gave me the impression it was at least two or three kilometres square, and this was just one of many camps spread across the vast desert of northern Kuwait.

'Listen in!' a sergeant from the RRF shouted from just beyond the tent entrance. I quickly joined the others inside. 'All of your kit has been placed carefully [yeah, right] on the ground behind the booking-in tent. Go and fish it out and report to the front of the tent.'

Fetching kit from 300 other bergens was easier said than done – they were all the same colour, for a start. A mass scrap broke out, with dust and sand flying everywhere. Bodies pounced on bits of kit, claiming possession, whilst others argued it was theirs. When the dust settled, the majority had grabbed their kit and were heading for the sergeant to await further instructions. A few stragglers, myself included, wandered around, desperately searching for bits of kit – a day sack, helmet, doss bag, webbing – which had been removed from the bergens prior to the flight from Germany. I found everything apart from my bergen. I couldn't believe it, I'd been in Kuwait for just over three hours and I'd already lost the main item of my kit.

I looked around in vain, scanning the remnants, trying to eyeball the last four digits of my service number, which were scrawled on top of every detachable pouch in black marker pen. I eventually found the bergen when I noticed some arsehole had decided to take mine without checking its identity first. After calling him a few choice names, I left him searching for his own. When I arrived at the tent entrance, the rest of the lads were already taking notes from the RRF sergeant, who was calling out names from his list and instructing them to fall in to different groups. Chris disappeared and joined others boarding a Bedford truck which would take them to their new home – 3 RHA, part of 7 Armoured Brigade, the Desert Rats, somewhere in the desert. That was the last I saw of him until he returned home safely six months later.

Mike beckoned me over. 'Kev, hurry,' he shouted.

I struggled to carry my kit in the soft sand. The straps either choked me or pulled my shoulders out of their sockets. I managed to reach the main group just as Mike picked up his kit again to move to another group. 'We're joining that lot,' he said, nodding his head towards some soldiers standing 50 metres to his right.

'Oh, bloody 'ell, I've only just reached you lot. Give us a couple of minutes.' I dropped my kit and rubbed my aching shoulders.

Mike let out a chuckle. 'C'mon, we're off to Camp Cambrai.' He dropped his kit on the sand and took out his notebook. 'We're to wait for the other coaches to arrive. Until then, we're to grab some rations and chill out.'

'Then what?' I asked, still rubbing my shoulders.

'Our units will be informed of our arrival and they'll pick us up from the camp.'

Half an hour later, our coach arrived and within a further half-hour we'd arrived at our final destination – Camp Cambrai. An apt title for the camp, which housed many units, including 2 RTR (2 Royal Tank Regiment) and the SDG. The camp took its name from Cambrai, the small town in northern France renowned because it is where the British first used tanks against German positions during the First World War. Other units, such as the Royal Engineers, RRF, REME and many other LADs (light aid detachments) used Camp Cambrai for desert training.

Tuesday, 11 March 0730hrs local We disembarked from the coaches and grabbed our kit, carrying it into one of the huge white tents, similar to those at Camp Centurion. As

I left the coach, the intensity of the sunlight hit me like a tonne of bricks. I'd never experienced a heat quite like it. I couldn't get into the tent quick enough. Our adopted units weren't expected to collect us until 1600hrs local, so we were told to chill out. This gave us plenty of time to grab rations and catch up on some sleep.

Predictably, the lads found a space at the far end of the tent. Inside, the floor had some kind of wall-to-wall carpeting, purple in colour. Not very tactical but then again, what does it matter inside a tent? Five wooden poles, equally spaced along its entire length, kept up the roof. Attached to each pole was a cluster of low-wattage light bulbs, dimly illuminating the tent. Either end had an entrance flap loosely closed to keep out the sun's glare but allow a breeze to enter, albeit a warm breeze.

I threw down my kit between Mike and Dave, and adjusted my bergen to use as a back rest, then lay against it. It wasn't long before I started to drift off, although I was still aware of people talking around me. My mind soon began to relax, rousing memories of home, family and friends. My thoughts began to play back like a video tape: standing in the kitchen talking to my mother just before leaving for Chilwell; explaining to my wife about the call-out; and the last time I played a game with my daughter, Rachel. As in a dream, I jumped from one scenario to another: the training at Grantham, the time we were all summoned to the office, Frammy telling us we'd been called out for Op Telic and the piss-up we'd had the night before it all happened.

'Kev! Kev!' Mike shouted, shaking my shoulders, trying to wake me up. So I had fallen asleep after all.

He threw an MRE (meal ready-to-eat) in my lap. MREs are the US equivalent of the UK ration packs, or 'rat packs' as we call them. The immediate difference was that the

MRE packs had only one meal inside them, while the British rat packs had a menu to cover a 24-hour period. The other important difference was the way the food was heated. While the British options were nothing more than 'boil in the bag' meals which required heating externally using a naked flame, each MRE was accompanied by strips of card with a kind of crystal coating which reacted in such a violent manner with water that they could heat it to almost boiling point. So, a small amount of water was poured into a plastic bag containing the card strips then the vacuum-packed meal was placed inside the plastic bag. A few minutes later, the meal was removed and, hey presto! This particular method saved on the amount of water used and there was no need to make a fire, which meant no smoke – a perfect eating system for tactical operations.

After working out how to use the MRE heating system and devouring its contents, a few of the other lads from inside the tent and I ventured outside to use the 'smoking area' and have a cigarette. I picked up my rifle and walked outside, only to be greeted by the searing heat and blinding sunlight, which automatically made me raise my right hand to shade my eyes.

'Oi! Buddy!' a voice shouted a few metres away.

I naturally turned towards the voice, which came from a Land-Rover painted in desert camouflage, where a squaddie was sitting in the driver's seat with the door wide open. I pointed to myself, to question if he wanted my attention.

'Yes, you. Gas! Gas! Gas!' he whispered quietly, but loud enough for me to hear. I realised what he meant. I quickly raised and lowered my arms in submission and ran back into the tent to grab my haversack, which contained my respirator. I clipped it around my waist, grabbed my rifle and walked back out of the tent only to be greeted by the same squaddie, who turned out to be a WO2 (warrant officer – 2nd class). 'You'll remember next time, won't you?'

I expected to be shouted at and given some kind of punishment but he just warned me of the situation and reminded me of the consequences should a gas attack occur. Pleased I had escaped a bollocking, I caught up with the others walking towards the smoking area and took a mental map of my surroundings. The camp was made up of many other smaller camps. Like all the other camps, we were surrounded by a three-metre sand berm. The tented area, with its half-dozen tents already covered in a light coating of sand, had its own lower two-metre berm boundary. Towards the rear of our tent, some 30 metres or so away, a smoking area had been cordoned off with white mine tape.

Next to the smoking area were four of many strategically placed 'Scud' or fire trenches spread around the camp, about one metre wide, three metres long and one and a half metres deep. These were to be used in case of any incoming, for example, shells, air bombardment, mortar fire, small-arms or machine-gun fire, or missile attacks. In the event of an enemy assault on the camp, they also became our 'stand-to' or emergency positions.

I placed my rifle on the ground (breach block side facing up to prevent sand from entering the working parts), sat on the dug-out sand surrounding a fire trench and lit a cigarette. I could feel the intense heat burning my scalp and dust blowing in my eyes, caused by the 'dust devils' (mini tornadoes) which appeared without notice and disappeared just as quickly. The sound of tracked vehicles in the distance and the sight of the fire trenches brought home the seriousness of it all, and here we were, sat in the middle of it. I thought of Chris and how when I'd asked him how he felt whilst we waited for our flight at Hanover Airport, he'd said, ask me in a week's time. I now understood why.

The fun and games leading up to our call-out were now over. The laughter of our pre-deployment training had suddenly ceased. I asked myself the same question many of the other soldiers had surely asked themselves when they arrived – what the fuck am I doing here?

I finished my cigarette, stubbed it out in the sand and threw it into the extra-large empty bean can used for cigarette stubs and made my way back to the tent. When I got inside, I noticed a few more fresh faces, about 30 or so, dotted around the sides, lying or sitting in small gangs, some asleep and some chatting quietly so as not to disturb the others. I made my way to my kit, took off my haversack and slumped against my bergen, setting down my rifle against my right leg. The guys from my unit were fast asleep and it didn't take long before I joined them.

It was early afternoon before I woke. Mike, Paul, Dave and Frank were already awake and sorting out their kit.

'What's happening?'

'We're moving out,' answered Mike.

I checked my watch; it was only 1420hrs local. 'What do you mean moving out? Have our units turned up?'

Mike paused from struggling with his doss bag before answering. 'While you were asleep, some sergeant came in and explained that none of our units were picking us up. We're to meet a couple of Bedford trucks outside in 20 minutes and they'll be taking us to our units.' So much for the rest of the day chilling out.

We all vacated the tent and were greeted by the searing heat once again. The hottest part of the day had passed and the temperature was in the mid-30s Celsius – a dry, suffocating heat we Brits were definitely not used to. We dropped our kit on the sand and waited for the Bedfords. The first one showed up as soon as we had settled down in a heap. The driver jumped out of the cab and reeled off some names and units. He didn't mention anyone from our gang so we stayed put and the rest jumped in the back of the Bedford. As it drove off, Mike noticed we were the only five left.

Half an hour later, the other Bedford arrived to take us to our new homes. Two other TA squaddies were already in the back, having been picked up from some other camp, and were all destined for the SDG. We introduced ourselves and settled down for the bumpy ten-minute journey along the dusty desert track. The sand was extremely dry and had been crushed to a fine powder by the wheeled and tracked vehicles rumbling over it. The air in the back of the Bedford was soon full of dust, which was something we would get used to over the coming months. The Bedford came to a halt just outside the SDG area. We threw our dusty kit out of the back and quickly followed it.

'Wait here, lads,' the sergeant called out. He held a clipboard in his left hand and was running his pen down a list attached to the board with his right. 'I'll book you in and grab the CO so he can greet and welcome you to his unit. Meanwhile, chill out.'

Fifteen minutes or so passed. 'I wonder what the hold up is?' mumbled Dave.

'God knows but you can bet there's a balls-up somewhere,' I replied.

'I get the funny feeling they don't want us,' Frank added.

A further ten minutes passed before the sergeant returned, accompanied by the CO. 'Welcome, lads, welcome. We have a slight problem.' He checked the list he had in his right hand. 'We only have room for two of you, two recy mechs. To make it fair, we've drawn two names out of a hat, so to speak. The names are L/Cpl Callolm and Cpl Clipston. The rest of you will have to find homes elsewhere.'

There were a few moans from the rest of the lads before we were ushered back into the rear of the Bedford. Before we climbed aboard, we said our farewells to Frank and Mike, wishing them all the best. We then drove off to other units on the camp whilst the sergeant desperately tried to find us homes before the night drew in.

We had stopped at various camp areas, none of which required any recovery mechanics, until we found a CS (close support) field hospital. The sergeant jumped out of the cab and approached the reception tent at the camp entrance. By now, the time was 1830hrs local and daylight was fading fast. After five minutes, he returned to the rear of the Bedford. 'Cpl Fletcher, out you get, this is your new home.'

'Good luck, Paul, all the best, mate,' I said, as Paul gathered his kit and threw it out of the Bedford.

'Yeah, keep your head down, OK,' added Dave.

'Cheers, lads. Maybe we'll bump into each other one day.' Paul jumped out of the back of the Bedford and lifted his bergen onto his back. He then walked off with the sergeant to the eagerly waiting CO of his new unit.

'Then there were two,' I said under my breath.

'What? Did you say something, Kev?'

'No, Dave, just . . .' I paused, not really knowing what to say.

We must have travelled for a further two hours, stopping at various camps and units, but no one wanted us. We returned to the SDG camp for the night, with hope of finding a new home in the morning. In the mean time, we tried to find Mike and Frank but they had been taken elsewhere within the SDG camp, so we spent the night amongst the CRARRVs (Challenger armoured recovery and repair vehicles) of the REME LAD to the SDG. The CRARRV is a huge tracked beast of 60 tonnes, used by the REME to recover Challenger 2 tanks and AS90 self-propelled guns, as well as for other heavy recovery tasks.

The morning came around too soon. We were woken at 0600hrs local to be taken to our new home. Apparently, the sergeant had been on 'the net' (radio) throughout the night looking for a unit that could use us. Dave and I packed away our sleeping systems and threw our bergens in the back of the Bedford. After a quick wash and shave, we grabbed some breakfast – well, if you can call it that: powdered egg scrambled into a splodge, part of an undercooked ten-man rat-pack sausage out of a tin and a boiled, skinned tomato. After breakfast, we were on our way to the camp of 32 Royal Engineers (Armoured).

A small ride later, we were there, but the news wasn't good – again. Out of the four of us, three stayed behind, including Dave. I wasn't needed, so the CO had to find another unit for me. Thankfully, he had a few contacts around the camp and found a position at 2 RTR BG (2 Royal Tank Regiment battle group). Finally, I had found a home. The cock-up certainly came as a surprise, considering we had been told many weeks in advance which units wanted us or, more to the point, which trade requirements they needed. But it soon became apparent that some units realised they had either overbooked or were short of manpower.

The Land-Rover from 2 RTR arrived a few hours later. I threw my kit in the back, wished Dave luck and introduced myself to the lieutenant and the split-arse lance jack driver. Lieutenant Pym, who couldn't have been any older than his early 20s, had a clear, baby-faced complexion and short black hair. I felt like asking him if his mother knew he was out here. The split-arse, Jane, was very nice. The first woman squaddie I'd seen whose arse looked sexy in CS95 trousers.

I jumped in the back of the soft-top 110 Land-Rover as the lieutenant chatted about my new home and asked me a few questions about my background. He said that the other recy mech I'd be crewed with was also a TA soldier. And just to make me feel slightly concerned, the Foden recovery vehicle I'd be using was the only one for the entire 2 RTR battle group.

The 2 RTR BG camp was just inside the Camp Cambrai boundary, so I'd gone full circle, arriving back where I'd started. The LAD was next to the main gate and beyond that, about 100 metres away, was the main dual carriageway, Route 6, code-named 'Route Tampa'. This led into Iraq, about 50 kilometres north.

The camp area was surrounded by the usual three-metre sand berms. The main entrance was a six-metre gap in the berm with a sentry either side, standing behind a pile of sandbags, one with an LSW and the other with a GPMG (general purpose machine gun), known as a 'gimpie' – a 7.62-mm belt-fed machine gun. Behind the gimpie was a Warrior CVT (combat vehicle tracked) with its turreted 30-mm Rarden cannon facing down the dirt track towards the dual carriageway. I should have felt safe with all this firepower at the main gate but I felt surprisingly uneasy.

I dumped my kit on the sand next to the reception tent, and Lieutenant Pym introduced me to the rest of the REME LAD. He showed me where everyone was and what they did. The LAD was nothing more than various armoured B-vehicles and box trailers parked in two rows covered in desert cam-nets. The CV (command vehicle), a Scimitar, had its four antennas pointing through the canopy of its cam-net. This was where all communications were sent and received. Any recovery tasks came in via the CV.

Walking back to my kit, I spotted the CRARRV opposite the LAD location, about 100 metres ahead, on top of a slight incline. There was a makeshift sunshade canopy made out of hessian fitted to the side of the armoured recovery vehicle. The lieutenant grabbed my webbing and brown grip whilst I carried the rest of my kit. As we approached the CRARRV, I noticed the diesel burner boiling water in a tin.

'Hi, Sir, is this our recy mech?' SSgt (staff sergeant) Phil Robinson asked.

'Yep. This is L/Cpl Mervin, Foden trained. I'll leave you to get acquainted. Anything you want, just ask Staff Robinson.' He dumped my kit on the sand and quickly walked back to his CV.

'What's your first name, mate?' asked the 40-or-so-year-old staff sergeant. He had a number one haircut which made him look bald, with his light blond hair. 'We don't go by rank here, not unless officers are present.'

'Kevin, or just Kev.'

'I'm Phil. Fancy a brew, Kev? The water's nearly boiled. I'll introduce you to the rest of the lads as soon as I've made the tea.'

'Yeah, please, two sugars.' I dug my plastic mug out of my day sack and passed it to Phil. 'Anyone smoke?' I asked, opening my cigarette packet, a sure way to break the ice. Five heads turned around.

'Yeah, cheers, mate,' they all said, seemingly in unison.

Phil let out a laugh. 'Bet you wish you never asked.' I offered him one. 'Oh, go on then, being's you're offering.' He took one, then continued to make the tea.

The apprehension I'd felt earlier quickly disappeared and I soon relaxed with that lot. It's a natural reaction to feel uncertain about new surroundings and new faces but at the end of the day, we were all there to do a job. I didn't mention I was in the TA, though, not straight away. I knew my being a TA soldier might rub some of the regulars up the wrong way. There has always been a stigma attached to the TA, like we're the 'Dad's Army' or 'plastic soldiers', and some of the regs regarded us as just that. Thankfully, I personally never came across it. At the time, however, I kept quiet, just in case. As it turned out, they were all a great bunch of lads and even bowed to my better judgement on many tasks, including how to drive properly off-road.

We sat around in a circle under the canopy drinking tea and smoking each other's cigarettes, swapping stories and generally having a laugh. Before we knew it, night was drawing in and the Foden still hadn't returned from a recovery task. Bobby, a L/Cpl, and Cpl Andy Dawson, both VMs, finished their tea and wandered off to complete a repair on a Warrior. Those that crewed the Warrior recovery vehicle followed to help the VMs with the job.

In the hour that had passed, the wind had picked up. I didn't take much notice but everybody else around the camp started battening down tent pegs and cam-nets, packing kit into vehicles and generally running around like headless chickens.

'There's a sandstorm brewing,' Phil said.

'A what?'

'We have them from time to time.'

I thought he was talking about a dust devil, which I had already experienced. 'A bit over the top for a dust devil.'

'This is no dust devil; a tad stronger than that.'

He packed away the brew kit and slung it on the back of the CRARRV, just as the Foden arrived from its recovery task. It parked next to the canopy as a strong gust of wind whipped sand against my face.

'Jump in, mate,' a voice shouted over the noise of the storm. I quickly climbed into the passenger side of the cab to escape the growing storm. It was Danny, a craftsman recy mech. He should have been crewed with the CRARRV but the original Foden recy mech had had some kind of accident and hadn't made it out of Germany. Phil was pleased then that I had come along and relieved Danny from the Foden. 'I'm Danny and this is Stuart, the STAB [sad Territorial Army bastard] recy mech.' Danny smiled as he said it, thinking I was a regular like him and would make some passing comment on STABs.

I leant over, close to Danny's face, and quietly said, 'I'm Kev, a STAB like Stuart.'

Danny's smile soon disappeared but Stuart laughed. I shook hands with both of them and settled down in the passenger seat, pushing Danny towards the centre of the cab.

'Not another "part-timer". Part-time, part-trained, that's all you lot are.' Danny said, jokingly.

'I'll teach you regs a thing or two,' I replied, half-jokingly.

Stuart let out a forced chuckle, sounding relieved another TA soldier was here to even the balance. He was about 40 years old and quite a senior lance jack. He was also a B2 recy mech, with probably as much training as me. He was a truck mechanic by civvy trade, so his experience definitely came in handy. He was about 5 ft 10 in. tall, slim and going grey at the edges. We had a lot in common: both divorced and remarried, both had kids and both had worked with HGVs (heavy goods vehicles) all our working lives. Danny was a young lad and at 19 years old had a lot to learn. The impending war was about to give him a crash course in life – and death. He was quite broad-shouldered and, at 6 ft, made perfect recy-mech material.

As time went on, the sun had well and truly set and the storm outside had gained strength. I could hear the canopy being whipped about as the pegs were ripped out of the sand. Danny jumped out of the cab to give some of the lads a hand to batten down. Stuart and I thought we'd better do the same but as soon as I opened the passenger door, the wind tried to blow it shut again; I literally had to force it open. The only light we had came from torches, but even then we couldn't see any further than a few metres.

My eyes started to sting from the thick dust and sand kicked up by the storm. I tried to shield my eyes with my hands but it was no use. I managed to pick up a few bergens and other bits of kit, leaning them against the track of the CRARRV, but that was all I could achieve. The others were wearing issued sand-goggles and *shemaghs* (a 'tea towel' that wraps around the face to protect it from sandstorms), so they could last a tad longer in the storm than Stuart or me. After a few more minutes, we couldn't take any more punishment and bowed out by climbing back into the Foden cab, which was an effort in itself. A few minutes later, Phil and the others gave in to the storm and climbed aboard their vehicles, battening down the hatches to sit it out.

'Welcome to the Middle East!' Stuart said, sarcastically.

'Yeah, cheers, mate.' I dusted down my clothes and removed sand from my ears, using the top from a ballpoint pen. 'How can we get hold of some goggles and shemaghs?' I asked.

'You'll be lucky, there's hardly any desert kit up here. Funnily enough, the GS [general support] guys seem to have it all. I can't even get any desert boots.' He looked at mine. 'I see you managed.'

'I paid for these myself,' I said, pointing at them. 'They

were one item I knew I'd have trouble getting hold of.'

We carried on moaning about the lack of kit and the fact that our desert clothing was stuck at the docks in Kuwait and swapped stories of our exploits during our pre-deployment training. After a few hours, the storm was still raging, so we decided to get our heads down for a few hours' kip until it burnt itself out.

6

I SPY WITH MY LITTLE EYE

Wednesday, 12 March 0240hrs zulu It was first light before I woke. The storm had raged on through the night whilst I'd slept on the passenger seat with my legs stretched over the dash. Stuart was curled up in his doss bag on the driver's seat. I wound down the passenger-door window to take in what was going on outside. The sun had started to rise and the camp was silent and still. I must have been one of the first to be awake. Stuart appeared from inside his doss bag wearing an expression that said, what the fuck are you doing up so early?

'Do we have to report for parade?' I asked.

'Do what? No, mate. Just get up, have a wash and get some breakfast down ya neck. Then just sit in the cab, and wait.'

'Wait for tasks, you mean?'

'Yeah. This is our job, innit. Everyone else is on training exercises but if they want us for anything, they'll let us know.' I relaxed a little after Stuart's reassuring words.

He climbed out of his doss bag and checked to see if there was enough water in the BV (boiling vessel), which was situated in the passenger footwell, for a brew and switched it on. Without the engine running, the BV drew so many amps from the vehicle's main batteries it would flatten them within minutes, so I started the Foden, leaving it to tick over. 'We'll have a brew before we do anything. What's the time?'

I checked my watch. 'It's 2.45.'

'A little early, reveille isn't until 0300hrs but it doesn't matter. You could sleep all day if you wanted to, until a job came along. They tend to leave us recy mechs alone.'

I couldn't get used to this laid-back attitude. I was so used to being mucked about at weekends that I never expected to be left alone to just get on with it. Our unit back home always seemed to be breathing down the back of our necks, never leaving us alone to get on with things. It seemed in reality, in a real war, the attitude was very different. The battle group expected us to be able to do the job, TA or not. Get the job done and you'll be left alone, fuck up and we fuck you up, regular-army style. That seemed to be the philosophy.

No sooner had we made the tea than there was a knock on my door. I wound down the window and found another young lieutenant standing beneath me at the foot of the cab, wearing a welcoming smile; another one not much older than his mid-20s. He had a vacant look about him, as if he didn't want to be there.

'Hi, you must be L/Cpl Mervin. I'm Lieutenant Connor.'

I nodded my head in response and acknowledged his presence. 'Mornin', Sir.'

'Well, you've been chucked in at the deep end; we have your first job.'

My heart sank and my stomach tightened. 'Oh, right. OK, Sir.'

I grabbed the piece of paper from him, which had a grid reference scribbled on it. And that was it – no details on vehicle type, call sign or what the problem was with the vehicle casualty, nothing. It wasn't even a proper REME recovery log sheet, just a scrap piece of paper.

Lt Connor walked back to his CV whilst I looked at the scrap of paper in a somewhat confused state of mind.

'Got a job, have we?' Stuart asked.

'Yeah, well, I dunno. Look.' I passed the piece of paper to him.

'Yeah, it's a job.'

'Do all jobs come written on scrap paper?'

Stuart smiled. 'I've only been here a couple of days myself and I've already done four jobs, including the one last night. You either get a bit of paper like this or you are summoned to the CV. Even then, you're only told the grid reference and the vehicle type, if you're lucky.' I slumped in the passenger seat, staring through the windscreen, unable to believe Stuart's words. This tour was going to be an eye-opener.

Before we set off on my first live task, we had a wash and brush up, then tucked into breakfast, which I was quickly getting used to. The cookhouse, situated in one of the large white tents, served the traditional powdered egg – scrambled, boiled – peeled tomatoes and the rat-pack tinned sausage. Queuing at the tent entrance, I was among many different regiments, some tradesmen, some infantry and some I wasn't too sure about.

I reached the tables serving the three-course breakfast. A plastic bowl of cereal with UHT milk (pasteurised milk wouldn't last five minutes in the desert heat), a paper plate of nutritious and delicious goo, followed by a piece of bruised and battered fruit. The idea was to wolf it down as quickly as possible before our taste buds had a chance to recognise what we'd eaten. Stuart, however, seemed to relish his breakfast; in fact, he'd go back for seconds.

Once the recovery kit was checked, we set off in the direction the second-hand GPS (global positioning system) receiver told us to. The one we borrowed belonged to Bobby, the VM. I hadn't any previous experience of such an instrument but thankfully Stuart had grasped the basic principles of marking grid references, planning routes, that sort of thing, thanks to his recent tasks. We also had a full set of maps covering the whole of Kuwait at 1:50,000 and 1:100,000 scale. They did, however, have one major drawback. The maps had been drawn up by a military organisation, so they showed only what they wanted us to see. This included power stations, land formations and so on. Unfortunately, in the middle of the desert there weren't many road signs to help you find yourself on the maps, so a GPS was vital. And, of course, our vehicle casualty of unknown type (although we knew it was a CVRT (combat vehicle reconnaissance tracked)) and origin was stuck in the middle of nowhere, close to the Iraqi border.

Stuart let me drive to get a feel for the desert terrain. I started the engine and checked my watch: 0610hrs zulu. We set off north, up Route Tampa. This was the first time I'd driven on the right-hand side of the road since I'd been on exercise in Germany back in 1997. As we drove up the carriageway, we overtook many convoys of British and American hardware, including tank transporters, Warriors, HumVees and troop carriers. I didn't notice at first but soon realised there was a lack of civilian cars. The only non-military vehicles I did see were occasional Mercedes water tanker or 4x4 Toyota Landcruisers with 'TV' or 'Press' written in big black letters on the doors and bonnet.

The television 4x4s, although full of camera and sound

equipment, also carried quite an arms cache: MP5 automatic machine guns, semi-automatic pistols and even grenades were common in the back of these vehicles. The weapons were also usually accompanied by an 'armed guard' (Special Forces variety). My conclusion was the assault on Iraq was imminent.

The smooth, relaxing drive on tarmac came to an end when we had to turn right into the desert. Up to that point, we'd travelled roughly 20 kilometres. Whilst driving on the constantly changing desert terrain, we had to put up with dust and fine sand being kicked up from the tyres and blown into the cab. If we'd closed the windows, we'd have immediately felt the effect of the sun's scorching heat beaming through the windscreen, making the temperature inside the cab unbearable, as if it wasn't bad enough already.

Stuart checked the map, then checked the grid reference on the GPS in accordance with our location. The problem with our GPS was it could only show a direct line from our position to the course grid reference; it didn't allow for obstacles such as a bend in a road, a river or, in our case, a sand berm surrounding a large disused camp area, which was suspicious in itself. We had to find the route the GPS laid out for us and get back on course as soon as the obstacle was cleared.

We must have travelled about five or six kilometres around the sand berm, which over rough desert terrain took us a good 20 minutes. The next challenge was to find a track of some description to follow; again, easier said than done. There were many vehicle tracks criss-crossing the desert, the majority of them made by Warriors, CVRTs and Challenger 2 tanks. They had no problem skimming across the sand but our B-vehicle, despite having a 6x6 configuration, struggled as the soft sand tried to pull its 27-tonne weight under the surface.

We had to try and find tracks made by B-vehicles so the Foden was on a more suitable surface for tyres, rather than use any old track and increase the chances of sinking in a pocket of loose, dry sand. At the same time, we had to make sure the track was going in our direction. The only way to do this was to get our 'tracking' heads on and try to recognise tyre-tread marks, which wasn't easy. We had to pick up a tread amongst dozens of armoured tracks and to make matters worse, the rising morning sun was now shining directly on our dust-covered windscreen. The only way we could concentrate on the tracks was for both of us to lean out of the cab-door windows and drive slowly until we came across some clues.

'Found one! Land-Rover tracks, I think,' Stuart shouted, as he pointed ahead of the Foden, slightly to his left.

I squinted my eyes to minimise the sun's glare and noticed the tyre marks, 20 or so metres ahead, and yes, they were from a Land-Rover. After making a slight detour towards the tracks and checking them against the GPS to make sure they were going roughly in our direction, we followed them across the desert for 30 kilometres, which took almost an hour. They criss-crossed our route but generally took us on the course we wanted.

We passed many British and American armoured vehicles, either parked up or travelling to and from recce (reconnaissance) tasks. In a way, the sight of these vehicles gave us some security, knowing that we had back-up should a situation arise. Our first concern, however, was to find the bloody vehicle casualty.

Many hours had passed and the sun's blistering heat finally started to ease off a little, which was the good news. The bad news was we couldn't find our casualty. The detour we'd made to avoid obstacles and rough terrain wouldn't allow us to find our correct bearings and rejoin the course the GPS had selected for us. The task was beginning to prove to be too difficult for a B-vehicle to undertake. And to add insult to injury, the radio inside our cab was playing up. Sometimes it would work but more often than not, it didn't, and, of course, we generally picked the occasions it didn't. Plenty of bleeps and crackling, but that was it. Over the hour which followed, we'd lost sight not only of other vehicles but also of tracks of any kind. All in all, my first live job was turning into a right bummer.

I stopped the Foden. 'Check our position, Stuart,' I said, massaging my face with the palms of my hands.

Stuart unfolded the map and lay it across his lap to give a better overall view of the area. Holding the GPS in his left hand, he ran his right index finger across the route we'd taken and calculated our position from the GPS; it wasn't looking good. 'Kev, according to the GPS, we're about one and a half Ks over the border.'

I couldn't believe it. He must have made a mistake. 'Check it again, you must be wrong, we'd have come across signs for the UN buffer zone.' This zone was five kilometres wide and stretched along the entire border between Kuwait and Iraq. Stuart checked it again but came up with the same grid reference.

I drummed the steering wheel with my fingers and scanned the barren desert horizon, trying desperately to think of a quick solution. 'Can you think of anything resembling a border crossing, cos I'll be fucked if I can.'

'Nah, nothing, apart from that gap in a sand berm we passed through, which must be about a K behind us.' Stuart indicated the direction by pointing his right thumb towards the rear of the Foden.

'Sand berm?' I asked, then remembered. 'But that was

another camp area of some sort, wasn't it?'

Stuart looked at the map once again, locating the grid position of the sand berm we'd passed through. 'That was no camp, that was the border. We've probably passed through the breach points of the buffer zone the engineers made for the assault.'

I still couldn't believe we could just wander into the buffer zone without noticing some sort of barrier – barbed wire, trenches, anything that would have given us enough reason to turn back. This particular position had only had a sand berm of similar size to the ones surrounding the camp areas of Camp Cambrai. Our only option was to get out of there but it wasn't just a case of turning tail and legging it back to the Kuwaiti side of the border. The UN buffer zone was the equivalent of no man's land between the trenches of the Somme in the First World War. If spotted, we could have been shot by the Iraqis, or even worse, by our own side. We also had to contend with the thought of landmines, and reconnaissance vehicles from Kuwaiti and coalition forces, let alone those from Iraq. Basically, we were in the shit.

We turned the Foden around and drove towards the Kuwaiti border, using the tracks we'd already made hoping we wouldn't drive over any delayed-action anti-tank mines. The idea of these was they would be fused by a first vehicle then detonated by a second, disrupting the rest of the convoy. The same result can be achieved by using anti-personnel mines against patrols. A detonated mine instantly separates the leading section of the group from the rest, making the task of probing the ground for further mines the responsibility of both parts of the patrol. This affects the soldiers psychologically and also slows their progress. Because of the volume of casualties, the number of personnel available to administer first aid is also reduced.

And Iraq supposedly had one-sixth of the world's planted landmines on its border with Kuwait – a statistic I didn't really want to remember from our pre-deployment lessons back in Grantham but which my subconscious decided to bring to my attention.

Because of the growing seriousness of our situation, Stuart and I decided to grab our rifles from behind our seats, load them with magazines of 25 rounds and make them ready. However, my webbing, containing the other three magazines, was placed inside one of the side bins. At this point, I called myself a few choice names for leaving it there. I was in two minds about whether to venture out of the cab, because of the risk of landmines. The psychological effect was already playing on my mind but I had no choice – I had to get my other magazines just in case I needed them.

Stuart could see the predicament I was in. 'Take two of mine, Kev, if you need 'em.' He grabbed his webbing from underneath the pile of crap he had on the bunk and was about to open his magazine pouches.

'No,' I replied. 'You never know what will happen, we may need all the rounds we can muster.'

Decision made. I climbed out of the cab and rested my right foot on the wheel hub. As I carefully lowered my left foot out of the cab, I slipped and landed in a heap on the soft sand. I shut my eyes and waited for a loud bang. Realising I was OK and wasn't sitting on any mines, I made my way down the side of the recovery vehicle, probing the surface with my boots. The side bin was only a few metres away but it might as well have been a few kilometres; it seemed to take hours to reach it.

Eventually, I got to the bin, stretched up to unlock the catch and opened the thin-skinned metal doors. Handfuls of sand and dust that had gathered in the bins poured over me, quickly followed by my webbing. Coughing and spluttering, I attempted to clear my eyes of the sand and catch my webbing but I lost my balance and fell backwards onto the ground. I shut my eyes once again but thankfully nothing happened. I began to sweat – this time with relief that I wasn't blown up, rather than from the heat of the sun.

Grabbing my webbing, I placed my arms through the yoke and snapped the belt buckle shut around my waist. I then gingerly shuffled my feet towards the cab, still trying to clear my throat and eyes of sand. Finally, I reached the front wheel and climbed into the cab. Stuart had already put on his CBA and helmet; I didn't waste time in doing so myself.

'You do realise one of us will have to act as a ground guide and walk in front of the Foden all the way back to the Kuwaiti line,' Stuart said softly, hoping I'd say I'd do it. 'And it was you who drove us to this position,' he added sarcastically.

'Now hang on a minute, it was you . . .' I stopped mid-sentence. A movement on the horizon had caught my eye. I diverted my eyes from Stuart and squinted to minimise the sun's glare through the windscreen.

'What's up? Seen something?' asked a concerned-looking Stuart.

'I don't know. I thought I could see a vehicle on the horizon, just to your left, about a klick [kilometre] or so away.' I pointed in the general direction of the movement.

Stuart scanned the area to see if he could make out any vehicles. 'I can't see a bloody thing, only sand being kicked up by the wind.'

'Maybe it's just a dust devil,' I said, half-jokingly, trying to convince myself it was. If it *was* a vehicle, enemy or friendly, we'd be in the shit – we were in the shit!

'You're right, Kev, there is a vehicle, and it appears to be coming this way.'

'Fuck this, we'll have to scarper, pronto, before they gain any ground on us. The further away we are from them, and the dust cloud we'll kick up, the less chance they'll notice who or what we are.'

I rammed the gear lever into first and started to turn the Foden around to regain our tyre tracks. It was now a case of fuck the landmines – either way, we'd end up dead. Adding to the cluster fuck, I'd picked a soft spot of sand and managed to travel only about 10 metres of the Foden's 27-metre turning circle.

'Stick all axles in!' Stuart shouted over the din of the engine.

I actuated all the differential locks, putting the vehicle into 6x6-drive, depressed the clutch and selected the crawler gear, making sure the revs didn't fall low enough to stall the engine. The Foden began to slowly crawl out of the soft sand but as the wheels turned, the sand pulled the vehicle in a little deeper, which caused the whole vehicle to shudder. With each shudder, the wheels locked intermittently, burying them even further and labouring the engine. I had to rev the bollocks out of the engine to keep moving, without bellying the axles, I hoped. If that happened, we wouldn't have had a cat-in-hell's chance of driving out, which would have left us with no alternative but to use the front self-recovery winch rope. For that, we needed time, which we didn't have.

Slowly but surely, the Foden pulled out of the soft sand and gradually gripped a harder surface but time was wasted, too much time. The other vehicle was approaching fast, and we still couldn't make out if it was friend or foe.

'It's stopped!' Stuart shouted, his head poking out of the passenger-door window, trying to keep an eye on it.

I glanced towards the passenger-side mirror but couldn't see anything. I was, however, more interested in getting the fuck out of there.

'Shit! It's the Iraqis, I'm sure of it,' Stuart screamed.

'What makes you so sure?'

'It's a wheeled vehicle, military, by the looks of it, but I don't recognise the type. Definitely not a HumVee or a Land-Rover, though, so it must be Iraqi.'

Stuart frantically searched for his binoculars as I continued to struggle with the Foden. He found them and quickly focused on the vehicle's position. 'They've stopped. Shit! They're getting out of the vehicle, and they are definitely Iraqis.'

We were finally facing towards Kuwait but it appeared we might have been too late. 'Do you think we should radio back?' I asked.

'Fuck off! We'll be up to our necks if we do that; besides, we'll look right tits. Leave it until we have to, providing the radio works.'

He had a point; we had to find a way out of this one ourselves. I raced up the gearbox – second, third, then fourth. There was no point selecting the range change for the rest of the gears, I'd have only ended up changing down again because of the grip of the sand around the tyres slowing the Foden down. It was best to leave it in fourth and keep a steady speed of 30 kph, which was our maximum speed on this terrain.

'Shit! They've got back into their vehicle and they're following us now. I don't fucking believe this is happening,' Stuart said, sounding a little more concerned.

'I'll keep driving, just keep an eye on them.'

The Iraqi vehicle was catching up but keeping at a cautious distance, about 400 metres behind, just visible in the side mirrors. Stuart leant out of the passenger-door window to keep them in view using his binoculars, watching their every move, or as best he could as we bounced along the rough desert terrain.

'They've stopped again, and they're getting out,' Stuart said. '*Fuck!* One of 'em has an RPG.'

I slammed on the brakes. 'Get the fuck out!'

We grabbed our rifles and jumped out of the cab, running a good distance away from the front of the Foden. I dived into the sand, quickly adjusting myself into the prone position. The undulation of the ground obscured my vision of the Iraqi vehicle, so I had to compromise and make do with squatting. Unfortunately, the Iraqi soldiers, especially the guy with the RPG, had us both in their sights. I glanced over to Stuart and could see he was doing the same, squatting down about ten metres to my left.

'OK, Stuart?'

'Yeah, now what?' he replied, sounding slightly pissed off, as if it was my fault we were in this situation.

By now, all of the occupants, five in total, had vacated the vehicle. The guy with the RPG (which is accurate to about 500 metres, or, to put it another way, well in range of us) had knelt down a few metres in front of the vehicle and the other three were scattered around the opened doors, using them as some sort of feeble cover and pointing their AKs directly towards our position. The fifth guy had a pair of binoculars and stood, legs astride, to the RPG guy's left, watching our every move and most probably wondering what the fuck a coalition recovery vehicle was doing in Iraq. I was wondering the very same thing.

Sweat began to drip from my eyebrows and into my eyes, stinging them and causing me to drop my rifle momentarily. I wiped the sweat from my eyes and hoped the Iraqis wouldn't open fire at that precise moment. By this stage, two or three minutes had passed, but it might as well have been two or three hours. This was crazy. What were we supposed to do now? I thought. With my next thought, I wondered if we were being pinned down whilst a second vehicle, maybe a BMP2 with a 30-mm cannon, was called in to assist them. With that in mind, I made a hasty decision.

'Stuart!'

'What?'

'I think they're pinning us down, waiting for assistance.'

There was a pause before Stuart answered. 'Yeah, I see what you mean. Will you take out the RPG or shall I?'

I thought for a moment, working out our next move after dropping the first target – the guy with the RPG, as he was the greatest threat. Then I played out their secondary moves, marking each target and anticipating their actions before they had the chance to realise what had hit them, not unlike playing a game of chess.

'What was your grouping on the ranges back at Grantham?' Stuart asked.

I frowned at his stupid question. 'Why?'

'Mine was 122.'

A grouping was when you fired 20 rounds at a distance of 100 metres into a number-11 target. The rounds were then counted as a group, measuring the distance between the two outermost hits, giving a maximum group measurement in millimetres. I thought to myself, 122, pretty shit. '88!' I replied.

'Bollocks!'

'No, honest,' I said, losing my concentration on our predicament slightly, feeling it was more important to defend my grouping score.

'You in the shooting team, then?'

'No.'

'Well, you should be with a score like that. If that was me . . .'

'Stuart!' He fell silent so I could continue. 'Forget about that. I'll take out the RPG and you take out the guys on your left, then I'll take out the guys on my right. As soon as I open fire, you'd better be right behind me, Stuart.' I glanced at him, I thought probably for the last time. All I could see was a big grin across his mush, which said to me, yes, he was right behind me. I had a funny feeling he was about to enjoy the next few minutes. I took two deep breaths and with the RPG guy lined up in my sights, was about to deliver my first live round in anger.

'Kev!'

I rolled my eyes, then diverted my attention to Stuart. 'What?'

'Should we wait until they fire the first shot? Otherwise we could be responsible for starting the war. And you do realise, by rights, they're not the enemy, not yet, anyway. Rules of engagement and all that.'

Stuart had a point, a strong and valid point. If we did open fire, it might not start the war but it would create further ammunition for Saddam's regime to use, and say to the media that we were the aggressors, making them the innocent party. We found ourselves in a precarious position and couldn't see an easy solution.

'So, what do you suggest?' I asked, still in the squatting position. By then, pins and needles had well and truly engulfed my right foot.

'I dunno!'

That wasn't the answer I was looking for. I also couldn't believe we were having an argument as we faced our first actual life-or-death situation. This wasn't how I thought I'd react to my first fire-fight – arguing over grouping scores and the politics of our position while desperately trying to think of a diplomatic solution to our crisis. Whilst we discussed what to do next, the RPG guy lowered his weapon. The other three guys quickly followed suit and lowered their rifles too.

'What the fuck?' Stuart said under his breath, loud enough for me to hear.

'Keep 'em in your sights, Stuart. If they get in their vehicle and drive straight for us, we'll have no choice but to open up.' I stretched out my arms to relieve some of the tension and reposition myself but still kept low and remained in the squatting position. The pins and needles were beginning to annoy me but my foot would have to wait a few more minutes.

We could hear his engine start, even over the noise of the Foden ticking over. Here we go, I thought, as I made a final adjustment to my line of sight. I glanced at Stuart to make sure he looked OK. Yep, he was all right. Two deep breaths and . . . what the fuck now? I relaxed my rifle from my right eye to get a better view of the Iraqi vehicle.

'It's turning away from us!' Stuart shouted.

I glanced once more at Stuart to acknowledge his remark but soon looked back at our retreating target. 'C'mon Stuart, let's get out of here, whilst we have the chance. There might be another vehicle joining him.'

I threw my rifle into the cab and jumped into the driver's seat. Stuart didn't hang about either, and we were soon tanking it towards the Kuwaiti border. As I gathered speed, Stuart unfolded the map across his lap, desperately trying to find our position against the grid marked on the GPS. I looked in my rear-view mirror every other second to see if the Iraqis had changed their minds and decided to follow us.

'Can you see anything?' I asked.

Stuart had a quick glance through his open window.

'Nothing, I think we're safe.' He then continued to scan the map.

As we increased our distance, we simultaneously sighed with relief. 'That is what I call a close shave,' I said, with a nervous giggle.

'There is one thing, well, a couple, really,' muttered Stuart.

I eagerly waited for his comments. 'Well?'

'The first thing is, I don't think we'll come across any mines.'

I frowned, confused by his comment. 'Why's that?'

'That vehicle didn't seem to drive down a pre-determined route.'

Good point, I thought. That made me feel a little more confident. 'And the second?'

'The second thing is, do you really think they'll just drive off without saying or doing anything?'

Another good point, which made me wonder if the answer he was about to give would be the one I'd want to hear. I prompted for an explanation. 'Well?'

'I think they radioed back our position and we'll start to see incoming from their artillery.'

At first I smiled and even dared a slight laugh, albeit somewhat forced. But he was being serious – bang went my attempts to rebuild our confidence.

Stuart looked up from his map and checked out the terrain in front of us, as if he was waiting for the impending incoming, mumbling to himself, 'Can you give any other reason why they fucked off without firing a single shot? After all, we were the ones in their territory.'

No, I couldn't, not immediately, anyway. For the next few minutes, we diverted our eyes from the rear-view mirrors and started to look up for any incoming, as if we could actually see artillery shells raining down on us.

It suddenly dawned on me. 'We are now roughly half a kilometre from the border, if not less.' I waited for a reply – not a murmur – so I continued. 'Do you really think they'll start raining shells on us when we're this close to the border?' I looked at Stuart, wearing a smug grin.

He looked up from his map and stared out of the windscreen, deep in thought. I could almost hear his mind ticking over, weighing up my question and trying to think of a clever answer. 'Oh, yeah, never thought of that,' was the best he could come up with. 'Dead ahead, gap in the sand berm,' he quickly added, changing the subject as he pointed towards the borderline.

I noticed the gap, about 300 metres ahead, and put my foot down hard on the accelerator. We couldn't reach the border quickly enough. Although we weren't exactly out of the woods, passing through the sand berm certainly made us feel a little safer. I drove for about another kilometre before I stopped the vehicle. I pulled on the handbrake lever and sat back in my seat, letting out another sigh of relief. I lit a cigarette and took in the surroundings, whilst Stuart checked our bearings and grid reference. We still had a vehicle casualty to recover and time was racing on.

I checked my watch – 1430hrs zulu. This meant we had about an hour of daylight left. Stuart found our position on the map and after half an hour managed to direct us to the casualty. It turned out to be a CVRT Scimitar on a reconnaissance task, seeking potential targets and movement of enemy vehicles just across the Iraqi border, but it had broken down with some sort of gearbox problem.

We disengaged the final drive and hooked it up to the back of the Foden using the hollibones – a V-shaped heavy-duty steel tube hinged at one end, allowing the other two ends to bolt either side of the CVRT using various adaptors. The casualty could now be steered by the recovery vehicle when towed. The pivoted end, with a forged towing eye welded to one side of the hinge, was connected to the back of the Foden via a tow pintle. With the CVRT hooked up and checked, the crew of three decided to stay in their vehicle rather than squeeze into our cab, which was fine by us. Not the usual practice, for health and safety reasons, but hey, there was a war on – well, nearly.

The drive back with the casualty would take a good few hours but not as long as it had taken to find the bloody thing. The sun had well and truly set by the time we completed the hooking up, which, of course, meant driving whilst under tactical conditions, which meant no lights. Stuart did ask the crew if they'd seen any suspicious vehicles, but they hadn't, thank God. We decided to keep quiet about our little escapade, as it could have ruffled a few feathers back at the CV. We didn't even mention it to Phil or his crew, just in case it got back to the ASM (adjutant sergeant major), because I was pretty certain what he would have said.

7

IT CAN ONLY GET WORSE

The law of averages made us think we'd had our quota of bad luck for one day. Surely, things couldn't get any worse. Although it wasn't entirely his fault, Stuart had lost our position on the return route. Or maybe it was my fault for not listening to his instructions. Either way, we were lost. The crew of the CVRT casualty were battened down in their vehicle and thankfully blissfully unaware of our predicament. Hopefully, they were getting their heads down for a kip.

I knew we weren't driving towards the border again because the compass on the dashboard gave a reading of south-south-west; the problem was the pitch dark. In the middle of a desert, there isn't a lot of ambient light – no streetlights or even a reflection from an animal's eye – just thousands of square kilometres of nothing. The only light we had came from the moon, and that was occasionally extinguished by the odd cloud.

Military jets screeched past at low level, flying at warp factor eight, momentarily interrupting the eerie stillness of the desert. They were most probably on reconnaissance sorties, or checking for recovery vehicles that had ventured into enemy territory by mistake. Although we couldn't see them, we knew they were military because commercial airlines had been banned from the no-fly zone. Besides, who'd be mad enough to fly around Iraqi airspace at the time of an impending conflict? We also knew they weren't Iraqi jets because: 1) they would have been shot down as soon as the undercarriage lifted after take-off; and 2) Saddam Hussein gave the Iranians most of his air force jets for safekeeping during the 1991 conflict – and when it was over, they wouldn't give them back. Isn't life a bitch!

Stuart checked and double-checked our position on the map using the green fluorescent glow of the GPS display screen. If he had used a torch or the internal cab lights, we would have been seen from miles away and become an easy target. My only option at that moment was to keep on our present course, preventing us from straying into Iraq, again.

A further hour passed. We'd travelled about 20 kilometres and had detoured around a soft sand dune, but still we couldn't pick up any sign of vehicle tracks. Then bingo – tracks galore. All we had to do was follow them until we picked up our route on the GPS. This brought a smile to our faces and a feeling that we'd finally turned the last corner – we were on our way home. Our smiles soon disappeared when 100 or so metres ahead and to my right we saw, silhouetted against the moon, a large vehicle, tracked, on top of the slight incline we were ascending.

Shit! We'd spotted it too late and had to think the worst – that its occupants had spotted us. The question was whether it was an Iraqi recce patrol. After all, we'd managed to penetrate the border unnoticed. No, it couldn't have been, otherwise there would have been a string of tracer rounds and God knows what else whizzing past us. So, who the fuck could it be? Friendly forces, perhaps? As I mulled over our predicament, Stuart decided to take the initiative and poked his head out of the cupola; at least now we'd have instant covering fire should any fireworks start – from friendly forces or otherwise.

With Stuart covering our approach, I made up my mind to continue driving rather than stop for three reasons: 1) If we could see them, sure as eggs they could see us, so coming to a sudden halt would raise suspicion and most likely attract incoming; 2) Whilst I kept driving, slowly but steadily, the natural tendency would be to believe we were friendly forces and that we warranted a challenge, rather than being fired at first; and 3) If they were to open fire, a moving target at a distance of 100 metres in the pitch dark would be harder to hit than a standing target, and would give us both a chance to take cover and leg it.

As we got closer, it became apparent it was a Russian-built BMP1 – a tracked, armoured personnel carrier complete with its 73-mm cannon mounted on a turret shaped like an upside down frying pan – and therefore an Iraqi vehicle. It was just sitting there, in the middle of the desert, now some 30 or so metres ahead of us. It looked as if it had seen better days and appeared abandoned but we couldn't be too complacent, especially in light of our day thus far.

We were now roughly ten metres away and couldn't see any signs of life, which certainly relieved some of the tension. I then noticed there weren't any tracks leading to the vehicle from the north, which would have been the case had it come from Iraq. Furthermore, the front of the vehicle was facing north. I came to the conclusion it had definitely been abandoned. Stuart must have decided likewise and sat back in his seat, the threat of being fired upon having lapsed. Instead, we were now just confused as to why this Iraqi armoured vehicle was in Kuwait.

Although it was dark, it was possible to make out that the ground surrounding it was disturbed and scarred with deeper, fresher tracks made by a heavier vehicle – a tank, perhaps. A BMP1 couldn't weigh any more than 15–20 tonnes, so they definitely didn't belong to this particular vehicle. The other tracks were wider and had therefore been made by a considerably larger piece of armour, which had approached from the south, indicating it belonged to the coalition. My second thought was that it had been abandoned during the last conflict and might have been dragged to its present location because it had been in the way of some military track or route.

A few minutes later, we came across another armoured vehicle. This time a BMP2, which has basically the same BMP1 chassis but a 30-mm stabilised cannon mounted on a two-man turret. We drove past, thinking it too had been moved by coalition vehicles, but something didn't seem right.

'Where are we?' I asked, trying to sound calm and collected.

'Not that far to go now. According to the map, we've about 9 Ks until we hit Route Tampa, it should then be—'

BOOM!

'*What the fuck was that?*' I shouted.

The Foden shook violently, all 27 tonnes of it, as the blast went right through us. My ears popped as the shock wave rushed past, momentarily deafening me and causing a high-pitched ringing in my ears. Stuart leant out of the passenger-door window to see if he could get any bearing on the explosion, which had come from somewhere behind us. At first, I thought we'd triggered a mine with the CVRT because I knew the Foden wasn't hit – we were still moving. I looked into the rear-view mirror and about 100 metres behind, I could see white molten steel and brilliant orange flames shooting out of the BMP1 we'd just passed. Shrapnel quickly followed the explosion and rained down on the roof of our cab. I dropped a gear and put my foot down in the hope of clearing any further explosions.

Stuart was straight on the radio. 'Hello Kilo 24, this is 24 Echo, over . . .' Stuart repeated his call but the only reply he got was static. 'Fucking heap of shit! I'll try again. Hello Kilo 24 . . .' But it was no use.

I managed to pick up enough speed to engage the range change and use fifth. The ride wasn't very comfortable but then again I suppose that didn't matter. The CVRT would have glided across the ground with only the occasional bump to contend with but the sound of the explosion had definitely grabbed the crew's attention. I could hear the crew commander shouting from his hatch. He must have been screaming like a madman for me to hear him over the noise of the Foden, but I chose to ignore him. Whilst he screamed and waved his arms, at least I knew he was alive.

'Where are we on that fucking map?' I shouted, as Stuart studied it once again, desperately searching for our position. 'That couldn't have been the Iraqis. They're bloody nuts if it was, we're well into Kuwaiti territory.'

Stuart studied the map and glanced outside, trying to pick up some kind of reference point, which was virtually impossible in the pitch dark. He then noticed something to his right, on the horizon, as we reached the top of another incline. It was a faint shimmer of street lighting lining a road, about five or six kilometres ahead, although it was difficult to judge such a distance at night.

'Kev, is that a road ahead of us?'

I diverted my attention and took a quick glance but couldn't really see anything. I was more interested in further explosions and avoiding the huge holes which suddenly appeared from nowhere and nearly swallowed us up along with the CVRT, as we had found out to our cost on a couple of occasions.

He checked his map and the grid reference on the GPS. 'Yes! It's Route Tampa.'

I had faith in his navigation and finally trusted my instinct that we had in fact reached safety – but I still had thousands of questions running through my mind, like who the hell was throwing shells at us?

'What d'ya reckon caused that explosion? Iraqi shells or what?' I asked.

Stuart paused to think before answering. 'Maybe it was a booby trap, or some dodgy abandoned shell we triggered somehow.'

'When we'd already passed it by about 100 metres? I don't think so. That was definitely incoming.'

'Must have been the Iraqis, then, unless . . .' He went deep into thought, studying his map again.

'Unless what, Stuart? Stuart!'

'I don't believe it.'

'Believe what, Stuart? Believe what!

The radio sprang into life, making us both jump. Stuart picked up the receiver. '24 Echo receiving . . .'

I didn't take any notice of Stuart shouting down the mic. I couldn't grasp the conversation anyway; it was difficult to hear over the noise of the engine. Whilst I concentrated on the driving, Stuart finished off his report on the explosion. When he'd finished, he started to laugh. 'You're never going to believe this, not in a million years.'

'What?' I snapped, not really too sure if I wanted to hear what he had to say.

'They've just confirmed what I thought. The CVRT we're towing reported the position of the explosion back to its CV.' He started to laugh again but took a deep breath, trying to compose himself before carrying on.

'Their CV contacted ours. We've just driven through an American artillery range.'

I lost my concentration for a second and struggled with the steering. 'A what?'

'Yeah, a live firing range. The Yanks are on a bloody night shoot! Those abandoned vehicles were put there as targets.'

I slowly shook my head, but sighed with relief at the same time. 'How the fuck did we end up in the middle of an artillery range, and why didn't they see us?'

'Beats me. The Yanks decided to extend their range but didn't tell anyone. The original boundary on the map is clearly marked and our position back there was well clear of it, but the extension put us well inside the boundary.'

I couldn't believe it. After all that had happened, the fact we'd nearly had a fire-fight with a bunch of Iraqi soldiers earlier in the day, it was the bloody Yanks who ended up taking pot shots at us.

The lights on the horizon grew bigger as we drove closer; it *was* Route Tampa. We reached the kerbside and the tall, orange-glow sodium street lamps illuminated either side of the entire length of the road, instilling in us the confidence that we were in a safe zone. Realising we'd be back in camp very soon, adrenalin stopped flowing through my veins and my body seemed to know I wasn't in any danger, making me tired and drowsy.

The time was nearly 2000hrs zulu. I drove towards the other side of the dual carriageway, passing over the wide sandy central reservation to turn left and head south. The sodium lights illuminated our vehicle casualty and I couldn't see any dramas, so I settled down in my seat and built up speed. All I could think of was grabbing a few hours' kip.

Just over half an hour later, we reached the entrance to Camp Cambrai. I passed the sentry, flashed my MoD 90 and came to a halt so Stuart could jump out and give our report to the CV. I then turned right towards the CRARRV, swinging around the back of it so I could pull up next to its offside. I turned off the engine, lit a cigarette and sat back in my seat, enjoying the fact we had made it back in one piece.

When Stuart returned from the CV, he told the crew of the CVRT they'd have to stay the night, until their unit decided what to do with them. He then jumped in the Foden's passenger seat and started to laugh.

'What's up now?'

'Nothing. I was just thinking, this was your first live job of your tour, right?'

'Yeah, and?'

'We managed to stray into Iraq and most likely drove into a minefield, came face to face with an Iraqi patrol and nearly had our first fire-fight, got lost in the dark, the radio's fucked and we virtually got blown to pieces by the Yanks. And the war hasn't even started yet.'

I looked at him and started to laugh myself.

'And it can only get worse,' he added, with a smug grin.

After that first live recovery job, I certainly quickly learnt that I wasn't on exercise – even though the days leading up to 20 March had felt like nothing more than just that. No enemy in sight (except the vehicle we had encountered across the border), no incoming artillery and no terrorist attacks of any kind, even though we were warned of such possibilities. We did hear about a bunch of paras making contact with an Iraqi patrol on the border, similar to our encounter. The paras, however, decided to approach them and gave the Iraqis a choice – either drop your weapons and fuck off, or stay and be killed. The Iraqis decided to fuck off, which was a wise choice, if I say so myself.

8

CALM BEFORE THE STORM

Wednesday, 19 March 1000hrs zulu Parked on the brow of a sand-dune facing the main track leading into the camp, I watched vehicle movements vastly increase. From our position and to our left, Route Tampa was busy with convoys of British and American hardware. Hundreds of artillery pieces – tanks, troop carriers and support vehicles – thundered past, travelling towards the Iraqi border. Above, flying at low level, Chinooks and 'Huey' helicopters followed the convoys, whilst Cobra gunships buzzed about like bees around a honeypot. I gave up counting when I reached 70, as more and more squads of them kept appearing from what seemed like nowhere.

Once, when walking back from the cookhouse towards my Foden with my paper plate of piping hot range stew, I first had to dodge the Warriors and CVRTs racing past, kicking up a wall of sand and dust. Thinking I was safe to continue across the track, I was suddenly strafed by an extremely low-flying F16. At the last moment, I could hear an ear-piercing screech coming from my right. I stopped and looked up at the fast-approaching jet, which seemed to be heading straight for me. All I could do was dive for cover, sending my range stew airborne as the F16 dive-bombed the camp, not unlike a Second World War German Stuka.

The pilot pulled out of his dive from a height of no more than 30 metres, leaving a trail of black smoke over the camp as the jet throttled back into a vertical climb. As I looked up at the bastard, coughing and spitting out sand and fumes, I saw him 'tip' his wings at us, waving them from side to side as if to say 'Gotcha!'. He was either returning from a reconnaissance sortie, in which case he would have been on an incredible adrenalin high, or he was on a training exercise using our camp as a pretend target. Either way, he was lucky nobody opened up on him; trigger fingers were beginning to itch.

Stuart, who witnessed the whole event from the comfort of the Foden, fell about laughing – as did everyone else nearby who wasn't affected by the dive-bombing. Another quick trip to the cookhouse was called for and I was soon back in the driver's seat of the Foden with a fresh plate of steaming stew – just the sort of meal you wanted in the desert sun.

Trying to catch a few hours' kip after that hefty meal was virtually impossible, not only because of the constant drone of heavy armour pounding the tarmac on the dual carriageway but also because of tracked vehicles deciding to pass through our camp. And our Foden, of course, was parked about 50 metres away from the traffic jam. There was also an uneasy feel around the camp that something was about to happen. We had had many dry runs before but something definitely felt different.

A knock on the passenger-side door woke Stuart and me from our afternoon snooze. ''Ere, take these, will ya!' a voice shouted from outside the cab, trying to make itself heard over the engine noise in the camp.

Stuart leant out of his window and grabbed the small, flat boxes from the soldier's hands, passing two of them to me. NAPS and BATS tablets. Oh boy, something was going to kick off, and soon. I placed them in my NBC haversack and sat back in my seat.

'What do you reckon then, Kev?' Stuart said, as he read the instructions for his NAPS tablets.

'Doesn't look good, does it?' I pointed to the NAPS tablets Stuart held in his hand. 'Will you take 'em, then, the tablets?'

'Dunno, what about you?'

I thought about it for a second. 'I don't think I'll bother.' We'd heard scare stories about the NAPS, which were rumoured to make you violently sick and cause a continuous headache. And to see some of the guys froth at the mouth after taking these tablets certainly convinced me not to bother. As for the BATS, they were new to us, and I assumed they would have the same side effects as the NAPS. After all, we'd already had countless injections and I for one didn't want to add to the cocktail of chemicals swimming around my body.

Stuart finished reading the label and placed his tablets in his haversack. 'Fuck it, I don't think I'll bother either.'

By now, the time was reaching 1130hrs zulu. We both became increasingly restless as we waited for the inevitable, although we didn't know when that would be. All we could do was sit and wait. The heat didn't help our restlessness either. The cab doors were wide open and the cupola lid was removed to try and capture a through breeze, even though the wind was just as hot as the sun. I switched on the radio but the only station on which we could find programmes in English was Radio Kuwait, and all we could hear on that was a broadcast about what to do in the event of an air raid. There wasn't any news of an 'invasion', so it seemed even the media fraternity were unaware of any imminent breach of the Iraqi border.

A further hour passed and still the convoys on Route Tampa thundered past. More and more troop carriers could be seen, with countless fuel tankers taking up the rear of the packets, quickly followed by endless convoys of HumVee utility vehicles with their roof-mounted 50-calibre machine guns. USMC (United States Marine Corps) Cobra and Chinook helicopters continued to pass overhead, joined by numerous Black Hawk troop carriers. Surely the shit was going to start soon, I thought.

There was another knock on the cab door, this time on my side. ''Ere, mate, I've been told to give you these.' The same soldier passed me a cardboard box.

'What's in this?' I asked, leaning out of the window to grab it from him.

'You'll see,' he replied, walking back towards the CV.

'What's he brought this time?' asked an intrigued Stuart.

I opened the overlapping flaps of the box to reveal two S10 NBC canisters, shrink-wrapped in foil, two large Mk5 NBC suits complete with boots and gloves, also shrink-wrapped, three atropine pens, three morphine pens and four menu-G 24-hour rat packs. I looked at Stuart for some kind of explanation but he too had a blank expression on his face. I passed him his share of the goodies when another knock at my door distracted me. This time a different soldier passed me a long cardboard roll and a bundle of maps wrapped in a polythene bag.

'You'll need these, mate. Have fun.'

I didn't say anything. I grabbed the roll and maps, and quickly ripped open the polythene wrapper. Stuart opened one end of the cardboard roll to reveal yet more maps of

Iraq: one at a scale of 1:50,000 and the other 1:100,000. As Stuart and I frantically placed the maps in some kind of order, thinking there was an urgent need to do so, there was a further knock at my door.

'O'group in two minutes at the CV,' the voice shouted. Without hesitation, we grabbed our haversacks and rifles and made our way there. The entrance was heaving with bodies, pens and notepads poised at the ready, everyone eager to find out if the balloon was about to go up.

'Gentlemen, be ready to move within one hour's notice,' the ASM ordered. 'Next location is at code-name 'Barnsley', grid 625–175, which is the FAA [forward assembly area] just over the border in Iraq where we'll meet with the rest of the battle group.' He then gave details of vehicle packets, which consisted of A1 and A2 vehicle movements. Call sign 24 Echo, my Foden, was the tail-end Charlie of the A1 packet, which consisted of eight vehicles. He finished giving his orders and asked if there were any questions. No reply. 'That's it, gentlemen. Fuck off and check your kit and vehicles.'

An eerie silence fell in the tent as we all looked at each other, caught out at the sudden urgency of the task ahead. Walking back to the Foden, Stuart and I remained silent, taking in what the ASM had said. Although he never actually mentioned when we would be moving forward, the inevitable was definitely drawing near, which gave me a strange feeling in the pit of my stomach. I wasn't scared, at least I don't think I was; maybe because I didn't know what to be scared of. After all, nothing had happened – yet.

We sat in the Foden contemplating the ASM's words.

'Start the engine, Kev, I'll make us a brew.'

I turned over the engine and set the hand throttle to 1,000 revs. 'I suppose we'd better check our kit. How many 5.56-mm rounds do we have?' I asked suddenly, as if it was the most important thing to remember.

'Sixty. The same ones issued to me when I arrived.'

'Yeah, me too.'

'Do you think we'll need more?' Stuart asked.

'You can never have too many.'

I turned off the engine when the BV boiled and Stuart made the tea. I sat back in the driver's seat and lit a cigarette as I watched the never-ending convoys driving up Route Tampa. 'I reckon it'll kick off in the next 24 hours, cos the Iraqis are bound to have noticed this lot moving towards them.'

'Nah, they wouldn't have noticed a thing,' replied Stuart.

I looked at him, frowning at his comment. 'What makes you say that?'

'Just look at the odds. They don't have any aircraft in the skies, no satellites, no radar left and no recce vehicles anywhere near the border, well, not to make any difference.'

Stuart had a point. Saddam may have known about the odd military vehicle movement, thanks to the biased Western media reporting details of coalition movements around the world without thinking of the consequences, naively giving Saddam and his generals delicate information. Thankfully, as far as I know, the Iraqi Army never knew the exact number or location of vehicle movements prior to the breaching of the border. In effect, he was militarily blind. Not the best position to be in – especially as he was on the brink of being attacked by some of the most powerful armed forces in the world. That would teach him to brag that he still had a mighty army at his disposal.

As we drank our tea, we checked and double-checked

our kit, including the recovery equipment on the Foden. The time was nearly 1515hrs zulu, which meant it was 1815hrs local. Checked and ready to move, it was now a case of playing the waiting game. Our minds started to create scenarios we'd have to face. I soon found myself thinking of my family back home – again. I had to try and stop such thoughts, otherwise they could have caused big problems. I had to concentrate on the job and be professional. We were trained soldiers, albeit 'part-timers', and still had a job to do.

Stuart and I had proved over and over again to the regulars that we could cope with recovery tasks, but what about under fire? How would we react to someone trying to stop us doing our job and actually trying to kill us? Or how would we react to killing someone? The ASM had warned us to expect to come under fire from small arms, automatic fire, mortars and artillery shells. How would we cope with the horrific casualties? Especially us recy mech crews out on a task in the middle of a battle. We were expected to look after ourselves without any kind of immediate back-up. Basically, we were on our own and had to fight our way out of any situation using the weapons we carried.

We were also told to expect to be ambushed. Not only by the Iraqi Army but also by militia groups dressed in civilian clothing. And, of course, not forgetting the real threat of a chemical bombardment. Recovery crews relied on themselves to figure out if an attack was chemical or not. Not easy when the enemy could throw in the odd conventional explosion just to confuse the situation. Unfortunately, we didn't have the luxury of having artillery support – or relying on a bunch of LI (Light Infantry) guys armed with 94-mm LAWs (light anti-tank weapons), .50-cal machine guns and gimpies. What we carried was all we had to defend ourselves.

The wind started to pick up. We ignored it at first but within an hour it looked as if it could turn nasty. By 1700hrs zulu, it had transformed into a sandstorm. All we could do was sit it out and pray that 1 Div (1 (UK) Armoured Division) decided not to make the move that night. By 1800hrs the daylight had almost disappeared, thanks to the sandstorm, which added to the difficulty of seeing anything outside the cab. As we battened down to ride out the storm, someone knocked on the passenger door. Stuart opened it slightly to acknowledge the person outside.

'Move your vehicle to the end of the A1 packet, buddy,' the voice shouted, just about audible over the noise of the storm.

Stuart turned to me once he'd closed the door. 'You'll love this, Kev, we're to move to the rear of A1.'

I didn't answer him. I knew something like this would happen, so in a way I was ready for any last-minute panic movements – this was the British Army after all.

Starting the engine, I slowly moved forward. It was a waste of time putting on any headlights because of the sand being kicked up by the storm. It was like using headlights in a severe snowstorm or thick fog – all I would have seen was a reflection of the beam from my headlights. So I switched on my sidelights instead, which helped slightly. I only had about 400 metres to drive but amazingly it took over 5 minutes to complete. If I'd run over some unfortunate squaddie, I wouldn't have known anything about it.

Once parked at the rear of A1 packet, I switched off the engine and sighed with relief that my little trip was over. It did indicate, though, that 1 Div had decided to start the push and wanted all battle groups to be ready.

The storm, however, was becoming unbearable. The cab doors of the Foden weren't exactly a good fit and every so often a strong gust would peel back the edge of the doors, allowing sand and dust to enter the cab and swirl around inside. Stuart suffered the worst of it because the windows were wound up and he had to put up with my cigarette smoke. Bless him, he never said anything and just sat back in his seat studying his German road atlas under his torchlight.

9

THE SHIT HAS
HIT THE FAN

Thursday, 20 March 0020hrs zulu I must have dozed off. One consolation of the sandstorm was that it cooled the air, which made it a little more comfortable for sleeping, if only for a few hours. I checked my watch – 0020hrs zulu – then looked up, distracted by the movement of two, three, five, then eight heavy tracked vehicles, Challenger 2s. I counted twelve in total passing our packet and heading for the camp entrance towards the carriageway, although it was difficult to tell in the dark. All I could see were the sidelights on the front of the tanks and, of course, I could hear the deep grunt of their engines, even above the howl of the continuing sandstorm.

'I wonder where they're going?' I muttered, straining my neck to watch them pass.

'Wonder what?' Stuart asked, lifting his head out of his atlas.

'Those tanks, I wonder where they're going.'

Stuart gave a half-interested glance towards the passing

armour. 'Dunno,' he replied, and returned to his maps, not really paying much attention.

As the tanks rolled by, a number of Warriors took the rear, maybe half a dozen or so. Then the distinctive sound of a CRARRV joined them; I think two passed our position. Over the noise of the armour and the storm, a rapid knocking came from Stuart's door. He lifted his head from the back of his seat once again and looked out of the window. The knocking continued, then the door opened.

'Let me in, lads!' a voice cried out, muffled by the sound of the wind as he clambered inside the cab. It was Danny. 'It looks like it's started,' he said excitedly, dusting himself off and making himself comfortable on the dashboard.

Stuart and I looked at each other wearing blank expressions, instantly thinking the worst, but gave him the benefit of the doubt.

'What's started?' Stuart asked, still looking blank.

'The war, the fucking war!'

Stuart responded with an 'Oh, fuck!'

I didn't say anything. I just felt the blood run from my head and a sense of foreboding rush through my body, kicking off that sick feeling I'd had earlier in the pit of my stomach.

Danny took out his cigarettes and lit a couple, passing one to me, before he explained what was happening. 'You see all this armoured shit racing through the camp, it's off to take out some T72s.'

'What?' I replied, choking on a lungful of cigarette smoke.

Danny took a drag of his before continuing. 'The Yanks have fired a bunch of cruise missiles at Baghdad. They had some kind of intelligence report that Saddam was on the move, so they blitzed the building he was in, along with a bunch of his henchmen.'

'Did the missiles get him?' I asked.

'Dunno. We haven't had any feedback yet.'

'So what about these T72s?' Stuart asked, more eager to find out about the tank movements.

Danny took another drag of his cigarette before answering. 'There've been reports of a massive movement of T72s heading straight for the Kuwaiti border, over 100 of them, I heard.'

'Bollocks!' I replied.

'No, straight-up. I'm only telling you what I've heard over the net. The T72s have been reported coming this way, using the sandstorm as cover.'

'The sneaky bastards,' replied Stuart.

'So, how come you haven't taken your CRARRV?' I asked.

Danny took a few more quick drags of his cigarette before flicking the stub out of the small gap at the top of the driver's-door window. 'They didn't want us, not yet anyway. But I'd better go, knowing my luck we'll be moving out any minute. See ya later, lads.' Danny jumped out of the cab and headed for his CRARRV. Stuart quickly closed the door after him to try and keep out as much of the sand and dust being whipped up by the storm as possible. I lit another cigarette, contemplating the news.

'You're putting away the smokes, aren't you?' Stuart commented.

'Yeah, but I don't think I'll bother giving up just yet.'

I sat back in my seat and rested my legs on top of the steering wheel, wondering what would happen next. I suppose the whole camp was wondering what would happen next. Many thoughts went through my mind, in much the same way that many describe life flashing before their eyes in a life-or-death situation. I began to imagine what we could expect to see as we crossed the border. The

Challengers wouldn't have any problem wiping out the T72s, even though they were heavily outnumbered. The T72s wouldn't stand a chance. It was the destruction left behind I wondered about, and the Challenger crews. I hoped they would return safely. I'd already met some of the crews and some of them were just kids. Only a handful had ever seen actual battle. The majority, like me, were still battlefield virgins.

It wasn't long before I dozed off once again. And after what seemed only minutes, I woke up to find it was daylight. Stuart was fast asleep curled up under his sleeping bag. Outside, the sandstorm had finally dispersed, giving way to a strong early-morning desert sun shining brightly through the windscreen. There was little movement of vehicles and only a few squaddies running around in a blind panic – something I had expected to see after the news we'd received from Danny. Or had I dreamt it? Yes, that was it, I dreamt the whole thing, I thought. But no, I hadn't. And what made it even more of a reality was the distinct gap in the sand where Danny's CRARRV once stood, leaving only its track signature heading towards the camp exit. I felt my heart miss a beat. I started the engine and switched on the BV, prompting Stuart to wake up.

'What's up?' he asked, as he stuffed his sleeping bag into its compression sack. I stared out of the windscreen, looking at nothing in particular. 'I'm wondering what the fuck's going to happen.'

'We'll be all right,' he replied, trying to reassure me.

'Do you really think that?'

'No, but ignorance is bliss.' His light-hearted comment managed to raise a smile on my face. We had to get used to the fact the war had started.

A quick wash and shave and a change of clothing was required – the combats I was wearing had taken a battering from the sandstorm, even though I had spent most of it inside the cab. The truck also needed a dusting down and the air-filter housing was almost full of sand and needed immediate attention. The last thing the battle group wanted was its only Foden recovery vehicle out of action just because we'd forgotten to clean the air filter. Our rifles needed stripping and cleaning too, due to the soft powder-like sand getting into the working parts, even though we used insulation tape to cover them. Attaching an empty magazine to the rifle to stop sand entering from underneath didn't work either. Our only hope was that this new improved SA80 (A2) rifle would function well in desert conditions. We still had to clean it three or four times a day to try and keep the chances of a stoppage to a minimum.

The time now was 0330hrs zulu. Breakfast consisted of our 24-hour rat packs. The cookhouse had packed up and gone, although the tents were still erect. I was surprised to see them still standing after the sandstorm. Stuart placed the foil-packed meals in the BV to warm them through – meatballs and pasta, for breakfast. As we tucked in, we could hear the distinct sound of an explosion in the distance, quickly followed by a loud thud. It came from the north, probably about five kilometres or so away.

'Gas! Gas! Gas!' someone shouted from a Land-Rover to my immediate right, quickly followed by his vehicle horn sounding one second on, one second off. Shit! This was for real.

I threw what was left of my breakfast out of the window, stopped breathing and closed my eyes, frantically fumbling around for my haversack, which was somewhere next to me. When I eventually found it, I managed to open the lid and take out my respirator, quickly pulling it over my face. I blew out hard, shouting, 'Gas, Gas, Gas!' as we'd been taught to do over and over again, then opened my eyes to see if Stuart was OK. Noticing he too had donned his respirator and didn't appear to be suffering from any symptoms, I wound up my window and sat back in my seat trying to catch my breath, which wasn't easy wearing a respirator. Stuart quickly wound up his window, instantly cocooning us in an already hot cab.

My worst fear had now been realised, only this time I couldn't remove the mask to catch a few sneaky deep breaths of unrestricted air. If I did, I would be affected by whatever chemical had been used in the ballistic attack. Amazingly, I took control of my fear and forced myself to calm down and be aware of our situation. Neither Stuart nor I were wearing our noddy suits. Did this matter? Should we put them on? Should we start the decontamination drill? I went over the training in my mind.

We were relatively safe whilst under cover or inside a vehicle, even though it was a Foden with a plastic cab and ill-fitting doors. A nerve agent won't penetrate skin, it will only affect the respiratory system, so there was no need to cover ourselves with DKP. If droplets were falling, for example from a blister agent, they wouldn't penetrate the vehicle's skin, therefore wouldn't land on us. The vapours, however, could still be effective, so a respirator was very necessary.

Forty minutes passed before the all-clear bellowed across the camp. I soon ripped off my respirator to catch a lungful of unrestricted air. Stuart quickly did the same.

'That was exciting, wasn't it?' he said sarcastically.

I didn't reply. I was too busy cleaning the inside of my respirator. Sweat soon built up in this hot climate, especially when the cab doors and windows were shut – and you were shitting yourself. Stuart opened his door to let the fresh-ish breeze inside and I opened mine, allowing the air to circulate around the cab.

'Our first gas attack; not what I expected, though,' I said, somewhat triumphant that I'd survived it.

Stuart let out a forced chuckle. 'What did you expect?'

'I dunno, just didn't expect that.'

He was about to comment but was beaten to it by the same voice shouting 'Gas! Gas! Gas!' again. Straight away, we donned our respirators, quickly closed the cab doors and wound up the windows.

'What the fuck is all this about? I didn't hear any explosions,' Stuart shouted, sounding muffled through the voice modulator on his respirator.

I acknowledged him by shrugging my shoulders. All we could do was sit it out. This time, however, the alarm only lasted ten minutes or so. But as soon as we took off our respirators, someone else shouted, 'Gas! Gas! Gas!' and yet again we repeated the IA drill.

Over the next five hours, I counted fifteen ballistic attacks, which meant fifteen chemical warnings, which meant carrying out the IA drill fifteen times. According to the instruction manual, we had only nine seconds to don our respirators. I think we managed to do it in about three or maybe four seconds, which included grabbing it from our haversacks.

The retaliation from the Iraqi forces didn't take us entirely by surprise. We knew they would do something and that it was just a case of when. We also knew there would be no chance of Saddam's army or air force travelling as far south as us and attempting some kind of attack on our camp, so missiles were his only option. It turned out the first explosion followed by the thud was a Scud missile being destroyed by a Patriot missile. Later, two more missiles could be heard, only this time they managed to penetrate our defences. One landed about seven kilometres away and the other hit Camp Rhino. The explosion, as far as we were concerned, wasn't the immediate problem. It was the type of warhead they carried that had us on edge. The other fear was an attack from suicide squads. Although none had been reported, we knew they existed and that it would take only one pick-up truck full of high explosives to disrupt an entire camp.

During the missile attacks, countless heavy armoured vehicles continued to thunder past our packet. The sight and sound of this 'heavy metal' train heading for Iraq was awesome. Challenger 2s from the SDG and our own 2 RTR passed by the dozen, with Warrior AFVs quickly following. Then passed CVRTs, AS90s, Warrior recovery vehicles, CRARRVs and support vehicles such as Bedford TMs full of ammunition for the tanks and AS90s, which no doubt included DU (depleted uranium) rounds – a lethal shell that has twice the density of lead and can penetrate any known armour, causing a vacuum of such extreme force it sucks out everything in its wake, including the crew, as it exits a vehicle. A tank commander once told me that if an armoured vehicle was hit by a DU round, the crew inside would end up like soup. A sobering thought.

The time was approaching 1000hrs zulu. We were beckoned for our last O'group before the move into Iraq. Of course, the first thing on the agenda was the importance of carrying our respirators at all times. I think we'd already got the message. As before, our Foden was to be tail-end Charlie of packet A1. We were given a brief about the immediate situation and took notes of further grid references, call signs and radio frequencies. We were also given BATCO (British Army tactical communication) cards, of which Stuart and myself had little experience. That didn't matter, we'd have to muddle through, the typical British Army way. BATCO codes were used over the net when signalling by radio. They gave details like grid references, formations and enemy locations, as well as other information relevant at the time. The cards were numbered and changed on a 12-hour rotation and if we forgot what card to use, tough.

Theatre passwords also changed every 12 hours. In fact, any information given prior to an engagement or during a battle would be valid for only 12 hours. One good reason for this was that if captured by the enemy, we were expected to hold out for the duration. After which, the information held would be of little use to anyone. The Iraqi forces knew this, which was why the interrogation of prisoners had to be swift and effective in order to gain any relevant information. The maps we carried with grid references, locations, call signs and radio frequencies pencilled on them would also have to be destroyed if capture was imminent but we prayed that would never happen. Besides, we were told that being captured by the enemy wasn't an option.

Nonetheless, the crews of the reconnaissance vehicles were told to strip their uniforms of any insignia, which included their Desert Rat flashes, Union Jacks, rank slides and even their dog tags. A lack of identification on uniforms contributed to time wasted by the enemy. The recce crews gathered information on enemy positions and target positioning, and relayed this to the battle group who passed it to the Challenger crews and the artillery and air-assault crews, British and American forces alike, so they were high on the Iraqi forces' list of targets to destroy or, better still, capture.

After our briefing, we walked back to our vehicles and talked about the impending drive into Iraq. Sitting in the cab, we once again prepared our kit and made our rifles ready for the off. The time was approaching 1100hrs zulu. In between the boredom and the waiting, the odd 'Gas! Gas! Gas!' was heard but they were mainly false alarms. However, we still had to carry out the IA drill, just in case. It was explosions from Challenger 2s and AS90s firing off practice rounds on the artillery range a few kilometres north that had caused the false alarms. Nobody else on the camp knew about the practice range, which was worrying – and sounded familiar.

In the mean time, gas attack or no gas attack, vehicle tasks soon started to roll in. Stuart walked back from the CV with details of a vehicle casualty we had to recover.

'What we got?' I asked, as he jumped back into the cab.

'Nothing much. Just another CVRT with a gearbox problem that needs taking to 3 Battalion's ECP [equipment collection point].'

The 3 Battalion REME workshops were situated about 50 kilometres south on Camp Centurion and the CVRT we were about to take to them was the same one we had collected from the border. Nothing had been done to it, except that a bunch of A'mechs (armoured mechanics) had looked around it with hands on their hips, tutting a lot and shaking their heads from side to side. We hooked up the CVRT using the hollibones and with the crew safely tucked up inside began our journey down Route Tampa. We reached the camp entrance and were greeted by a US Army sentry. 'Where you headin', buddy?'

'Taking this CVRT to the workshops,' I replied, quickly showing my ID. He checked the mug shot on my ID card and nodded his head, beckoning us through. On reaching the ECP workshop, I pulled up next to the 'dead vehicles' on my left awaiting further repairs.

'I'll check in,' Stuart said, as he jumped out of the cab.

The workshop, comprising commercial garages

designed to house large commercial vehicles, was surrounded by a large courtyard roughly two kilometres square. It was probably last occupied by the Iraqi Army during the invasion of 1990 and now looked a little 'battle-damaged'. It had been left derelict until we decided to take it over. Three-storey office buildings surrounded the area, their outer walls peppered with small-arms fire. Open-air hangars made of steel pillars and corrugated-iron sheets were fixed to the front of the office walls. Additional inflatable workshops had been brought in by 3 Battalion, complete with air conditioning, specially constructed for NBC attacks and to allow VMs to carry out repairs whilst under a chemical threat.

I jumped out of the cab to tell the CVRT crew we'd arrived but I was too late, they had already vacated their vehicle and disappeared to find the cookhouse. Stuart came out of the building which housed the ops (operations) room for the workshop. As he walked towards me, the distinctive warble of an air-raid siren, not unlike those heard during the Second World War, burst into life from an outdoor public-address system, followed by a warning: 'Ballistic attack, find suitable shelter!' repeated three times in quick succession. I jumped into the cab and grabbed my rifle, helmet and haversack. Stuart, being the switched-on soldier he was, already had his with him.

'Where the fuck is some suitable shelter?' I asked, donning my respirator and checking my CBA's Velcro was secured at the front.

Stuart didn't answer, he was too busy running around trying to find some cover. 'Over 'ere, Kev!' he shouted, running into the ops room, which was better than no cover at all.

As I ran across the courtyard, VMs and other squaddies who worked at the workshop compound were running to pre-determined shelters. It was only us strangers that were left to fend for ourselves, frantically searching for some decent cover. Remember what I said about recy mechs looking out for themselves? I reached the outer door of the ops room and heard a loud, powerful explosion that sounded as if it was only a few kilometres away. Too close for comfort, as far as I was concerned. I quickly slammed the door shut and raced towards a further door a few metres ahead. The door was closed but not for long. I pulled it open and a body nearly fell onto me. It was an officer.

'What the fuck?' he shouted, as I stopped him mid-fall.

We sorted ourselves out and I shut the door behind me. Whilst I struggled to get my breath back, I noticed the one and only window in the room was boarded up. The single light bulb hanging in the centre of the ceiling dimly lit the room, revealing a desk in the far-right corner. Next to the desk was a pile of engine parts, all in plastic bags with ID tags attached. Stuart was sitting in the corner leaning against them.

It was a tight squeeze with seven squaddies crammed together in a room no more than three metres square. The temperature outside had reached the mid-30s. In the small space with our bodies huddled together, it must have exceeded the mid-40s. The sweat poured down between the leather band of my Kevlar helmet and my forehead, gathering on the top of my respirator before running down the sides of my face. Inside my respirator, the area for my chin quickly filled with sweat. Although I had managed to regulate my breathing, I began to feel light-headed from the heat and lack of oxygen inside the room. I then realised only Stuart and I were wearing our respirators.

'Why isn't anyone else wearing respirators, Sir?' I asked the officer who had fallen on me.

'You don't need 'em; it's a ballistic warning, not a chemical warning.'

I frowned at his reply. I'd never heard such crap. 'How do you know it's not a chemical attack?'

'Because the warning said so, didn't you hear it?' he said, sarcastically.

Fuck you, I thought. One thing I had learnt was to cover all options. I'd be damned if I was going to use any of my atropine pens on him. If it was a chemical attack, tough shit.

I flinched when another missile exploded but it sounded further away the second time.

We all stood with our heads bowed, waiting for further explosions and praying we'd be safe in the tiny single-skinned brick room. There was nothing we could do but hope the Iraqi Army was a crap shot. Twenty minutes passed before the all-clear signal bellowed from the sirens. I soon extracted the respirator from my face and made my way outside.

'You kept your face welly on, then. I thought you'd have taken it off when I said—'

I interrupted the officer, a second lieutenant, 'Sir, did you go through all those attacks yesterday without carrying out your IA drills?'

He had a confused expression on his face. 'What attacks?'

He'd inadvertently answered my question. 'Doesn't matter, Sir. I wasn't taking any risks, that's all.'

He still looked confused, but then again he was an officer, and a young one at that. Yet another in his early 20s.

'Did you experience chemical attacks, then?' he asked.

'Luckily, they weren't chemical, just conventional shit.'

'Where was this?'

'Camp Cambrai.'

'Oh right, you're from up there. I didn't know. Yes, I did hear about some excitement at your end.'

Some excitement – that was an understatement. Once outside, I took a few lungfuls of warm, fresh air whilst I held my respirator upside down to pour out the sweat.

'Arseholes!' Stuart said sternly.

'What's up with you?' I asked.

'This lot. That could have easily been a chemical attack, then what would have happened to them? Fucking arseholes, the lot of 'em.'

I laughed at his comments. 'You could hear that officer, then?'

'Yeah, he must be from the Planet Mong.'

'C'mon, we'd better uncouple the CVRT and get the fuck out of here. You can drive back for a change.'

I helped Stuart uncouple the CVRT and stow the kit, then we made ourselves comfortable in the cab. A few minutes later, we were on our way back up the dual carriageway heading for Camp Cambrai.

We later discovered the two explosions were Scud missiles targeting Camp Centurion and Camp Rhino a few kilometres further south. Thankfully, they missed their targets. The one targeting Camp Rhino was again intercepted by a Patriot missile, which exploded the Scud in mid-air. No chemical warheads were used but at the time the psychological effect of chemical warheads potentially cracking above our heads was definitely keeping our nerves on edge.

When we arrived back at Camp Cambrai, there was a lot of activity. Cam-nets and tents were being rolled up and packed away and even our CV had had its cam-nets removed and the antennas taken down. Stuart parked in the same spot as before, at the rear of the A1 packet. I jumped out of the cab and reported to what was left of the CP (command post) in the CV.

'Glad to see you back in one piece. I heard about the ballistic attack. Everything OK? No dramas to report?' the ASM asked.

'No, Sir, none.'

'Good. Sort out your admin and be ready to move in one hour, at 1500hrs. We're heading to our next location. Three guesses where that is,' he said, raising his eyebrows.

I walked back to the Foden where Stuart had already moved into the passenger seat and was making another brew. 'What's the word, then?' he asked.

'Move out in one hour to the next location,' I replied, as I jumped into the driver's seat.

Stuart didn't say anything. He made the tea whilst I checked the recovery kit and completed a fuel check. Three quarters of a tank was plenty (the capacity of the fuel tank was over 360 litres). Stuart had already marked the grid reference of our next location on the map, folded it and wedged it between the dash and windscreen ready to use. The only task left to do was give our rifles a quick dusting and lightly oil the working parts. And because we were heading for hostile territory, we loaded a fresh, live magazine and made the rifles ready, leaving the safety catch on. As for the radio being repaired – fat chance of that happening.

I checked my watch, 1430hrs zulu – half an hour to go. I realised I no longer felt apprehensive or scared, which was different from how I thought I'd feel before we headed into Iraq. Why I felt nothing, I don't know. Maybe because I had been eased gently into the war by the ballistic and the false chemical attacks, and the artillery shell just missing us, and nearly having to open fire on a bunch of Iraqi soldiers. I suppose it all added up to acclimatisation. What I hadn't experienced, as yet, was being shot at, shooting someone myself or witnessing anyone being blown up. Until such time, I had to put up with feeling numb and at that moment, it suited me not to have any feelings.

Our packet started its engines and I quickly followed suit. The CO of A1 packet, Captain Schaffer, walked up from the front and made sure everyone had managed to start their engines. He must have been close to his mid-50s, with a well-worn and weathered face on top of his broad 6-ft frame and plenty of grey showing through his close-cropped black hair. He'd worked his way up the ranks before taking his commission and becoming a captain. He was a down-to-earth bloke and definitely one of the lads, even with his south London accent.

When he reached our Foden, he gave the thumbs-up. I returned the gesture, signalling to him that everything was OK. Content with my answer, he walked back to his Land-Rover at the front of the packet and jumped in the passenger seat. Seconds later, the A2 packet began to move. After a few minutes, A1 followed on, passing the sentries at the camp entrance and turning right onto the dual carriageway. The rush of heavy armour had chewed up the tarmac and ripped the reflective cat's-eye lights protruding from the road's surface from their housings. But what the fuck, we were off – destination Iraq.

10

SO THIS IS IRAQ

The drive to the border was slow and frustrating. The hundreds, if not thousands, of military vehicles in front of us, all in their individual packets, repeatedly either slowed down to about 20 kph or just stopped because of a 30-kilometre tailback leading up to and beyond the border. It seemed every type of military vehicle was on this dual carriageway, from US HumVees to Bradley AFVs and Abram M1 main battle tanks.

We couldn't have travelled more than 20 kilometres when we noticed a Bedford TM towing a trailer either suffering from binding brakes or a slipping clutch. Whichever, it had left a trail of a distinctive burning stench. The driver pulled over onto the hard shoulder and I instinctively did the same, stopping a few metres behind. Stuart jumped out of the cab and had a look at the trailer, then at the eight-tonne truck, feeling the wheels first to see if they were hot, which would indicate binding brakes. He then moved towards the front of the vehicle and poked his head between the front nearside wheel guard and tyre to see if he could spot anything odd from the engine.

The driver, an LI soldier, was talking to Stuart as he did his checks. It looked as if the LI guy was desperately trying to explain what had happened and was giving some feeble excuse that it wasn't his fault. Stuart ignored him whilst he worked. I shook my head and chuckled to myself as the driver desperately fought his corner.

Stuart made his diagnosis: a burnt-out clutch. Luckily, the engine was ticking over, so the easy option was to tow the vehicle and trailer using the straight-bar and leaving the driver in the truck to steer. We soon hooked up the vehicle casualty and left the crew sitting in the cab, after giving the driver strict instructions to follow the steering of the Foden and not to use his brakes. The young soldier seemed a little nervous with the instructions, so I tried to reassure him I wouldn't travel any faster than 50 kph. Stupid boy, I had to do at least 100 kph to catch up with the packet.

With everyone ready, I pulled away from the hard shoulder and built up speed, the extra weight – the truck and trailer were overloaded with ammunition, well over its design weight – forcing a few grunts from the Foden. After 5 minutes or so, I managed to reach a speed of 100 kph, passing convoy after convoy, but I still needed to go faster to try and make up for lost time. I continued to put my foot down, which in turn made the vehicle casualty sway from side to side a little, but the young LI guy must have quickly learnt what to do and soon corrected it.

As we passed each convoy, we could hear the odd cheer coming from the backs of LI Bedford troop carriers. No doubt they recognised the crew in our vehicle casualty. The Land-Rovers at the front of the packets were less impressed. A recovery vehicle towing an 8-tonne truck and trailer full of ammunition at 120 kph wasn't a sight they were used to. But hey, this was war! No time to be obeying the Highway Code.

Unfortunately, the clean, newly laid but slightly damaged dual carriageway soon came to an abrupt end. It turned into a single-lane potholed road as we passed a sentry post on the border, guarded by Kuwaiti soldiers. Because we had stopped to recover the truck, we'd fallen behind our packet and became the tail-end Charlie of a US Army convoy of HumVees, complete with their 50-calibre roof-mounted machine guns.

Once again, we came to a halt. A bottleneck had been caused by the traffic trying to get through the border gate and a further three checkpoints ahead. Stuart grabbed his camera and took a photograph of a sign saying 'No cameras allowed in the demilitarised zone'. He then started to snap away at road signs saying Basrah and Baghdad. The demilitarised zone stretched for five kilometres. UN buildings, surrounded by sandbags and barbed wire, were scattered on either side of the road. They lay derelict from the last war, stripped of air-conditioning units and most probably the furniture inside. Burnt-out military B-vehicles and civilian tractors were just dumped on the side of the road, along with tonnes of litter left to blow about in the wind. Stuart had just decided to switch on the BV when a knock on the passenger door startled us.

'Who the fuck is that?' I asked.

Stuart looked down through his window at whoever it was. They had an exchange of words then he opened his door. The passenger of our vehicle casualty wanted to join us.

'All right, mate,' he said, making himself comfortable on the bunk behind our seats. 'That arsehole of a driver is doing my head in.' Our new passenger was Corporal Mike Moffat of the LI, a stocky lad about 35 years old.

'I thought he was your mate,' I replied.

'Nah, I was told to go with him. We're attached to you

lot but he's to deliver the ammunition somewhere else, then drop me off at my next grid before joining his own packet.'

'We'll have to take you to our location anyway,' Stuart said. 'The radio's fucked, so we can't contact our CV to find out what we should do with you.'

So we not only had to hope the grid reference for the FAA was correct, we now had to bring the vehicle casualty with us. The driver of the Bedford, a chubby young lad in his 20s called Mark Johnson, now nicknamed 'Stupid Boy', didn't know where he was supposed to go. He hadn't bothered to write down the grid reference of his next location or the radio frequencies of his packet when briefed at his last O'group. He told us he intended to follow the vehicle in front, so didn't think he needed to write anything down – stupid boy.

The convoy started to move, slowly at first, but it soon gathered pace. 'Shithole, innit!' Mike said. 'And we haven't got through the buffer zone yet.'

When we reached the end of the five-kilometre zone, there was a deserted Iraqi 'Checkpoint Charlie' peppered with small-arms fire. The concrete building looked as if it had been fired on by tanks, with chunks blown out of it. The battle damage looked old, probably from the last conflict, but the area did present traces of more recent occupants. Abandoned military vehicles such as BMP1s and BMP2s were left intact and piles of shells were left next to S60 anti-aircraft guns. AK47 assault rifles and helmets were also abandoned on the side of the road, looking as if they had been hastily discarded.

The road was almost as straight as a Roman road, with a slight incline towards the horizon. The orange flashes on top of the vehicles in our packet were a dead giveaway as they drove up the gradient in the distance, about a kilometre way.

SO THIS IS IRAQ

The fluorescent orange flashes were nothing more than pieces of plastic sheeting. The idea was to attach them to the top of the vehicles to give coalition aircraft a sign that we were on their side, basically saying 'Please don't shoot me'. Our packet seemed to be the only convoy fitted with them on this stretch of road, which made them easy to spot. In between them and us, though, was this bloody HumVee convoy. Mike buzzed his radio in the hope of relaying a message to our packet. The only problem was its limited range; it was just a small, compact radio. On a good day, it might have had a three-kilometre range but in this environment and with masses of vehicles in front of us, Mike received nothing but garbled signatures and static.

By this stage, we were in Iraq – time to 'switch on', if we hadn't already, and look out for all the danger signs. Mines, booby traps, ambushes, militia and even children carrying RPGs and AKs. We couldn't help but look at everything with a suspicious eye but, then again, I suppose that's one element of survival in a war. The road opened up into a dual carriageway once again and at a junction a few hundred metres ahead of us, it joined a flyover intersecting another main road which, fortunately, the HumVees decided to take. This gave me the chance to catch up with our own packet. As we passed under the flyover, I gathered speed and was soon fast approaching our convoy.

Mike tried his radio once again, with better success. He talked to his mate who was in another Bedford truck somewhere ahead of us. 'They've reached the boundaries of Safwan,' he said, relaying the message from his mate. Stuart had a look of fear in his eyes. 'This is it, then,' he said, scouring the road ahead.

'First time? Doing this for real, I mean,' asked Mike, overhearing Stuart.

'Yeah, for the both of us,' I replied.

'Me too,' added Mike. 'I never thought I'd be doing this, and I've been in the army for nearly 15 years. I never even made it to the Balkans.' He then let out a snigger. 'My dad said I should keep my head down, as if he'd know what to do. He was in the TA. A plastic soldier, you know, a part-timer.'

'Not too keen on the TA, then, Mike?' I asked, noticing a grin growing on Stuart's face.

'Well, they're all right, I suppose, but they're not real soldiers, are they? No good for the real thing. They should be left at the rear, that's what they're good for.'

I slammed on the brakes and came to a sudden halt.

'What the fuck are you doing?' screamed Mike.

'You'd better get out and walk. Stuart and me should turn around and go to the rear; after all, we're only TA.'

Mike's jaw dropped. He didn't know what to say. I was trying my hardest not to laugh but the grunting noises from Stuart's pathetic attempt made me lose concentration.

'TA, really?' replied a surprised and slightly embarrassed Mike.

I started to move again, before I upset any of the convoy behind us. As I raced through the gearbox, Stuart explained who we were and what we did. This gave Mike a chance to apologise and he had soon changed his mind about the TA.

We forgot his comments as we approached the outskirts of the small town of Safwan, just north of the Kuwait–Iraq border, and straight away we witnessed what a war can do to a town. The main road through the town was lined with flat-roofed shops and houses, which reminded me of a Spanish village I once visited whilst on holiday in Malaga. The big difference being the shops in Spain weren't shot to pieces. The road had mortar splats blown into it, caused by a shell's impact; trees, or what was left of them, had their trunks blown in two, leaving branches and half-trees falling on buildings and cars; and the streets were covered in shrapnel and splinters, the result of shelled military vehicles.

Thick, acrid black smoke spiralled from T55s and T62s scattered on either side of the road, left as burning hulls with bits of their crew sprawled on the side of the road. The sights I'd seen up to then hadn't bothered me, then a bad odour hit my nostrils like a smack in the mouth. A mixture of burning oil, bad body odour and shit is the only way to describe it.

'Smell that stench, that's war, mate. That's the smell of burning tanks and corpses. You can even taste it, can't you?' commented Mike.

He was right; I could feel it hit the back of my throat like a bitter-tasting dose of medicine. I thought I'd vomit but for some reason I didn't. I didn't feel anything, not even remorse for what we'd done – until I noticed the children lining the pavements.

It seemed the whole of the town's population had lined the streets, cheering and waving, all pleased to see us. It gave me a tremendous buzz but the looks on the children's faces will haunt me for the rest of my life. Bright, wide brown eyes looked directly at me but at the same time stared into infinity with the proverbial thousand-yard stare only seasoned soldiers are supposed to have. I tried to divert my attention to something else but everywhere I looked I could see children, from toddlers to those in their early teens, all wearing the same stare. Some were dressed in rags, whilst others wore what seemed like their Sunday best, but it was still dirty and tatty.

A little girl, no older than four years old, caught my attention. She was wearing a pretty pink and red dress but had bare feet. Her long, dark, matted hair looked as dirty as her face. I noticed where tears had run down her cheeks, causing two clean streaks through the dirt, but she wore a beautiful smile. She had no idea what this was all about and we couldn't have any idea what she had gone through in her short life, especially during these first few days of the war.

The convoy drove through the town extremely slowly, slower than I liked. I wanted to get through this place as quickly as possible; I'd seen enough. As we drove closer to the little girl standing on the kerb to my right, she looked up at me with her wide, brown, innocent eyes burrowing into my skull. All I could do was return a pathetic wave. She immediately began to smile, showing off her white teeth, and waved back. I had to do something; this beautiful innocent child had put me under a tremendous, powerful spell. I quickly rummaged through the 24-hour rat pack sitting next to me and pulled out a half-melted bar of chocolate. I threw it at her in a feeble attempt to ease my guilty conscience.

Before the chocolate bar landed on the dusty road, a bunch of young boys, no older than ten or twelve, rushed towards it and knocked the little girl clean over. She rolled into the dirt, messing up her pretty dress, but she didn't cry or throw a tantrum, which would have been the immediate reaction of my three-year-old daughter. She just sat on the kerb, leaving the boys to fight over the chocolate. My heart went out to her. This was quickly followed by a rush of anger surging through my veins – I couldn't let these kids get away with that.

'The little bastards!' I blurted out. I stopped the truck and grabbed my rifle as I clambered out of the vehicle.

'Where ya going?' shouted Stuart.

'Back in a minute,' I replied.

I ran the few metres back to the scrapping kids in the hope of salvaging the bar of chocolate but it was too late. The vultures had legged it down a side street. I could see them fighting over their booty as they ran a safe distance away from me.

'I'll show them,' I muttered under my breath. Reaching for one of the side bin doors, I took out a complete 24-hour rat pack and handed it to the little girl, who was still sitting in the gutter. 'Take it, go on, take it.'

She was reluctant at first but soon gave in to curiosity. She struggled with the parcel's taped lid, so I gave her a hand to open it. I took out one of the two bars of chocolate, opened one edge of the wrapper and revealed another half-melted chocolate slab. Her eyes once again lit up. The expression on her face was like she had regained her faith in the 'grown-up people'. After a few mouthfuls, she looked up and gave me a smile, complete with melted chocolate around her mouth. Sitting on the kerb with her legs outstretched into the gutter, showing off her dirty grazed knees, her feet wobbled from side to side with the excitement of eating the chocolate.

This precious child must have thought everything was OK now. No more terrible loud bangs, no more fear and no more pain and suffering. I wished I had a magic wand to make everything all right but I was regrettably powerless to do anything. A bar of chocolate was all I could give to try and make things better. I knelt down in front of her and could feel my emotions build up inside. I desperately wanted to help this little girl, but how? The emotions were too strong for me to control and I felt a tear or three run down my cheek. Tears of guilt? Tears of failure? I don't know. Whichever, they just poured out.

A woman, who I presumed to be the little girl's mother, approached and knelt down behind her daughter, putting her hands either side of her shoulders. The girl looked up at her mum and gave a big grin as she passed her the rat-pack box, then continued to tuck into her chocolate. Her mother passed the box back to me.

'No! You keep it,' I said, as I pushed it back in her hands.

'Thank you, thank you,' she replied.

I was gobsmacked. 'You speak English?'

'I learnt at school, not good at very English,' she said, slightly embarrassed.

Good or not, I could understand what she meant, and she could understand me. 'You OK?' I asked.

'Will now, thank you. Saddam gone, thank you.'

Oh boy, more bloody tears welled up in my eyes. She was bound to notice. I rubbed them to make out they were full of dust.

'C'mon, Kev, the convoy's moving,' Stuart shouted, as he leant out of the driver's-door window.

'Yeah, be right with you.'

The little girl carried on with her chocolate bar, still smiling and waggling her feet. I rubbed the top of her head with my right hand and winked at her. Her mother, who was most probably younger than me, but looked as if she'd had a hard life, thanked me once again as I stood up and walked back to the Foden. The boys that mugged my new friend noticed her eating her chocolate. I aimed my rifle at them to show that I wasn't happy with what they had done and to warn them they'd better watch out. They all froze to the spot and two of the four raised their hands in surrender. Shit, I thought, they'd probably done that for real.

'Go on, fuck off!' I shouted, as they turned tail and ran back down the street. I jumped in the driver's seat of the Foden and moved off without saying a word. Luckily, my tears had dried up, otherwise I'd have faced a barrage of piss-takes from Stuart and Mike.

'You soft git, but I'd have done the same,' said Mike.

I turned to acknowledge him and noticed his eyes were a bit waterlogged. He quickly moved his head to avoid eye contact.

We continued driving through the town, stopping after a few hundred metres, then moving a few hundred more. The pavements were still lined with people of all ages and not one showed any animosity towards us. The older kids, however, seemed to be aware of their impoverished appearance and exploited the situation. 'Mister! Mister!' they'd shout, and point to their mouths or stomach, indicating they were hungry. I wasn't about to fall for this put-on, not after the episode with the little girl. Some of the kids who were begging certainly didn't come across as being starving. They only wanted something to sell on to other unsuspecting squaddies further down the convoy, preying on their benevolent nature to raise easy cash.

Stuart threw some boiled sweets from his 24-hour rat pack to the kids on his side of the road. 'Fucking 'ell, they're killing each other over these sweets, look!' he said excitedly, pointing at the kids. 'Go on, boy! Smack the bastard, that's right,' he shouted, as they virtually murdered each other.

Thank God the end of the town was approaching. Mike buzzed his radio to keep up with what was happening further along the convoy. 'It's all clear ahead, we should be able to drive straight through without a—'

Crack! Crack! Crack!

'That's fucking small arms!' He quickly shouted back into his radio to report our situation, then stood up and put his head through the cupola to get a better all-round view. 'Came from down one of these side streets,' Mike confirmed, as he poked his head back in the cab. 'I'll try and get a better fix.'

The convoy rapidly gathered speed in response to the small-arms fire, with me tight behind, making it difficult for Mike to spot the incoming. He talked into his radio again, desperately trying to gather as much information as possible. The spectators lining the streets dived for cover, screaming and shouting. A young child, not much older than a toddler, was left on the side of the road crying and screaming in fear and lifted his arms in the hope of being carried to safety by some passing adult. But he was ignored by people diving for cover over low-level garden walls and into doorways. Mike returned a few rounds at a suspect target, heightening the tension amongst the locals. It didn't do me any good, either.

'What the fuck are you firing at?' I shouted.

'I'm keeping their heads down but I don't think they were aiming at us.'

He continued to blat out a few more rounds just to show anyone that wanted to take pot shots at us that we meant business, then gave a sit-rep (situation report) on his radio.

'Did you see anything, Stuart?' I asked.

Stuart was scanning his side of the road with his rifle resting on the open window, pointing towards the battered buildings ahead of him. 'I didn't see anything. This is unreal, Kev. Is this really happening?'

I didn't answer him. I was concentrating on getting the fuck out of there. Being shot at seemed to be our trademark of late. If it wasn't artillery shells or missiles, it was bloody small-arms fire.

We made it to the other side of the town's border. Open ground lay ahead of us with only the odd group of locals on either side of the road. I took a deep breath to relieve some of the tension that had built up inside me and lit a cigarette.

'Are you OK, Kev?' asked Mike, now lying behind me on the bunk, chilling out after his action-man antics.

'A bit scary, wouldn't you say, back there?' I replied.

'Nah, you'll see a lot worse than that over the next few months, believe me.'

'Oh, thanks, very reassuring.'

Mike checked his GPS to see how far we had to go before we reached the FAA. 'About another 50 Ks, Kev, so time for a brew. What d'ya reckon, Stuart?'

Stuart was too busy concentrating on the locals walking on his side of the road. 'Eh, what?'

'Time for a cuppa?'

'Yeah, OK.' Stuart rested his rifle upright on the floor of the footwell, as he continued to scan the area.

'Leave it, mate, chill out. The danger's over, for a while anyway,' Mike said, trying to ease Stuart's nerves.

Stuart shook out of his trance and put a little trust in Mike's words. At least for the time being.

Nearly two hours later, we finally reached the FAA – Camp Barnsley. It was nothing more than the occupation of part of the desert on the side of the road. It had a slight incline, which went on for about half a kilometre, before it reached a ridge. On top of the ridge was a joining road, which met the main Route 6 highway we'd just come off. A couple of buildings and a chain-link fence stretched along the ridge and what seemed to be a garden centre sat on the far left – a bizarre sight in the middle of the desert. I parked behind our A2 packet just off the side of the road and switched off the engine. Stuart and Mike checked in at the CV so Mike could give a sit-rep on his Bedford truck and see what we were supposed to do with it. In the mean time, Mike put Stupid Boy on stag (guard). I noticed him on prowler-guard duty when he walked by my driver's-door window.

'Oi, mate,' I shouted, as he walked by. 'How did you get on with driving on tow?'

He smiled before answering. 'Not bad, there was a few scary moments, especially when someone opened fire on us from that town back there.' His facial expression was nervous as Mike and Stuart walked back from the CV. 'I'd better fuck off. See ya later, Kev.'

Mike shook his head as he and Stuart walked closer to the Foden, with what looked like bad news. 'What's happening, then?' I asked, leaning out of the window.

Stuart explained the situation. 'He's to stay here. Bobby's going to have a go at changing the Bedford's clutch overnight.'

'Well, that's all right, innit, Mike? You'll be back on the road by tomorrow.'

Mike shook his head again but smiled at the same time. 'It means I'll be with Stupid Boy for at least another 24 hours. I was hoping to be rid of him today.'

Not being really bothered if Mike was stuck with Mark or not, I jumped out of the cab to help Stuart unhook the vehicle casualty.

'Where to now?' I asked, stowing the last of the recovery kit.

'To join A1 packet at the other side of the FAA.'

The other side of the FAA was about two kilometres away. As we drove around the area, it seemed like the entire 7 Armoured Brigade was there: there was row after row of Challenger 2s, Warriors, 432 AFVs and 432 ambulances; CVRTs, including Scimitar, Samson and Sabre armoured fighting and reconnaissance vehicles; CRARRVs and the Royal Engineers' armoured vehicles, including the

CHAVRE (Chieftain armoured vehicle Royal Engineers) and CET (combat engineer tractor); countless support B-vehicles, Foden recovery trucks, Bedford TM troop carriers, fuel tankers and Land-Rovers. Hundreds of vehicles in one huge area, not forgetting the tonnes of stores, fuel, rations, medical supplies and ammunition. If the Iraqis had had an effective air force and we hadn't had control of the skies, almost the entire forward 7 Armoured Brigade could have been wiped out with one single strike.

At last, we found our convoy. I pulled up to the rear of the packet and halted a few metres away from the VMs' Bedford truck. Stuart switched on the BV to boil some water for a brew before I killed the engine. The sight of all these vehicles was amazing. I also noticed we were right at the very rear. We were the last vehicle of the last packet on the last corner edge. This made me feel a little vulnerable at first but I soon noticed a couple of Challenger 2s about 200 metres behind and a couple of Warriors patrolling our left flank.

The BV started to boil. I switched off the engine and Stuart began to make the tea, then there was a knock at my door.

'We've an O'group, Kev.' It was Stupid Boy pointing towards the front of the packet.

'What is it?' asked Stuart.

'Just an O'group. You can stay here, if you want. There's no need for both of us to go.' I jumped out of the truck, wearing my helmet and CBA, and grabbed my rifle and haversack. These four essential pieces of kit were to be with me for the duration of the war, never leaving my side 24/7.

Five minutes later, I returned to the Foden. The O'group was nothing more than a quick brief on our situation and grid references to our next location. The only concern was that we were being watched. Probably the local civilians, but it could easily be the Iraqi Army or local militia on a recce. Whichever, we had to treat them as hostile and if in doubt 'shoot to kill'. Bit of an eye-opener, but it highlighted the position we were in and reflected the reality of war. For some reason, this news put a smile on Stuart's face. I was beginning to worry about the lad.

When evening fell, there was an eerie silence around the camp, apart from the odd engine ticking over to boil a BV. The idea that we could be being watched prevented both Stuart and me from sleeping, even though we were knackered. The LI guys patrolled the area with a sense of anticipation. It seemed as if they were concerned that we were about to be bumped. Their trigger fingers had become so itchy, I didn't dare venture too far from my vehicle, even to take a piss. A few over-anxious soldiers had already mistakenly shot half a dozen stray dogs. Any sudden movements resulted in a magazine of 25 rounds being emptied, before the question, 'Who's there?' was asked. Our only option was to urinate up the side of the vehicles and even then we were constantly looking over our shoulders.

No light whatsoever was reflected anywhere around the camp; not even a red torchlight could be seen. We were stretching our field-craft training to the limit, taking no short cuts, but then again our lives depended on it. Throughout the night, I could only take the odd snooze, a 'power nap' of ten minutes or so, every other hour. I now knew what it was like to sleep with one eye and one ear open. I listened to every sound and my overactive imagination amplified it tenfold. At one point, I thought an entire Iraqi infantry company was walking past my Foden. In reality, it was only Stupid Boy on stag. But that is how our minds react in such extreme conditions. I didn't dare light a cigarette that night, just in case. I thought of that 'third light' saying which came from the First World War trenches: first light, the sniper is aware of your position; second light, he has you in his sights; and third, you're dead.

The sun began to rise, thank God, bringing with it a sense of security. A feeling of relief shuddered through my body. We'd survived another night but we now faced another day. We went through the usual morning rituals: wash, shave, shit (shovel recce) and a brew. A quick check over the Foden and recovery kit, then it was a case of sit and wait. For breakfast, it was menu G of the rat pack once again – meatballs and pasta – what a lovely combination for first thing in the morning. And, as usual, I could only manage a couple of mouthfuls. The time was 0430hrs zulu by this stage. We weren't moving out until 1300hrs zulu. This gave us plenty of time to prep the vehicles, carry out any repairs and catch up on some much-needed sleep, which I exploited to the full.

'Oi! Wake up sleeping beauty, we're moving in half an hour,' shouted Stuart as he climbed into the cab. It was always the bloody same – as soon as my head hit the pillow, some arsehole woke me up. He'd been to yet another O'group. I checked my watch, 1225hrs zulu. I'd slept longer than I'd thought.

'What's the latest?' I asked.

'We're preparing to move.'

The next location was roughly 120 kilometres north-north-east, where we'd stay the night to hold and secure before pushing further north to our next objective.

'What's the rush, we're ready to move anyway,' I said.

'Yeah, I know, but we have to pick up Mike and Stupid Boy's truck. Bobby couldn't repair it. He didn't have a replacement clutch.'

'Oh, great. We'll end up towing that truck for the rest of the war.'

'C'mon, we'd better get it hooked up. It's where we left it yesterday.'

Mike and Stupid Boy were waiting at the side of their Bedford truck to give us a hand. Ten minutes later, the straight-bar was secured and we were ready to move. Mike opted to keep Stupid Boy company whilst he steered the vehicle casualty. I moved behind our packet and waited for the off. The surface of the sand had a crust of two or three inches but underneath it was soft, so it took a couple of hours to move all the vehicles off the camp area. The B-vehicles in particular struggled, which wasn't helped by the tracked vehicles churning up the surface and creating deep troughs and ridges. After only a few minor dramas, we'd cleared the camp area and were soon on the tarmac.

11

FIRST TIME FOR EVERYTHING

The dual carriageway was full of military hardware travelling north and Iraqi civilians in chogie wagons (pick-up trucks generally used by militia) with all their worldly goods strapped on the back travelling south. And, once again, the road was chock-a-block with British and American military convoys, some heading our way while others veered left or right onto other routes but still basically headed north. The journey so far had taken its toll on some military vehicles but we couldn't do anything about it because of the casualty, or 'hook', we had already. All we could do was take their grid reference and vehicle details, and give them to an RMP (Royal Military Police) at the next VCP (vehicle checkpoint).

Four hours later, we turned off the main dual carriageway and onto a dirt track, then came to a halt. By then, it was 1700hrs zulu and night-time had well and truly drawn in. All vehicle lights remained switched off apart from the convoy light, which is a dim, three-watt light reflected on a white painted spot on the differential, or a rear-side panel of the bodywork. All other lights, including panel lights inside the cab, became inactive. Warning buzzers, such as the low-air-pressure warning buzzer, or the vehicle horn, became inoperative when the convoy light was in use.

Half an hour passed and there was still no sign of movement. I switched off the engine and noticed the other vehicles had done the same. An eerie silence followed; all I could hear was the faint rumble of military vehicles on the dual carriageway half a kilometre behind us, muffled by the undulation of the ground and the bushes lining the dirt track. To our immediate left, there was a farmhouse of some kind set back in a large front garden, or rather what was left of a house and garden. It looked as if someone had had a good time with a few tank rounds. A dog started to bark from inside the garden and broke the silence, but after a few minutes it got on my nerves. One consolation, though, was that whilst the barking continued, we knew we weren't under any chemical attack, a telltale sign we soon used to our advantage.

I became agitated and slightly nervous as we waited for . . . whatever the reason was. As the minutes ticked by, feeling like hours, my nervousness changed to frustration. I went to light a cigarette to calm myself down but found my Zippo had run out of fuel so I had to use one of the 'all-weather' matches from our 24-hour rat pack. The problem with these was trying to conceal the glare of the flame. Once the match is struck, it will continue to glare like a flare for about ten seconds. I tried to cup the match with my hands to hide the flame but all I managed to do was burn my palms, fill the cab full of smoke and illuminate my face, making a perfect target for the enemy. Stuart, however, found this amusing and sniggered like a naughty schoolboy. I threw the match end out of my window, nearly hitting a squaddie walking towards the Foden.

'We'll be here for about another hour or so,' he said quietly. 'Two T62s have been spotted in the area and they may have been following us. They're about two Ks away.' He pointed to our left, in the general direction they had been spotted. 'The LI have gone out on a recce, so sit tight,' he added, and walked back to the front of the packet.

I let out a nervous giggle.

'What's he say?' asked Stuart.

'There's two fucking tanks following our packet. The LI have gone on a recce to suss them out.'

'Must have noticed your fag,' he replied, with a muffled chuckle.

I threw my cigarette on the floor of the cab and stamped on it. 'I'd better tell Mike about the situation. That squaddie didn't notice our vehicle casualty hooked on the back.' I put on my helmet, strapped my haversack around my waist and slowly opened the driver's door, trying not to make too much noise. Grabbing my rifle, I carefully climbed out of the cab just as that dog started to bark again, only this time it was from my side and sounded very close. I chose to ignore it, which wasn't easy, as its deep, booming bark gave the impression it was a large dog.

I tapped on the Bedford's driver's-side door and a head appeared from the open window. 'All right, Kev, what's happening?' a voice whispered. It was Stupid Boy.

'We'll be here for about an hour. Two T62s have been spotted in the area. Your guys are doing a recce, so stay alert.'

I walked back towards my driver's door, making sure I didn't slip down the ditch on my right. Suddenly, the night sky illuminated with a brilliant bright light, complemented by a loud thundering explosion coming from the other side of the Foden. I didn't have any choice about the ditch and dived straight into it, rolling head over heels in the sand. A few seconds later, there was another flash of light, quickly followed by a loud explosion. Instinctively, I thrust my face into the sand and clasped my hands over my ears to try and stop them from popping with the shock wave. But I was too late. The first explosion had already initiated the familiar high-pitched ringing I'd experienced before. The point of the explosion couldn't have been any more than 100 metres away.

I crawled towards the straight-bar between the Foden and the Bedford casualty and lay face down on the ridge of the ditch. Stuart, Mike and Stupid Boy soon joined me as bits of shrapnel rained down on us.

'OK, Kev?' Stuart asked as he crash-landed beside me.

'Yeah, fine. Just taken by surprise, that's all. Where the fuck did that come from?'

'*Stand to! Stand to!*' a voice cried out from the front of the packet. The other crews soon followed suit and jumped out of their vehicles to take cover in the ditch. The immediate problem was that none of us had any stand-to positions and the whole scenario became improvised. Mike bellowed down his radio, which never seemed to leave his side. I made ready my rifle and pushed the safety catch to the off position. All around, I could hear others doing the same. Something was going to kick off and we weren't in control. Our makeshift stand-to positions in the ditch might have been pre-sighted and marked as a killing zone. Unfortunately, we didn't have a choice of cover and had to use it to the best of our ability.

'What's happening, Mike?' Stuart asked.

'It looks like the LI have taken out one of the tanks but they compromised their position when they used a 94 [94-

mm light anti-tank weapon]. The second tank then fired a round on their position.' Mike was in close contact with his LI mates further up the packet. They, in turn, had details relayed to their vehicles from the battle group. The tank the LI guys hit answered the question as to where the shrapnel had come from. So much for the T62s being two Ks away.

Crack! Crack! Crack! Rapid small-arms fire whizzed over our heads, quickly followed by bursts of automatic.

'*Return fire!*' a voice commanded. 'My tracers, on bushes dead ahead, rapid!' He quickly opened up with an LSW, using his tracer rounds to locate the enemy position. A split second later, 30 or so SA80s, LSWs and GPMGs along the line of the ditch opened up on the enemy position.

Further bursts of automatic came from the bushes on our left, about 100 metres ahead of the vehicle at the front of the packet, which was about 150 metres ahead of our Foden. I couldn't get a fix on any muzzle flashes but I certainly knew the general direction of the bursts, indicated by the enemy tracer rounds whizzing over our vehicles.

Stuart, Mike, Stupid Boy and myself crawled underneath the straight-bar to get a clear arc of fire on the enemy position. We trained our weapons on the enemy tracer rounds, which thankfully continued to fall short or pass high above our heads, and soon joined the others letting rip into the bushes. Within seconds, I had emptied my magazine by using small bursts of automatic fire and it soon became apparent I had to conserve my rounds, because I only had a further three magazines left, which were in my webbing on the back of the truck. I had no alternative but to climb on the back of the Foden and retrieve them. Unfortunately, we didn't have the same rifle magazines as those used in Hollywood blockbusters, the ones which never seem to run out of ammo. In reality, it's surprising how quickly they empty.

'I'll have to get my webbing, I've run out of rounds!' I shouted over the din of automatic fire.

As I crawled back from under the straight-bar, Stuart shouted, 'Get mine!' I couldn't believe what he had said.

I opened the driver's door, took a deep breath before climbing in and grabbed Stuart's webbing. Why I took a deep breath I don't know but it seemed a good idea at the time. I threw his webbing behind me and out of the open cab door. I then clambered out of the cab and climbed along its side using the grab rails. I made my way towards the centre of the truck where my webbing sat on top of my bergen, next to the base of the jib. In this position, my head was in clear view of the enemy, so I tried to stay low and keep my silhouette to a minimum. I hung by my right hand on the grab rail but couldn't release the webbing strap, which was caught behind the fuel-tank filler tube. I had to stand up straight, creating a greater target for the enemy, in order to use both my hands to free the webbing strap.

The packet continued directing their fire towards the bushes as I struggled on top of the Foden. Stuart and the others were totally oblivious to my predicament but thankfully continued to return fire, inadvertently covering my position. I gave one last tug and the webbing came free from the filler tube. I jumped backwards, holding onto my webbing as I fell, and landed on the dirt track with such a thud I fell backwards into the ditch, rolling towards the front of the Foden and dropping my webbing.

I was lying in the ditch trying to catch my breath when half a dozen enemy rounds fell onto my position, kicking up sand and dust just above my head on the ridge of the ditch. I had wondered how long it would be before the enemy noticed a stupid Brit squaddie prancing about on the roof of a Foden recovery vehicle. I still had to grab Stuart's webbing but I wasn't in a good position to retrieve it. When I had thrown it out of the cab, it had landed about a metre in front of the offside wheel.

If I raised my head above the top of the ditch, I risked being hit, so I had to crawl further down the ditch towards the centre of the truck – so far so good. The only option I had now was to crawl towards the truck and continue along its side towards the front. The ground clearance of a Foden recovery vehicle is about 400 millimetres – high enough to expose me. I hoped the enemy was either satisfied they'd hit me or too busy to notice what I was doing.

I managed to lie along the base of the front offside wheel so I could clasp the butt of my rifle and use it as an extension to reach Stuart's webbing, hooking the straps with the foresight. My first attempt failed but the second was more successful. I quickly pulled back the rifle and grabbed the webbing belt, then shimmied back into the ditch, which gave me cover whilst I put on my own webbing and crawled back to the others.

''Ere, and don't say I never do anything for ya!' I shouted at Stuart as I threw him his webbing.

He didn't thank me; he just crawled back a little and rolled on his webbing, clasping the belt buckle around his waist.

'Not at all, Kev. Thank you for risking your neck,' I muttered under my breath, as I positioned myself back under the straight-bar.

'Say something?' he replied.

I ignored him as I removed two fresh magazines from one of my pouches. I reloaded my rifle and tucked the other down the front of my CBA to save time when reloading. I continued to return fire but still couldn't visual any targets, so it was a case of giving blind suppressive fire and keeping the enemy's heads down.

Stuart ceased firing and pointed to his left. 'I can hear some heavy shit coming up the track!'

I strained to hear the armoured vehicles over the noise of Mike and Stupid Boy firing only a few inches from my head, but yes, I could faintly hear something. I tapped Mike on his right shoulder.

'What!' he said sharply, firing off a few more rounds.

'Armour, coming up on our left!'

Mike shifted back a little and shouted into his radio. A few seconds later, he returned to his position with a huge grin across his face. 'Warriors, two of them and a Challenger coming this way to sort the bastards out!'

'*Cease fire! Cease fire!*' a voice cried from further up the packet.

We stopped firing and within a matter of seconds the cavalry arrived. We stayed under the straight-bar and bowed our heads in the dirt to try and prevent the dust kicked up by the tracked vehicles getting into our eyes. The armour didn't hang about as they thundered by, considering there wasn't a lot of room to pass. Because the Foden took up over half of the width of the track, they had no alternative but to drive past with one side of their vehicle in the one-metre-deep ditch opposite. It didn't seem to hinder their performance, though.

The bursts of automatic from the enemy position suddenly ceased and there could be only two explanations why: 1) They'd noticed the armour racing towards them and legged it; 2) We'd finished them off with our blind suppressive firepower. Whichever, the whole episode couldn't have lasted any longer than five or six minutes.

Still, it was too early to get complacent and start relaxing. The only way we could be certain it was safe was after the Warriors and the Challenger 2 had done their job and secured the area.

Boom! A huge explosion, quickly followed by another. A gigantic firework display appeared immediately ahead of us from across the dirt track, roughly 100 metres away – the Challenger had hit the second T62. The gap in the hedgerow revealed a spectacular silhouette of a dying tank, complete with brilliant-white phosphorous, molten metal and an orange flame shooting out of the tank's hull and decking plates. The fireball allowed us to see the turret blown clean out of the hull and tilted to one side, resting against the top. A series of blasts followed quickly afterwards, caused by exploding magazines. A few seconds later, the distinctive sound of a Warrior's 30-mm cannon could be heard ripping through some target, then silence, apart from the burning T62 sounding as if it was screaming in agony. All we could do was lie still for a couple of minutes, wondering what was going on.

'Yeah, nice one! Cheers, Steve,' Mike said, speaking into his radio. 'Both T62s destroyed and the Warriors have just annihilated an Iraqi gun position. Eight dead, no survivors. My guys are just checking out the rest of the area, so we're to sit tight.'

Captain Schaffer swaggered down the dirt track like John Wayne, with a 9-mm pistol in his right hand and holding the barrel of an SA80 slung over his left shoulder.

'Get the fuck up and sweep the area!' he commanded.

'We'd better have a wander, then,' Stuart said, in a disturbingly calm manner.

I changed my magazine for a fresh one and climbed to my feet to join the others. Mike and Stupid Boy were already with the other LI guys and were advancing through the enemy position to 'mop up', whilst Stuart and I searched the immediate area towards the rear of our Foden and casualty vehicle. Every few minutes, I could hear bursts of automatic from SA80s coming from a few LI guys opening up on anything that moved, most probably wild dogs. Ten minutes later, a further four bodies, armed with AKs, had been recovered from the enemy position. Two of them were found next to a Russian-built 7.62-mm belt-fed machine gun, not unlike the GPMG in its performance.

'All clear! All clear!' a voice shouted out.

It seemed the area was safe for us to proceed to our hide, only a few kilometres up the dirt track. We returned to our vehicles, checking them for any small-arms damage sustained in the fire-fight. Although it was difficult to see in the dark, it looked as if the Foden had escaped unscathed. Thankfully, no casualties on our side were reported during the skirmish, although some of the vehicles in the packet weren't so lucky and suffered the odd hole in the bodywork.

It was assumed we'd bumped into either an enemy position or a bunch of retreating Iraqi soldiers resting for the night. Either way, it seemed we had surprised the Iraqis more than they'd surprised us. If it had been a planned ambush, we would have faced RPGs, mortars and sustained machine-gun fire from many positions, and most certainly anti-personnel and tank mines, the results of which would have been very different. As for the T62s, they may have been stalking us, or they may have been in the wrong place at the wrong time. In fact, the conclusion was that the retreating Iraqi soldiers didn't even know about the tanks. Total confusion, to say the least. I climbed back into the Foden and lit a well-deserved cigarette, using my emergency all-weather matches. I figured the glare from them wouldn't matter now, as we'd made enough noise to wake Tony Blair at No. 10.

I couldn't stop shaking, but not from fear; that faded when the fireworks started. It was from sheer excitement. The adrenalin refused to stop racing around my veins. I wondered if I'd killed anyone myself. It was difficult to tell, as I couldn't even pinpoint the enemy position. One thing was for sure, they had suffered fatalities caused by our sustained fire, so some of us must have killed them.

'John Wayne' walked back down the packet signalling a thumbs-up to start our engines – we were moving.

'That was incredible,' commented Stuart. 'I've never experienced anything quite like it.'

'I know what you mean, but it's not over yet. We have to reach our next location somewhere up this track, and fuck knows what we'll bump into.'

Stuart seemed to come back down to earth at the thought of going through it all over again. 'How do you feel?' he asked.

'Like you. I can't stop shaking, look.' I raised my hands in front of me. They were both trembling.

The convoy started to move. Mike stayed with Stupid Boy to keep him company, as well as to give fire support if it was needed. Stuart did the same for me, only this time he decided to poke his head out of the cupola. After six or seven kilometres, the steady incline and twists of the dirt track became a straight and level, although slightly damaged, tarmac road leading to our next location. The road was lined with BMP1s and BMP2s blown up by either an air strike or tank rounds. We then drove past a couple of coaches on our right, which were definitely taken out by some HE (high explosive) round. They were used at one time to ferry Iraqi soldiers, judging by some of the occupants left in the seats, although they looked a tad the worse for wear after being hit by a tank round.

After a further two kilometres, we approached the end of a road which must have been some sort of long driveway. A sentry standing at the end of the road used his red-filtered torch to signal us to turn left into a compound. We drove through some narrow gates, which had tall concrete pillars on either side, and entered a huge courtyard with a two-storey flat-roofed building ahead of us. It was difficult to get any idea of the scale of the courtyard because of the dark but I could just make out a two-metre breezeblock boundary wall surrounding the entire courtyard. If we were attacked, at least there was some kind of obstacle to slow down the enemy.

I was directed to stop behind the fitter's truck from our A1 packet parked at the far end of the courtyard. Because of the truck and trailer I was towing, I had to make sure I had enough of a turning circle to swing around the other vehicles. Luckily, the courtyard seemed ample in size to accommodate the length of my vehicle, including the dodging of another battle-damaged coach left in the middle of the space. I turned off the engine and was welcomed by more wild dogs barking and the sound of a diesel pump, or donkey engine, coming from a sanitation plant some fifty metres behind the two-storey building. We had to wait until first light to take in our surroundings – until then, it was time to get our heads down for a few hours' sleep, or so I thought. Stuart, still looking through the cupola, was talking to a figure on the nearside of the Foden.

'Guess what?' he said, leaning back inside the cab. 'We're on stag tonight.'

'Fuck off! Doesn't he know recy mechs don't do stag?' I replied abruptly.

Stuart climbed back into the cab and sat in the passenger

seat, resting his rifle in the footwell. 'Apparently not, but he's got a point, especially after what we've just gone through.'

That was true. I suppose none of us could sleep anyway. Whilst we had the chance, we made a brew and had something to eat. The last meal from today's menu-G rat pack was chicken and dumplings in some kind of vegetable soup. It may sound appetising but it did become monotonous after a while. We also grabbed the chance to clean our rifles, which raised the question of our ammo situation. Although we had scrounged extra rounds before leaving Kuwait, we were now running dangerously low and the chance of any replen at that particular moment was practically nil. So, just like REME soldiers, we exploited the fact we were towing an eight-tonne Bedford TM and trailer crammed full of assorted ammunition.

Of course, we couldn't just blatantly nick ammunition, we had to do it sneakily and slyly behind everyone's backs. And, of course, we only took what we thought we'd need. So, doing a bit of stag wasn't such a bad idea after all. Besides, we saw it as redistribution of MoD property for use by key military personnel in a war situation and not for personal gain. I think we were getting the hang of this war.

Saturday, 22 March 0001hrs zulu Time for our one-hour stag which only involved walking up and down our side of the A1 packet, reporting back to the CV every half-hour with anything suspicious. The other packets had their own guard duty list. We also had the chance to be nosy and have a look around the courtyard, which was at least 200 metres square. The donkey engine chugging away in the sanitation plant next door sounded as if it was on its last legs but it was also a clue as to how recently the place had been occupied. Prior to our gatecrash, it was used as some kind of assembly area for the Iraqi forces.

Towards the end of our stag, Stuart climbed into the back of the Bedford and handed me an ammunition box of 5.56-mm rounds. The lead seal on the lid was already broken which made us feel less guilty. The rounds inside the box were in bandoliers containing ten clips, with ten rounds in each clip. Stuart climbed back out of the Bedford and took the box from me so I could give our report at the CV whilst he jumped back in the cab of the Foden with our booty, giggling under his breath. When I returned to the Foden, Stuart had already recharged his empty magazines and made one ready on his rifle. I soon caught up with him and did the same.

'Right, time for some kip. It's reveille in a couple of hours,' Stuart said, and I couldn't have agreed more. The adrenalin rush and our excitement had passed and tiredness soon caught up with us. We'd just about made ourselves comfortable under our unzipped doss bags when I had a visitor knock at my door.

'What!' I shouted through the open window.

'Dress-state-four, immediately,' the voice replied, then it carried on to give the good news to the others in the packet.

'Did he say dress state-four?' Stuart asked. Although I think he'd heard, he just couldn't believe it.

'Yep. Must be expecting something.'

Our 'rocket packs', a nickname we used for our day sacks, were already in the cab for just this scenario. One of the two rocket packs housed a charcoal-lined Mk5 NBC suit, the noddy suit, which tends to make you sweat a bit, so it was a blessing to have a shout early in the morning before the sun had warmed up the air. Dress-state-four meant we had to wear our noddy suit as well as our gloves and over-boots. And trying to put it all on in the confined space of a Foden cab was easier said than done. I should have put it on outside but as I'd already started, I thought I might as well finish. It must have taken me three times as long.

Although it was only 0130hrs zulu, I was already sweating, mainly down to the struggle I'd had putting the suit on. I placed a sheet of one-colour detector paper on the bottom of each of the cab's side mirrors and one on each of the jacket sleeves of my noddy suit, in order to detect any chemical agents. If there was an NBC attack, the detector paper would turn blue.

We wound up the windows and clamped down the cupola cover on the cab roof. The chemical-attack warnings we'd had earlier were for nerve agents, so the order for us to don our suits could mean only one thing: we were expecting blister- or blood-agent attacks, like mustard gas. A chemical agent of this nature contaminates in the form of mist or droplets, which can enter through the skin as well as the respiratory system.

An hour passed with no warning of an attack and by this time we were getting pretty bored, and concerned we would end up wearing that shit for the rest of the day. A second hour passed, then out of the blue, 'Gas! Gas! Gas!'

We went into the IA drills and donned our respirators. As I pulled mine over my head, one of the straps broke, leaving the left side of the respirator with a poor seal around my face. I continued with the IA drill and secured the hood of the jacket around my respirator, still holding my breath and with my eyes shut. With my hood secure, I could hold the left side of the respirator tight against my face using my left hand, which allowed me to blow out hard, open my eyes and take a desperately needed lungful of filtered but restricted air. I now needed to decontaminate myself with my DKP1 pads, but this was difficult with one hand.

Stuart could see the predicament I was in and took out a DKP1 pad from my haversack and started to 'blot, bang, rub' over the required areas of my gloves and respirator: the 'buddy–buddy' system, as it's called.

'I'm OK,' I said, puffing and panting through the voice modulator. 'Look after yourself, I can cope with the rest.'

Stuart decontaminated himself whilst keeping a watchful eye on me. I think he was concerned I might have started to suffer the effects of a chemical agent.

After the decontamination drills, it was a case of sitting it out. The time was close to 0400hrs zulu and the sun was climbing rapidly – so was the temperature. I'd already drunk all the water in my army-issue water bottle, which had a straw adapter fitted into the screw cap. The NBC straw on my respirator pushed into the adapter, saving me from having to remove the respirator to take a drink. The only option I had left was to use the civvy bottles of water lying around the cab, which I could have poured into my army-issue bottle. However, a chemical agent could have easily contaminated it during the transfer, so I opted to leave it until absolutely necessary.

A further hour passed and my left arm was aching from pushing the respirator against my face. I may have been pressing too hard but I didn't want to risk allowing any agent to enter my respiratory system by relieving the pressure; I had to grin and bear it. Another half an hour passed and my left arm had finally gone numb; I could no longer tell how much pressure I was putting on my face. The only option I had was to lie down on my left hand and allow gravity to assist. And the only object I had to lie on was the HF radio set. I clumsily placed my rocket packs against the hard metal surface of the radio to cushion my hand and carefully lay against it. I noticed Stuart was lying back in his seat, either asleep or just dozing, so I thought I'd try the same.

Then, suddenly, I woke up – not from anyone shouting orders of all clear but because of the rise in temperature inside the cab and the aching pins and needles in my left hand. I couldn't have dozed off for more than 20 minutes but I still didn't dare move just in case I broke the seal around my respirator.

'All clear!' a voice eventually shouted, which was music to my ears. But I now faced another problem. I'd been lying in an awkward position for so long, coupled with the fact my arm had gone numb and I had pins and needles in my hand and couldn't move it voluntarily, that when I sat up, my arm remained in the same position, stuck to the side of my face.

'You can remove your respirator, you know.'

I attempted to turn and face Stuart. 'I know but I can't move my fucking arm!'

'What do ya mean, you can't move your arm?' Stuart replied, letting out a chuckle.

'I can't move it! I've had it in this position for so long it's stuck.'

'I'll go and get a medic.' Stuart was about to jump out of the cab.

'You won't,' I snapped. 'There's no way I want anyone to see me like this, I'll never live it down.'

Stuart could hold back no longer and started to laugh. ''Ere, hang on a minute.' He mooched around the back of the cab. 'I'm sure I've got my camera around here somewhere.'

'You can fuck off!'

'You'll just have to wait for the feeling to come back.'

I heard a knock on the driver's-side door. I couldn't believe it. That's all I needed, a bloody audience. I slowly shifted position with my arm stuck to the side of my face to see who it was. It was Mike, looking at me with a puzzled expression.

'You can remove your respirator, you know.'

'Yes, I know!' I snapped.

'Oh, right. You can take off the suits, that's what I've come to tell you. There's an O'group in 15 minutes.' He walked off, still wearing that bewildered expression.

Stuart removed his suit and packed it away in his rocket pack whilst I was still stuck with my arm up in the air. I did, however, manage to remove my respirator, much to Stuart's disappointment.

After a few minutes, I could just about move my arm, although it was slow and painful at first. I missed the O'group, so Stuart had to endure the ASM whilst I struggled with my noddy suit and replaced the broken plastic buckle on my respirator head strap. The following is part of the ASM's briefing:

> Many enemy forces have been destroyed through the night around our area. This was due to the countless explosions we heard in the distance caused by air strikes, artillery and our battle group. The area is now deemed safe, but, and isn't there always a but, we're moving out of this safe area and into an uncertain hostile area further north. The location is a GOSP [gas oil separation plant] 50 kilometres north of here and 14 kilometres south-west of a town called Az Zubayr. The location will be known as GOSP1. The GOSP was taken last night and it's our job to secure the area. It is likely we'll meet pockets of resistance, as this is a major prize. The GOSP oil tanks have been taken intact, including most of the plant, but it is thought they are primed with explosives and it's the enemy's

intention to detonate them when we get within range. Luckily, the majority of enemy forces have lost their bottle and fled the area but the threat is still very much a real one. The area is swarming with mines and booby traps, and it's likely we'll come under some kind of counter-attack, most likely in the form of hit-and-run tactics, which either the Fedayeen militia or Iraqi forces, dressed in civvy clothing posing as militia, will execute. So, the shoot-to-kill policy remains enforced. If it moves, kill it! A large section of the BG will be using the area as a retreat from Az Zubayr to service and repair vehicles, as well as rearm. The GOSP is well equipped with workshop facilities, which we will exploit to use as a forward repair workshop by our REME LAD. And, of course, the recovery section will be extremely busy. So far, there have been 15 oil fires counted at the GOSP and the surrounding area. These mainly consist of ruptured oil pipes, rather than oil wells. We'll be moving out of this location at 1200hrs zulu.

Preparations for moving out didn't take any longer than fifteen minutes, let alone the six hours we'd been granted before the 1200hrs zulu deadline. The constant banging of the donkey engine, the distant shelling and bombing through the night, the thought of the chogies retaking this position and the fact we'd just gone through a dress-state-four drill seemed to put a little urgency on the move.

12

PREPARE TO DEFEND YOURSELVES

The morning sun revealed the full extent of the courtyard and its surrounding area. Eucalyptus trees had been planted around the perimeter, which, I was well informed by Stuart 'the botanist' Richards, had been specially imported, since there are no native trees in Iraq. A small number of the trees were treated well enough to adapt to the conditions and grow, which is probably why we tended to see exotic trees around government buildings, palaces and the like. A sponge of information was our Stuart.

The coach in the middle of the courtyard had been hastily sabotaged, rather than hit by a shell. Typical clues were the ripped-out battery, ignition barrel and relays; slashed tyres; and a punctured fuel tank. Opposite the main entrance, we could now see the two-storey building which looked like some kind of house, maybe an office or a caretaker's living accommodation. The area outside the perimeter wall was nothing but desert. The only feature on the horizon was the odd battle-damaged T55 and T62.

Picking up any souvenirs from the area was a big no-no

and we didn't need telling twice about booby traps. We treated everything with suspicion. The thought of losing a limb would come rushing to the forefront of our minds if we came across a pile of small arms and artillery shells, for example, leaning against a wall. On one occasion, we found a crude automatic detonating device made from a hand grenade placed under some shells, clearly visible but obviously meant to be out of sight. The theory behind the device was that if the shells were disturbed, they would topple over and release the grenade firing pin. *Boom!* Even an empty Coke can left on the ground made us think twice.

Stuart had mentioned a few times that I was hogging the driving seat, leaving him to the role of 'brew-bitch', so to keep the peace and shut him up, I thought it best to let him have a go. This meant I became the brew-bitch.

The Bedford had to stay with us until we could unhook it at the GOSP and, as before, Mike and Stupid Boy stayed in their cab. When my wristwatch read 1159hrs zulu, we started to move to our next location. The route was mainly dual carriageway with the odd shell crater and burnt-out military vehicle to detour and, once more, it was full of American and British convoys. Again, the only traffic going south was civilian: people carriers, white and orange taxis, and countless donkey-drawn carts made up of old pieces of wood and car wheels. The donkeys couldn't have been any bigger than a Great Dane; their poor skinny legs going ten to the dozen pulling a cartload of household possessions. We soon came across other forms of transport which had been begged, borrowed or most likely stolen to transport families out of the war zone. We encountered tractors, battered trucks and even a gas-powered fork-lift vehicle with a family of about seven desperately clinging to the back and sides. Thousands of people were also escaping the war by foot, all walking south on both sides of the dual carriageway, carrying everything they owned, which wasn't a lot.

You'd think it would be possible to complete a journey of only fifty kilometres in less than an hour, including a piss break, but under battle conditions it took us a little over three. It was either traffic jams or suspicious situations, such as an abandoned BMP1, that held us up. The BMP1 was believed to be booby-trapped, so we had no alternative but to sit and wait for the engineers to blow up the obstacle and check the immediate blast area for mines or further booby traps before we could carry on – a 'better safe than sorry' policy.

We carried on down the dual carriageway, where abandoned plant vehicles and Nissan pick-up trucks had been left in the bushy, overgrown central reservation, until we reached a roundabout. There, the road split: driving straight ahead took you to Az Zubayr, whilst the right turn veered towards the main entrance to the GOSP. The amount of military traffic heading up the dual carriageway, however, had caused a bottleneck on this section of the journey. As Stuart edged his way through the narrowing of the road caused by the roundabout, we met two chogie wagons coming from the opposite direction. Behind them there appeared to be a brand-new white Toyota 4x4 Landcruiser. The occupants of these vehicles seemed agitated, but we didn't take any notice at first; they didn't open fire on us and certainly didn't appear to be carrying any arms. It wasn't until we parked up in our hide area that I realised these vehicles were either being stolen or recovered by their rightful owners, who were saving them from being misused by us. Other 4x4s were left in the middle of the road, some still with their engines ticking over. The Iraqis had obviously been disturbed by our uninvited appearance and had decided to leg it rather than risk getting their heads blown off by some trigger-nervous squaddie. We'd had plenty of prep talks regarding such behaviour from the locals and also about the possibility that deserting Iraqi soldiers would swap their uniforms for civilian clothes and steal vehicles so they could escape capture, from their own officers more so than from us, and disappear into the civilian population. Looting was also going to be an ongoing problem, but hey, who could blame them.

We reached the GOSP at 1500hrs zulu, by which time daylight was fading and night was gradually drawing in. And, of course, we were driving under tactical conditions. The only artificial source of light came from street lamps on the side of a road leading to Az Zubayr situated at the back of the GOSP. Brick security-guard buildings stood at either side of the entrance with a roundabout in the centre of the tarmac which looked like it had previously housed each end of a security barrier. It was difficult to see where exactly we were supposed to park. I'd only noticed that we were the lead vehicle ahead of the two Foden flat-bed 'drops' trucks parked behind us. We were blocking a driveway to an office block surrounded by those eucalyptus trees Stuart had kindly pointed out earlier. The rest of the A1 and A2 packets were opposite our position in a disused car park. The 2 RTR BG armoured vehicles were then parked on a large, hardcore surfaced compound area half a kilometre around the corner, complete with en-suite workshops, alternator and starter-motor repair shops, and other outbuildings. There was even a tyre-fitting centre.

The night belonged to the LI guys, which meant we could grab some well-deserved sleep. Once again, though, this proved to be easier said than done. All through the night, the constant drone of tracked and wheeled vehicles could be heard driving past, along with the sound of Challenger 2 tanks shelling some poor bastards. The odd explosion of falling bombs from an air strike nearby didn't help matters either. The following morning at 0300hrs zulu, A1 packet was on the move yet again. Destination: half a kilometre down the road to an unfinished petrol station.

The building was almost complete, minus running water and mains electricity. The pebbledashed shop and kiosk building was an empty shell, which made good office space for the boss and his disciples. The petrol pumps hadn't yet been installed but at least we had a concrete canopy above our heads, which gave us ample shade from the sun. A radio mast amazingly stood intact to the right of the entrance. Masts such as these, including TV, mobile-phone and communication masts, had been blown to pieces as part of a tactical move to blind and deafen the enemy.

The petrol station was in an area of about 200 metres square, surrounded by a chain-link fence. The grounds around the building hadn't yet been landscaped and piles of building sand and rubble were scattered around the site. North and west of the area was scrubland, with the odd shell-hole-infested building in the far distance. To the north, there was a second entrance leading to a road that reached the dual carriageway heading north-west towards Az Zubayr. To the south, next to the kiosk/shop building, a deep hole had been dug ready for the three huge petrol/diesel tanks which stood towards the south entrance. The top of the flat-roofed shop/kiosk building gave us a clear 360-degree view of our surrounding area and became one of three gun positions. The two other positions, placed within a horseshoe-shaped sandbag wall about one and a half metres high, were situated at the north (gun position two) and south (gun position one) entrances.

PREPARE TO DEFEND YOURSELVES

The ground positions were reinforced with earth and rubble, whilst the rooftop position just had a sandbag wall standing about one metre high. The positions on the ground were armed with the duty soldier's personal SA80 rifle, a gimpie with one box of 7.62-mm belted rounds and a 94-mm LAW. A night-vision sight was also supplied to all positions during dark hours, plus three flares. The rooftop position's weaponry consisted of only the individual soldier's SA80 rifle, because the rooftop was merely used as a recce platform.

Contact between each position was by radio, centralised at 'zero' in the shop. In the middle of the three gun positions, two roaming patrols consisting of two soldiers guarded the area. Sentries on stag had strict instructions as well as normal sentry duties, including a 12-hour password and orders to adopt the discipline of firing two rounds into the air as a warning for any challenge before any engagement – yeah, right!

Every other location scattered around the GOSP would have done the same, covering an area of about ten kilometres square. Countless Warriors and Challenger 2s patrolled the outer perimeters accompanied by 500 or so soldiers of the battle group, protecting not only themselves but also the oil tanks and refineries from any retaliation attacks. Such heightened defensive activity reflected the importance of the GOSP. Attacks were also expected on the armour returning from Basrah and Az Zubayr for repair and maintenance, not forgetting the vast stores of food, water, ammunition and spare parts for the tracked and B-vehicles. All in all, the enemy could have classed us as a prized possession – one effective strike on our location could have significantly slowed down the push into Basrah, if not postponed it entirely.

Across to our left, some 500 metres to the east, a

different battle had commenced. A gaggle of MLRS (multi-launch rocket system) vehicles were delivering their deadly salvo to an enemy position, most probably one towards Az Zubayr. Each salvo packet destroyed an area of one kilometre square and left little chance of survival. Scores of jet fighters and bombers – British and American – screamed overhead at low altitude as we completed our 'digging in' and all-round defences. On occasion, we could feel the roar of the jets and even taste their exhaust fumes as they passed, praying they could see we were friendly. There had been plenty of rumours flying around that many of the 'blue on blues' (friendly fire) were caused by air strikes on coalition positions.

The harbour area within the petrol station's perimeters was made secure and it was time for our evening meal. During the day, it was difficult to eat anything because of the heat but when the sun went down our appetites went up. We chilled out after our delicious meal of chicken and dumplings, again, and watched the firework display in the distance lighting up the night sky as Iraqi positions took a pounding just a few kilometres up the road. But we soon discovered we had a few uninvited guests of our own. Reports had been signalled to our CV that half a dozen chogie wagons, complete with mortars and 50-calibre machine guns mounted on the back, had been seen driving around the GOSP area: a typical style of pick-up truck with the hallmarks of the Fedayeen militia. Warriors and Challenger 2s screamed around the area to seek them out. We'd heard explosions close by, caused by the Challengers' pounded targets, but they were not necessarily the chogie wagons. Further explosions started to close in around our location, close enough to cause vibrations on the ground, and we could feel the pressure of the blasts rumble through our bodies. The incoming came from enemy mortars and artillery fire and it was definitely getting closer.

'*Stand to! Stand to!*' a voice cried.

This time our stand-to positions were clearly marked. Stuart and I grabbed our shit and ran to our location, about ten metres to the right of the north entrance. My rifle was made ready and I had two full magazines stuffed down the front of my CBA for quick access. Stuart and I settled in a pile of builders' rubble and within 30 seconds we were all in position, ready and waiting.

Heavy calibre machine-gun fire and the exchange of small arms were now closing in from the east but once again I couldn't see any muzzle flashes. My heart was soon racing ten to the dozen and the sweat began to drip uncontrollably in between the leather headband of my Kevlar helmet and forehead, then down into my eyes. I took a deep breath to try and calm myself down. I was determined to see this one through, just like the last contact.

The constant explosions and exchange of sporadic machine-gun fire became louder and more intense. Shells and mortar rounds lit up the night sky, landing 200 or 300 metres from our location. We lay still, in total darkness, with our rifles trained ahead, not daring to move a muscle in case the enemy was close enough to spot any movement.

Four Warriors raced past me and headed out of the north entrance turning east towards the enemy positions. I could feel the vibration caused by these 25-tonne monsters as they rumbled along the concrete road circling the petrol station. Within seconds of leaving the north entrance, the Warriors opened up with their 30-mm cannons and chain guns, and mowed down enemy movements. I then noticed muzzle flashes coming from the enemy, returning fire as they came under attack from the Warriors. They were closer than I'd thought.

Within a few minutes, the area fell silent, apart from the sound of Warrior and Challenger engines ticking over in the distance. They'd done their job and were now re-securing the area. We lay motionless in our stand-to positions for a further 20 minutes. I only wore a T-shirt underneath my CBA and now I'd calmed down a bit and stopped sweating through fear, I started to shiver with the cold, the first time I'd done so since arriving in the Gulf. Someone tapped my right shoulder. 'All clear!' a voice whispered. It was one of the LI guys.

'What's going on?' I asked.

'The threat has been dealt with. A couple of chogie wagons and some mortar and artillery pieces have been taken out. There's an O'group in five minutes in the shop.' The LI guy carried on around the perimeter, giving his message to the rest of the stand-to positions whilst his mates helped secure the immediate area on foot.

We walked back to the shop for the O'group, which was nothing more than a warning to stay alert – you don't say. Although the threat had been dealt with, the sentries were double-manned for the rest of the night. We were advised to sleep outside our vehicles just in case we were hit by any incoming but the thought of scorpions and camel spiders soon put me off that idea. Camel spiders can grow as big as your hand and are quite nippy, injecting an anaesthetic into their prey. They then munch on the flesh whilst their victims sleep. And as far as I was concerned, creepy-crawlies were far worse than a barrage of artillery shells, mortars and large calibre machine-gun fire.

Daylight soon began to break. The time was 0300hrs zulu. During the night, we'd only managed to grab the odd ten- or fifteen-minute snooze in between wild dogs barking and sudden bouts of paranoia about enemy attacks. One minute I'd be grabbing forty winks, the next I'd be fully alert to any alien sound from outside the cab. Tension was at an all-time high.

I started the engine so Stuart could boil the BV for a brew. Luckily, the cooks parked opposite had the 'Lazy Man' burner on the go, which meant ample hot water for a strip wash. The Lazy Man is a metal bin filled with water and heated up by a round steel tube in the base of the bin into which drops of ignited petrol fall from a reservoir, causing the water to heat up. It's quite an efficient source of heat. One of the downsides is the build-up of soot from the chimney, which flakes off and falls into the water. Another is the potential for a black face and singed eyebrows when lighting the petrol initially. If you're not careful, you can get a backdraught caused by releasing too much petrol from the reservoir. And, yes, it's happened to me on more than one occasion.

Stuart finished washing with our one and only plastic washing-up bowl and handed it to me. I filled the bowl with fresh warm water and started my strip wash as jets screamed overhead and bombed targets a few kilometres east, mopping up from last night's activities. Explosions continued to rumble in the distance whilst I brushed my teeth. Some of the targets were either extremely close or the bombs were falling short of their objectives, because we could feel the repercussions from the blasts. Either way, I was past caring. I didn't know if I was getting used to the war but I was certainly beginning to accept it.

After our wash and breakfast (meatballs and pasta – what else?), it was a case of get our heads down and wait for any jobs to come in. The lull of tasks was welcome because the past 24 hours had certainly taken its toll on the packet, let alone Stuart and me. A few hours of undisturbed sleep would work wonders, and that's as much as we got before a knock on my cab door woke us up.

'All right, mate.' It was one of the LI guys, Corporal Andy 'Stag' Thompson, grinning at me. He was known as Corporal Stag because of his eagerness to find volunteers to fill his notorious sentry-duty rotas. No one could escape his grasp – unless you were a recy mech . . . well, almost.

'Yeah, what's up, Andy?'

'You and Stuart are on stag in half an hour.'

'What? We're recy mechs. We don't do stag,' replied Stuart.

'I know that but this is an order from the boss. We don't have enough bodies to go around the clock, so everyone has to chip in, including the VMs.' He then walked away to give his news to some other unfortunate who'd been volunteered for the job.

The time for our sentry duty was 0600hrs zulu. Each of us had a one-hour stag in pairs. As usual, Stuart and I took the same stag at our stand-to position, which was gun position two. Bobby and Tony were to relieve us at 0700hrs zulu. I think the idea was to get the recy mechs and VMs out of the way and relieve them for any trade duties that came in. The previous staggies, a couple of LI guys, were waiting for us and looked relieved as we approached them.

'Thank fuck you're here, I'm starving,' said the first, who appeared to be slightly overweight.

'Nothing to report, apart from a red chogie wagon kept passing us on the road ahead. I think they were being nosy. Two in the cab and four riding in the back,' his mate said.

'Oh, a gimpie and a 94-mm LAW. Bit over the top, innit,' I said, as I pointed at the hardware lying on top of the sandbags.

'Ever used these before?' Chubby asked.

'The gimpie? Yeah, once, but not the LAW.'

'Yeah, me too,' added Stuart.

Chubby went through the firing drills of the LAW and gave us a quick recap on the gimpie just to allay any doubts. The last time I'd used one was on a firing range six years previously, so the lesson was much appreciated. Stuart hadn't used one for a couple of years so also benefited from the demonstration. As for the LAW, I decided to give it a wide berth. I would have ended up blowing us to bits if I'd picked it up, but Stuart had that look in his eyes once again. He couldn't wait for the chance to blow up something with it. I'm sure I could see a slight dribble running down the side of his mouth.

The heat of the sun was already taking its toll. Combined with the obligatory combat shirt we had to wear under the CBA, along with a helmet and webbing, whilst on sentry duty, it wasn't long before the sweat began to saturate my shirt and drip down my back. Thankfully, the last two guys had left a couple of unopened bottles of water. Although slightly warm, the water quenched my thirst, for a while anyway.

Because of the previous night's excitement, we had to radio the CV every 15 minutes, without fail. It didn't matter if we had seen anything or not, we had to give a report. We were three-quarters of the way through our stag and still nothing had happened, except that the red Nissan pick-up truck Chubby had told us about had driven past a couple of times. On each occasion, it would slow down at the junction 15 or 20 metres ahead of our gun position. When it passed, it would speed up and disappear down the road towards the main junction, heading towards Az Zubayr.

Slightly to our right and 30 metres in front of us was the 50-metre-high radio mast, with a flat-roofed single-storey brick station building at its base. Sandwiched between the road and our gun position were tall dry bushes and thick shrubs, which obscured our view of the road ahead. I radioed the CV about the red pick-up truck and was told to keep an eye on it. If they decided to get brave and tried to enter our position, I was to fire two warning shots. If that didn't work, I was to chew 'em up with the gimpie. Fair enough, I thought.

A further fifteen minutes elapsed and our sentry duty was finally over, although we'd actually done an extra five minutes waiting for Bobby and Tony. They'd do anything to waste time on their stag. As for the red pick-up truck, we hadn't seen it for about 20 minutes, so had put it down to looters or locals just being plain nosy.

'About time!' Stuart shouted as Bobby and Tony walked slowly to the gun position.

'What's up?' Bobby replied, as if he didn't know.

I gave Bobby a quick report. 'Bog all's happened. Only a red chogie wagon driving past now and again, and it hasn't been back for about 20 minutes.'

'So it's all yours,' Stuart said, with a smile.

'Cheers, mate,' Bobby replied, sarcastically.

Stuart and I started to walk back to the Foden but didn't get ten metres before I heard a vehicle approach. I turned around knowing it was the red pick-up because I recognised the sound of the engine.

'Is that it?' Bobby asked, pointing in its general direction.

'Yeah, I think it's just stopped behind those bushes, dead ahead.' I pointed towards the sound of its engine ticking over.

The engine picked up a few more revs as it slowly edged towards the mouth of the north entrance. I didn't like this situation; it felt like it was happening in slow motion whilst the rest of the world continued on an even keel. Stuart was oblivious to it all and continued to walk back towards the Foden but he soon turned around when he heard the engine revs increase, as if the vehicle was about to start a race.

'Stuart!' I shouted. 'Take cover, this could turn nasty.'

He nodded in agreement and ran towards the opposite side of the entrance, into the ditch, well in view of the red pick-up. Bobby crouched down facing the entrance and leaning on the corner of the sandbags. I ran to take charge of the gimpie. Tony had crouched down to my left with his rifle over the top of the sandbags and the LAW in easy reach, just in case we needed it. I was in two minds whether to shout out 'stand to' but it was too late. The red pick-up started to move forward, slowly at first but quickly increasing its speed, heading straight for us. From my position, I still couldn't see it, but Stuart could.

'Twenty metres, heading straight for us!' he called out. Automatic fire from the back of the pick-up filled the air.

'*Return fire!*' Bobby shouted.

It was now in sight, so I returned fire with a few bursts from the gimpie with Tony, Stuart and Bobby joining in with the exchange. The rest of our camp soon realised what was happening and were quick to join in, including gun position one. The gimpie chopped into the front of the pick-up, stopping it instantly. The windscreen and the off-side panels were peppered with holes from the 7.62-mm rounds of the gimpie and the 5.56-mm rounds of the LSWs and SA80 rifles.

The two chogies in the cab slumped in their seats instantly, after receiving countless rounds. I never knew how much damage a gimpie could actually do.

The four chogies in the back dived out and took cover in the bushes as soon as we returned fire. Seconds later, they emerged from their hiding places and threw their hands in the air, shouting what could have been obscenities, pleas of surrender or requests for mercy.

'*Cease fire!*' Bobby yelled, as four LI guys came running past the gun position and into the bushes to escort the four occupants of the back of the pick-up truck so they could be interrogated for any information they might have had. Somehow, they'd miraculously survived without a scratch. The two occupants of the cab, however, didn't stand a chance.

13

THE STORY SO FAR
. . . 20–25 MARCH

After the fire-fight, the camp area was buzzing with a mixture of excitement and fear. Captain 'John Wayne' Schaffer wanted to know all the details, so Bobby and I obliged, then we were asked to carry on with our duties. Bobby and Tony had to finish their stag, which didn't please them. I think they were concerned there might be further attacks.

I climbed back into the Foden where Stuart was already boiling the BV for a brew. I lit a cigarette and sat back in my seat with my legs resting on top of the steering wheel.

'How do you feel?' I asked.

'Still a bit fired up. How about you?'

I took a long drag of my cigarette before answering. 'I'm beginning to realise you shouldn't dwell on such things; just get on with it, that's what I say.' Boy, was I bullshitting – I had virtually crapped myself and I thought I was getting used to the war? I started to think how we had come out of it unscathed and if we would be so lucky next time. It wasn't long before my subconscious, yet again, began to throw images of my family to the forefront of my mind. The thought of them receiving a telephone call informing them I was injured or worse was too much to bear. I made the tea and chilled out for a few minutes, gathering my thoughts.

As always, when I started to chill out or tried to grab a few hours' kip, someone disturbed me. 'What?' I shouted, replying to the knock on my door.

'You've got a job.' It was Chubby, the LI guy. 'You've to go to the CV. They've got some details or something.' He shrugged his shoulders, not really having understood the message.

'Yeah, all right, mate, I know what they want.'

'A job, is it?' asked Stuart.

'Yeah, I'll go and see what it is.'

I took one more swig of my tea, grabbed my haversack and rifle, and headed for the CV. A few minutes later, I returned to the Foden with the details of our task: A2 packet wanted to 'borrow us for a few minutes'. In army terms, that meant anything from a few hours to a full day.

We finished our tea, put our trade hats on and made our way to A2, parked in the large compound next to the workshops. The road leading to this area came to a T-junction, opposite which was the PW camp – thanks to the previous night's activities, it already had quite a few inmates. A painting of Saddam Hussein on a sandstone monument greeted us as we turned right into the compound (the following day, a Warrior took it out with its 30-mm cannon). It was already filling with heavy armoured vehicles, with Challenger 2s and Warriors undergoing minor surgery. Most of the 'accidents' were caused by overambitious drivers damaging tank tracks or breaking vehicle lights. Some of the commanders were even upset about the paintwork on their precious tanks getting scratched.

Our task was to drag as many of the plant vehicles as possible out from the workshop and courtyard area to make way for our own vehicles and kit. These included earth graders, dump trucks, earth removers and an old Russian decommissioned 4x2 fuel tanker. We also had to drag a 40-tonne tracked crane out of the way, which caused a few problems when one of the tracks seized and made the crane jib tip over to one side. After a few choice words, we got the job done, although not entirely by the book.

SSgt Phil Robinson beckoned us from his position next to his CRARRV, parked at the other end of the workshop, offering us a brew, which we accepted. As we chatted, Phil suggested we have a 'cheese cutter' – a length of 50x50 mm angle iron with the leading edge sharpened to cut through garrotte wire – fitted to our roof. Stuart and I looked at each other none the wiser, so Phil explained the situation. The American forces had reported that the Fedayeen militia were laying garrotte wire across tracks and roads to sever the heads of soldiers sitting up through their cupolas. The idea of the cheese cutter was to cut the wire before it cut off unsuspecting heads.

I rubbed my neck and looked at Stuart with a slightly concerned expression. 'I think we'd better have one fitted, don't you?'

Stuart nodded in agreement and positioned the Foden further up the workshop, towards the metal-smith bay, where they were busy making these cheese cutters.

Danny, the TA-lover, acting as the brew-bitch, was eagerly awaiting our entrance so he could give us all the gossip about what had been happening over the past few days. He ushered me to some deck chairs around the other side of the CRARRV. Cpl Andy Dawson was sitting drinking his tea and appeared relieved he had company.

'He's collared you, then, Kev. We've had to endure his

storytelling for the past 24 hours, so I'm glad some other poor bastard has to put up with it. He's like a bloody woman.'

When I arrived in the Gulf, I decided to take any gossip from the 'battlefield bush' with a pinch of salt, but on this occasion Danny seemed to have fallen on some interesting facts, which actually filled in the gaps, as it were, from our O'groups and briefings. In between his overexcited tongue reeling off one story after another, and ignoring the added 'fuck's, 'fucked's and 'fucking's mentioned after every other word, I managed to gather information relating to the 'action' which had taken place since we'd crossed the border. I transferred this into a daily report for my diary, along with other tangible information I had written down from other sources.

I made myself comfortable and let out a sigh. 'Go on, then, Danny, let's hear it.'

20 MARCH: D-DAY

At 0300hrs zulu, Tomahawk cruise missiles from six US warships hit selected targets in Iraq, aimed at senior members of the regime and at Saddam Hussein himself. Other strikes hit air-defence systems and SAM [surface-to-air] batteries. Surface-to-surface missile sites and artillery batteries are also targeted. Elements of 7 Armoured, including 2 RTR BG, and 16 Air Assault, with other parts of 1 (UK) Division, breach the Kuwait–Iraq border and start a major ground offensive against Iraqi positions.

Within hours of the conflict starting, Scud missiles hit coalition forces in southern Iraq. Fifteen missiles hit Camp Cambrai alone, with the possibility that chemical warheads had been used. Soldiers are ordered to wear respirators at all times during the air raids.

THE STORY SO FAR . . . 20–25 MARCH

A huge sandstorm engulfing southern Iraq potentially delays any push over the border. A large number of Iraqi T62 and T72 tanks have been reported travelling towards the Kuwaiti border using the storm and their knowledge of the terrain as cover to attack British forces. Twelve Challenger 2 tanks are tasked to destroy the approaching enemy threat.

21 MARCH

Cruise missiles continue to hit strategic targets in Baghdad; 3 Commando, the Royal Marines make an amphibious assault on the Al Faw peninsula in southern Iraq, where the oil infrastructure is taken virtually intact; 42 Commando, the Royal Marines block positions and destroy Iraqi forces at Al Faw; 7 Armoured Brigade, with 2 RTR BG, muster at the FAA before continuing their push towards Az Zubayr and Basrah; 3 Commando, the Royal Marines and US troops push towards the seaport of Umm Qasr, close to the Kuwaiti and Iranian borders.

UK Special Forces, Royal Marines, elements of 7 Armoured, and US troops secure oilfields and GOSPs around Basrah, capturing them almost intact. As predicted, the GOSPs and oil refineries are booby-trapped, causing a huge headache for British and coalition forces attempting to secure them.

Fedayeen and local militia, including suicide bombers, become a problem with their sporadic attacks on roadblocks and checkpoints. Scud missile attacks continue to hit British forces along the Kuwait–Iraq border; US 3 Infantry Division quickly advance towards Baghdad.

22 MARCH

A massive air assault is launched with 3,000 sorties against various targets throughout Iraq. US troops encounter strong resistance from Republican Guard and regular army units at Al Nasiriyah in southern Iraq. The 51 Mechanised Division of the Iraqi Army defending oilfields and the surrounding area of Basrah surrender to British 7 Armoured Brigade and elements of 2 RTR BG. US and UK Marines, along with other coalition troops, secure the area.

Supplies and humanitarian aid enter the seaport of Umm Qasr with the Royal Navy RFA [Royal Fleet Auxiliary] ship Sir Galahad, *the first vessel to bring much-needed food, clothing and medicines to Iraq. US and Royal Navy minesweepers continue to scan the seaport and surrounding waterways.*

Many oil fires are now seen around Basrah and other regions, caused by retreating Iraqi forces setting oil pipelines, storage tanks and refineries alight.

Two Royal Navy Sea King helicopters collide, with no survivors. A total of six British and one US crew members were on board the helicopters.

23 MARCH

Whilst humanitarian aid and supplies dock at the seaport of Umm Qasr, British soldiers continue to fight Iraqi forces, trying desperately to cling to the port and the Al Faw peninsula. PW camps are beginning to overflow, as thousands of Iraqi troops surrender in huge groups around southern Iraq. Further camps are being constructed to cope with the ever-increasing PWs.

Twelve US soldiers have been reported missing. Some US soldiers have been captured and paraded on

Iraqi television. An RAF Tornado is shot down close to the Kuwaiti border by a Patriot missile battery as it returns from a sortie in Iraq. Both aircrew, from IX (B) Squadron, are killed.

Two British soldiers are reported missing after their Land-Rover and other vehicles from their packet came under attack in Az Zubayr. The Land-Rover's occupants, of 33 Engineer (EOD) Regiment, are later confirmed dead. 2 RTR BG, along with other 1 (UK) Division units, capture a GOSP a few kilometres outside Az Zubayr but soon come under attack by defiant Iraqi forces, desperately trying to regain the ground and, more importantly, the oil plants. A battle commences, with air strikes called in to assist with securing the GOSP.

24 MARCH

US forces advance past Al Nasiriyah, where two Cobra helicopter gunships had been brought down by a supposed RPG attack. Also, in separate incidents, two other British soldiers are killed in action in Az Zubayr as they patrol close to an area nicknamed 'RPG Alley'.

The first, a sergeant from 2 RTR BG, is tragically shot and fatally wounded in an incident involving an Iraqi suspect being held at a checkpoint. A second Iraqi suspect had approached the sergeant with a brick and was about to hit him over the head with it. Another British soldier quickly reacted by shooting the attacker, reportedly using his Warrior chain gun. Unfortunately, the fatal burst, which killed the Iraqi prisoner, went straight through him and killed the sergeant.

The second soldier, a lance corporal from

1 Battalion, the Black Watch is killed in action near Az Zubayr after coming under attack from Iraqi forces.

RAF and US aircraft continue to attack Republican Guard formations near Baghdad. British forces continue operations to secure Umm Qasr seaport. British artillery pounds Iraqi mortar and artillery positions, which had opened fire on British troops and Iraqi civilians near Basrah.

It is reported that three US Abram tanks have been destroyed – one by Iraqi forces using an RPG and two in a blue-on-blue incident involving two Cobra gunship helicopters.

25 MARCH

British Commando forces, with support from 16 Air Assault Brigade helicopters and coalition ground attack aircraft, successfully defeat 19 Iraqi T55 tanks. All are destroyed.

During multiple engagements with Iraqi forces, two British soldiers are tragically killed in a blue-on-blue incident involving Challenger 2 tanks belonging to 2 RTR and the Queen's Royal Lancers in Basrah.

The squaddie sense of humour was at that moment difficult to sustain. The previous four or five days had certainly been busy for some units, and it hadn't exactly been a bed of roses for us. Ever since we'd crossed the border, we'd witnessed more than enough pain and suffering but I couldn't help thinking at the time that things would only get worse.

Over the days which followed, the GOSP area quietened to

an eerie silence. Assisting with the odd Warrior engine-pack change or fixing non-starters with flat batteries was all we had to contend with. During the lull, we re-supplied on shower gel and toothpaste from the EFI (Expeditionary Forces Institute) shop tent and grabbed the chance to buy a few treats, including a crate of warm Coca-Cola and some tubes of Pringles. I also replenished my dwindling cigarette supply, and at $15 for a pack of 200, I couldn't grumble.

The lack of work was a mixed blessing. The excuse 'we're needed at the workshops', which we used to avoid any general duties and to just mooch around, was wearing thin with Captain Schaffer. We managed to convince him for a couple of days but he soon clocked on to our antics and threw us at the mercy of Corporal Stag Thompson for sentry duty with A1 packet, which included three or four one-hour stags over a twenty-four-hour day. Captain Schaffer, however, decided to put Stuart and me on the rooftop position. He thought it best to keep the 'real' soldiers on the other gun positions and give us part-timers the easier option – the cheek of it!

I also had the chance to write a few blueys home, one to each of my parents and eight to Helen, in one day. The usual 'wonder what they're doing now' thoughts soon gripped my mind. Writing blueys gave me the chance to escape the war for a few hours and concentrate on the family. Stuart had already received at least ten letters, some of which were emails sent to his BFPO (British Forces Post Office) address. So far, I'd received bog all, which made me wonder what the wife was up to back home. Poor Danny had only received two blueys – both had been redirected from his bank, letting him know his account was overdrawn. Still, at least he'd received something.

Writing letters back home was easier said than done. It was bad enough leaving loved ones at home to go and fight a war thousands of miles away, but to have them watch bullshit news bulletins on the television and read overexcited crap in the newspapers made it worse. So it wasn't a good idea to reiterate the news reports and make matters worse. We felt we had to tone things down a bit and make a joke of the weather, or write about how bored we were. We would also tell them that we ate three square meals a day and brag about how varied they were.

What we didn't do was write about the fire-fights, the Scud attacks, and the artillery and mortar bombardments. Or even how squaddie Smith's left foot got infected because a camel spider crept into his doss bag and feasted on his big toe, otherwise there would be grandparents keeling over having heart attacks, wives checking life insurance policies to see if they included acts of war and parents divorcing because mothers blamed fathers for sons or daughters joining the army in the first place.

So, what could we write about? First, soften the content – make a joke about the whole thing but don't shoot ourselves in the foot, as it were, and make too good a joke. If we did, it would make the family back home think we were having an easy life, spending all day getting a suntan. The reports on the 24-hour news channels would suddenly start being ignored because relatives would have written proof of what the war was really like, which in turn would make the BBC and suchlike look to be fabricating the whole thing – in many ways, as far as I am concerned, they were anyway. Even granddad would start moaning about the cushy number we were on and compare it with a 'real war', like when he fought the Nazis during the Second World War. So, you see, the humble squaddie was knackered whichever way he turned.

Our post office was part of the EFI, which was nothing more than a 12x12-foot tent, manned by two squaddie

TOP LEFT: My Foden 6x6 recovery vehicle having a 'cheese cutter'
fitted to the cab roof by one of the LAD guys in our makeshift
workshop at the GOSP near Az Zubayr, Iraq. The cheese cutter was
nothing more than a length of angle iron, about 1,000 mm in
length, with a sharpened edge towards the tip to act as a wire-cutter.

TOP RIGHT: The Foden in profile. This picture was taken in
Kuwait just before the start of the war.

BOTTOM LEFT: A Foden recovery vehicle in its DPM camouflage
colours of the BAOR (British Army of the Rhine) parked in my
platoon's hangar.

BOTTOM RIGHT: Last-chance saloon on the ferry to the Hook of
Holland – the packages wrapped in hessian are weapon bundles of
SA80 rifles and LSWs (light support weapons). It was my turn for
sentry duty and I needed some squaddie literature to occupy my
mind!

TOP LEFT: A view from the back of our reception tent at Camp Centurion the morning we arrived in Kuwait. The Bedford four-tonne troop carrier in the centre of the picture was one of the vehicles used to transport arriving squaddies to various camps.

TOP RIGHT: A Royal Engineers CRARRV – the canvas skirt around the base of the vehicle is supposed to minimise the dust kicked up by the tracks of this 60-tonne brute.

BOTTOM: I took this picture when Stuart and I returned from a task recovering a CVRT, which had taken most of the night to complete. On our return, we caught the CRARRV crew asleep. The time was about 0400hrs zulu.

TOP: A CVRT similar to the one Stuart and I recovered near the Iraqi border. This particular vehicle is being serviced by one of our LAD VMs.

MIDDLE: The FAA (forward assembly area) at Camp Barnsley where 7 Armoured Brigade assembled 24 hours before the push towards Az Zubayr. In the foreground the Royal Engineers, while in the background, 2 RTR light and heavy armour.

BOTTOM: Three of the four militia PWs captured after their failed raid on our position at the GOSP.

TOP LEFT: Me grabbing a rest in the back of the CV (command vehicle) after the failed attack by the Fedayeen militia. The muzzle of an LSW can be seen at the bottom of the picture.

TOP RIGHT: One of many pictures of Saddam Hussein at the GOSP near Az Zubayr. Soon after this photo was taken, a Warrior AFV destroyed it with its 30-mm cannon.

BOTTOM: A picture of the 'toilet kit' we had to take with us every time we wanted to 'pay a visit'. It consisted of an SA80 rifle complete with full magazine; haversack with respirator; a shovel; a 25-litre oil drum with top and bottom cut out; and a roll of toilet paper. The CBA and Kevlar helmet had to be worn at all times (hence they're not in the picture).

TOP: Another prize from a nearby airfield. One of the original plans was to repair the fire-tender and donate it to the Az Zubayr fire service. What actually happened to it remains a mystery, although I do know it was put to good use.

LEFT (top): Ready to move from the GOSP with the CET hooked up using the hollibones.

LEFT (middle): The Foden and a 20-tonne Tasker trailer hooked up on the taxiway at Shaibah Airfield. It's ready to transport a Cobra attack helicopter with a gearbox problem to an American workshop in Kuwait.

LEFT (bottom): Steve and me next to his HumVee during a halt to Shaibah Airfield. The smoke in the background is coming from sabotaged oil pipes on the edge of

TOP LEFT: Enjoying our chill-out period at Shaibah Airfield –
note the 25-litre oil drum hanging on the jib hook – our toilet!

TOP RIGHT: Propaganda left at a Republican Guard barracks at
Al Amarah.

BOTTOM: A Russian-built recovery vehicle used by the Iraqi
Army for their tanks and other heavy-armoured vehicles. The T62
tank at the left of the picture is the one Phil failed to recover.

posties who were responsible for the collection and delivery of all the blueys and parcels for the entire 2 RTR battle group. To say they were kept busy would be putting it mildly – bless 'em!

The sheer amount of mail delivered to the land forces was incredible. Controlled by the 98 Postal and Courier Squadron of the RLC, it employed 50 TA soldiers to sort and deliver not only squaddie post, but also important signals and intercommunication details to all 1 Div battle groups. And because blueys and parcels under 2 kg could be sent for free, a tremendous strain was added to an already overstretched and undermanned postal system – yet they somehow coped with their ever-increasing workloads.

Towards the end of the conflict, over half a million blueys and a further half a million e-blueys managed to reach their destination. E-blueys, although sent in an instant via email, still had to be printed and sealed, and took roughly two days to deliver. Ordinary, handwritten blueys would usually take a further two days, which wasn't bad considering they mostly came from the UK and Germany. Our continual movement around Iraq, however, meant that it was difficult to locate certain battle groups, which resulted in further delays. Stuart and I fell victim to this and often received mail which was two or three weeks old.

The morale parcels and other small packages and letters topped the 500-tonne mark towards the end of Operation Telic, resulting in a building having to be constructed to house the parcels before sorting and delivery.

When the conflict started and the coalition forces were about to cross the border into Iraq, we were ordered to either burn or hand over to our units for safekeeping all personal items, including family photographs and blueys sent by loved ones, mobile phones, driving licences and anything else which could relate you to your home address or personal contacts. The threat of capture by Iraqi forces was very real for all soldiers, not just the more clandestine squads involved with target recognition, or platoons of Special Forces positioned ahead of the advancing coalition battle groups. And if any of us were captured, as a few US soldiers were, it was common practice for the Iraqis to exploit such possessions and use them to extract any information during interrogation.

Personal possessions, such as a bluey, which may have included family names and address details, or even a family photograph, could be easily linked to make an individual profile. And a mobile phone confiscated by your captors would give them all the information required to telephone your loved ones and convince them that their husband, son or boyfriend had been brutally tortured and murdered. Likewise, captors could use psychological torture and convince soldiers that their family were about to receive a visit from a terrorist if they refused to cooperate.

The only personal items we were permitted to carry were an MoD 90 ID card, dog tags, a list of the 'laws of armed conflict' and our PW Geneva Convention card, which gave our 'big six' details: rank, name, number, date of birth, blood group and religion. If we wanted our chequebooks to withdraw money or our satlink phone cards to call home, or anything else we had handed over, we had to ask our platoon sergeants or RSMs to retrieve them from our HQ, which took days.

Unofficially, and I'm sure I wasn't the only one, I did keep the odd personal possession, including a couple of photographs of my wife and kids. Well, what did they expect!

14

IN THE NAME
OF HUMANITY

We were getting increasingly frustrated. The war seemed to have somehow lost its momentum, perhaps due to the sudden lull we were experiencing within our battle group. The unforeseen speed with which we had taken our objectives and the fact that we now found ourselves suddenly having to bring forward our planning for the assault into Basrah may have contributed to this. However, there was a little excitement for us recy mechs when we were tasked to recover some civvy vehicles from a lock over the River Tigris, between the locations known as Bridge Four and Bridge Five. The entire task took two days to complete.

The lock, which allowed ships to pass up and down the Tigris, was big enough to carry a single-carriage tarmac road, so the retreating Iraqi Army had blocked the road with civvy trucks. All they did to disable them was smash the ignition locks and remove some of the wheels, which they left in the vicinity – the fuel tanks were left intact and some were even full of diesel. No booby traps had been found, so it was easy for us to make them roadworthy and 'borrow' them for humanitarian purposes.

We managed to start a Scania 4x2 18-tonne 'cattle wagon', which was used for transporting PWs. Two nearly new bright-orange Mercedes 18-tonne water tankers were also taken, one of which had to be recovered with the Foden so the workshops could play with it and make it roadworthy. We even managed to start a Mercedes 24-seat coach, complete with air conditioning, which was used by the A1 and A2 packets for fetching and carrying whatever. We decided to leave the two cement mixers behind, as we couldn't really think of how else they could be used for humanitarian work, other than transporting cement. We did, however, borrow a radio-cassette player from one of them and soon had it wired up in our Foden.

Stuart spotted a garage housing three brand-new white Toyota Landcruisers with leather seats and air conditioning. We couldn't leave them there, and at least one of them had to come back with us but it soon disappeared within the battle group; pinched, no doubt, by those further up in the hierarchy. We also managed to bring back four flat-bed semi-trailers for the articulated truck units; we found two LPG-powered fork-lift trucks and a diesel one, which definitely came in handy for the guys in logistics shunting stores around.

By far the best prize had to be the airport fire-tender, though, originally used for extinguishing aircraft fires. We found it lying on the side of the road after dropping off a Bedford TM at ECP 4 of 2 Battalion REME at Shaibah Airfield, ten kilometres north-west of our then-current location. It was just sitting there and we had an empty hook, so we borrowed it. The fuel tank was empty and there was evidence of an attempt to sabotage it by breaking the ignition lock and ripping out some of the relays in the fuse box, but apart from that it appeared to be fine.

As we drove into the GOSP compound with this bright-red, nearly new Scania airport fire engine worth about $1 million, the ASM could only shake his head in disbelief and manage an 'I don't believe it' smile. I parked in the workshop yard and gave Stuart a hand to unhook it. The VMs couldn't hold back any longer and pounced on it like a pack of hyenas. It wasn't until the following day we noticed it was missing from the workshops; the VMs had been working on the repairs through the night. At first, I thought this was because it was needed as soon as possible for humanitarian purposes but the truth soon came out – the VMs wanted it to go joyriding, I mean, road test it. Rumour was it had been given to the Az Zubayr fire department.

Our efforts were soon rewarded, though, as we saw these civvy vehicles put to a more beneficial use. Whether it was true or not, we were told (unofficially) our unit was the first to supply civilian vehicles for the transportation of water and humanitarian aid during the conflict.

Whilst we were skiving around the workshops, yet again, Second Lieutenant Connor walked over from the CV with another task for us. A Mercedes Actros tractor unit had been spotted in Az Zubayr which could be used for pulling water-tanker semi-trailers. Our task was to bring it back. Location: area code 'Fulham'; grid reference: 633–622. The vehicle casualty was behind the hospital in a compound; safe route available but armoured escort was required – so far, so good.

We waited for almost an hour until our so-called 'armoured' escort arrived, which turned out to be a bloody Land-Rover. Not only that, the armoured escort was supposed to lead the way but because the two squaddies in the Land-Rover, a couple of LI guys, didn't have the appropriate map and didn't want to inadvertently lead us down 'RPG Alley', we ended up leading most of the way.

We drove down the 14-kilometre dirt track past the GOSP, which led to a single carriageway road into Az Zubayr. When we reached the end of the dirt track, we turned left onto the road, leaving only a further six kilometres before we hit the outskirts of the town. The road was littered with Scimitars, Warriors and Challenger 2 tanks from 2 RTR Falcon and Cyclops squadrons, and the SDG. The Irish Guards and the RRF carried out countless foot patrols up and down the main roads, along with 1 Battalion, the Black Watch.

We'd travelled only four kilometres when we came across a VCP surrounded by locals whose vehicles were being searched by the military police. The RRF looked on from a distance, standing next to a Warrior with its 30-mm cannon pointing towards the crowd, just in case something sparked up. There was also a Challenger 2 parked opposite, adding extra muscle to the VCP. A young corporal RMP beckoned me through the chaos so we could continue with our task without any unnecessary hold-ups. He tried to keep the crowd back but his efforts were wasted as we approached. By now, I'd slowed down to about 10 kph.

''Ere we go,' Stuart shouted. 'Hold on to your valuables.'

I knew what he meant. Within seconds, the kids were standing in front of the Foden, jumping up the side of the cab with their sticky fingers and poking them through the open windows. 'Mister, Mister! Water, water!' I could hear them shout. Luckily for us, we were sitting in a cab two metres above the ground. The Land-Rover behind us didn't stand a chance and was swamped by kids.

I looked in my rear-view mirror at the poor LI guys

sitting at eye level; easy prey for the kids. It was time for the LI guys to deploy Plan B (the original 'Plan A' had been to just plough straight through them, but we couldn't really do that without a reasonable excuse since it would warrant an arrest by the RMPs, weird as it may sound in the middle of a war). Plan B was to throw as many rat-pack chocolate bars and boiled sweets as far away as possible from the vehicle, making the kids run after them and fight over the booty. This would give us the chance to drive off quickly. Then again, we would only be ambushed by more kids further up the road. Plan B was therefore limited to how much 'ammo' we carried.

We generally took a light-hearted approach to carrying out crowd-control plans where possible and although some of our plans may have appeared heavy-handed, it was a case of knowing how far we had to go to ensure our safety, as well as the safety of the crowd, especially the kids. In a way, I suppose it was our fault we caused such crowds in the first place. But you simply cannot stop a British soldier from having a laugh with the locals; it's in our blood to make friends and help where we can, and always will be. Winning the hearts and minds, I think it's called.

And so to plan C, which was for when we ran out of sweets and had to resort to shouting 'Ali Baba! Ali Baba!' out of the window. This gave the kids the shits, big-time, because shouting it signified that there was a thief amongst them. They didn't want to be accused of theft because under Iraqi law they would have had their hands chopped off. Immediately, they would leg it and scatter, and deny having been anywhere near us. Sometimes it worked but the kids were beginning to realise what we were doing and had soon clocked on to our trick.

Plan D was a somewhat desperate measure, consisting of firing a few bursts of automatic in the air. It was effective, if only for a minute or so, until the excitement died down and the kids realised, yet again, that it was nothing more than a bluff. Plan E was for when all else failed – shoot the bastards! This particular solution, although highly effective for crowd control, didn't win any friends or gain the confidence of the locals, so Stuart came up with Plan E1. This was slightly effective but could result in our vehicle being attacked with rocks and stones, so it was best to use this plan when on the move. Perversely, it was also good fun and a tension reliever.

Stuart devised a catapult using a U-shaped metal-bearing holder with a stalk welded at the bottom, which he found in one of the workshop garages. He used an elastic strap nicked from a pair of sandstorm goggles to launch the projectiles. The best projectiles we found were the boiled sweets from our rat packs. They could travel at a fair rate of knots and resulted in quite a sting on a bare leg or arm.

Whilst we were waiting for the LI guys to execute Plan B (because there's a lot of complicated calculations to work out before lobbing sweets out of a window), a scruffy boy about ten years old, shouting at the side of my cab, caught my attention. 'Mister, Mister!'

I looked down at this dirty, scruffy-looking kid wearing urine-stained brown trousers and a dirty white T-shirt. He was using the international sign language for 'I want a cigarette' by mimicking himself smoking one.

Fuck it, I thought. ''Ere, mate,' I said, as I leant out of the window holding one. He was just about to grab it when a hand from a woman behind boxed him around his right ear. I could see the huge smile on his face disappear in a flash and become contorted with the sudden sharp pain from a well-positioned right-hander. He then faced a grilling from the woman I supposed was his mother. The boy started to shout, although I couldn't understand a word he was saying. I guess he was making some sort of an excuse; after all, he had a reputation to salvage after being hit by his mother right in front of his mates.

The woman stared at me and started to give me a right mouthful. Again, I couldn't understand a word she was saying but I knew I had a look of guilt on my face, not unlike her poor son. No matter what squaddies face in a war, we still have a boyish, guilty look on our faces when being told off by a woman, and this bollocking was no exception.

The LI guys finally executed Plan B, which took the kids' attention away from our truck. They soon headed for the booty left behind by the Land-Rover, which had itself made its getaway successfully and cleared the 'killing zone' in one piece.

'Quick, go for it, Kev, before the Land-Rover catches up with us and has to slow down again,' Stuart shouted.

I picked up the revs and moved off as fast as I could in a 27-tonne beast. I checked the rear-view mirror and noticed the boy's mother was still ranting and raving and waving her fists in the air; boy, was she annoyed.

The last few kilometres went unhindered until we reached a huge Y-shaped road junction just on the south edge of Az Zubayr, where there was an off-white brick compound surrounded by a wall to my left and wasteland to my right. Immediately ahead of us, there was a surprisingly clean mosque surrounded by dirty streets and battered buildings. I checked my rear-view mirror to see how the LI guys were doing and noticed they had come to a halt about 100 metres behind. I stopped and checked the mirror again.

'We can't stay here,' Stuart said, with a hint of apprehension in his voice.

'No shit, Sherlock,' I replied, and reversed towards the parked Land-Rover. 'Go and see why they stopped.'

Stuart grabbed his rifle and jumped out of the cab to ask the LI guys why they stopped. He returned a few minutes later.

'Why did they stop?' I asked.

'They flashed us a couple of times but we couldn't have noticed. They received a signal we're in an unsafe zone, so we've a new route.' Stuart opened the piece of notepaper given to him by one of the LI guys. 'I'll check the new grid reference against the map,' he added.

The locals started to gather around us, although they stopped at a safe distance. I didn't know who was more intimidating, them or us. I put on a brave smile and waved at them. The younger kids and some of the women returned the gesture but the older teenage boys and young men just stared at me. I made ready my rifle in clear view of the crowd gathering to my right, hoping it would send a clear message: I'm not going to be fucked about. In our latest O'group, we had been instructed that if it moved, shoot it, and that's exactly what I was prepared to do if one of them so much as picked up a pebble.

'Right, found it, but we'll have to go down the road ahead.' Stuart pointed to the road going through the centre of the town, roughly 400 metres ahead.

'But that's RPG Alley! You'll have to find a better route,' I snapped.

Stuart checked the map. The only alternative was to turn right at the junction and go round the back end of the town. He jumped out of the cab and made his way over to the Land-Rover to tell the LI guys which route we were going to take. Less than a minute later, he returned with a further problem.

'You'll never believe this, they're heading back to the GOSP.'

'They're what? They can't do that, they're supposed to be our armoured escort!'

'I know, calm down. They radioed back to the CV for one of the Warriors in the town to take us en route. It's a bit dodgy for the Land-Rover.'

'And, of course, you said we'll be perfectly safe in our plastic cab.' I replied, sounding slightly panicked.

'They'll hang about until the Warrior arrives.' Stuart said, trying to reassure me.

I wasn't having any of it. I didn't like this situation; it had the classic hallmarks of rapidly escalating into something nasty. The crowd started to disperse, most probably through lack of interest, but I couldn't stop thinking they were under instruction to disperse by hidden militia with RPGs pointing in our direction. Some of the kids opted to stick around just in case any freebies were thrown out of our windows. Fat chance of that, apart from some cigarettes I had and I wasn't risking having my head bitten off again by some irate mother.

My main concern was the unseen prying eyes of the Fedayeen militia and the Iraqi force's snipers hidden in the dark windows of nearby buildings. Whilst we stood still, the danger of being hit increased. Stuart thought we should give the loitering kids some water, just to show the adults we were friendly. I was reluctant to give anything away whilst we were in this town. In the past, adults had intervened and beaten up or even killed children just for a litre-bottle of clean drinking water. After all, water was more important than the odd boiled sweet.

I checked my watch: 1115hrs zulu. The Warrior escort finally arrived and within a split second of its arrival, the Land-Rover disappeared in a cloud of dust. I followed the

Warrior, turning right at the junction, and we drove down a potholed road, in desperate need of resurfacing. Stuart had his rifle made ready and poked the barrel out of his open window. Our eyes were scanning every inch of every building on each side of the road. We couldn't help but think of the two British soldiers who had been captured and brutally killed a few days earlier, not 200 metres from our present location. A Warrior is well protected against such an attack, but there was very little chance of us escaping an RPG or even a small-arms ambush because of the bloody plastic cab.

'How you feeling?' I asked.

'Fucking brown-trousers time, mate,' he replied, still with his eyes fixed on the streets. 'I feel more scared now than I've ever been,' he added.

He wasn't alone; I certainly felt the same.

The road turned to the right and the buildings gave way to wasteland. A railway track met the road on our left, leading to some sidings. The area of the sidings was scattered with burnt-out Russian-built military trucks and the odd S60 anti-aircraft gun hit by HE rounds from Challenger 2s, turning them into nothing but a mound of twisted, burnt metal. We crossed the railway line and entered the east side of Az Zubayr. Five minutes later, we reached the hospital compound on the side of a main road. The whitewashed hospital boundary walls were about three metres high with a narrow, arched gated entrance, just big enough to allow our Foden through. I parked a few metres from the gate, blocking the pavement. Grabbing my rifle and haversack, I jumped out of the cab and walked to a man waiting to greet me behind the gate.

'You pick up truck?' he asked, in broken English.

I placed my right hand through the bars of the gate to shake his hand. 'Yes, can you let us in?'

'No keys. Gone look for them,' he replied.

Fucking great, I thought. Talk about being an open target – again. I offered him a cigarette, which he accepted. And in typical Iraqi fashion, more of them came out of the woodwork. I quickly placed my packet of Benson & Hedges back in my trouser pocket and pulled out a packet of Silk Cut Ultra Low from the other – my 'giveaway' cigarettes. I offered the other five scrounging gits a Silk Cut, which, of course, they accepted.

A few minutes passed and the obligatory crowd of kids soon gathered around the truck, waiting and hoping something exciting was about to happen; the thought of freebies also must have entered their minds. One little boy, no older than four or five, was curious about the contents of my haversack. I crouched down next to him and opened it up, pulling out my respirator. He seemed a little frightened of the 'scary' mask, so I showed him it wasn't a monster by putting it on.

The other kids in the crowd started to giggle, so I jumped up and raised my arms in a monster-like fashion, growling and moaning like some deranged nutter. The boys thought it was funny when I made the girls scream and run away. Boy, was that a bad move. All of them wanted to try my respirator and scare the girls. I looked at Stuart hoping for some support but he just laughed, saying, 'You started it, mate, you can sort them out.'

'Found that bloody key yet!' I shouted to the guy behind the gate. He just smiled and shook his head.

Ah! I know. I walked a few metres along the pavement and picked up a stone as the kids looked on, bemused. I marked out an outline on the light-grey pavement slabs and sectioned off a number of equally sized squares in the shape. I then drew numbers in the squares for a game of hopscotch.

'Bloody 'ell, you can tell you have kids,' Stuart commented.

I ignored his sarcasm and searched for a suitable stone so we could play hopscotch. When I found one, I threw it on number one and began the game, hopping up and down the squares. At first, the kids were bewildered at this squaddie prancing about on the pavement, but they soon came round to the idea of playing the game themselves. After four or five attempts, they picked up the general idea. I didn't really care if they played by the rules or not, I was just satisfied that our truck was now a kids-free zone.

The Warrior's crew, parked on the other side of the road, clapped when I walked back to the Foden. I stopped and took a bow, although I felt slightly embarrassed.

I leant on the driver's-side wheel of the Foden and lit another cigarette, watching the kids play hopscotch. I chuckled to myself as they argued over the rules and made up teams. No matter where you are in the world, a group of kids playing a game involving two teams will always end up with the boys versus the girls.

Ten minutes later, and finally the keys were found and the gates unlocked. I walked ahead of the Foden and watched Stuart drive slowly through the compound entrance. As soon as he cleared the gates, they were immediately closed and locked to prevent any looters or militia racing into the compound. The Mercedes Actros truck, a 6x2 tractor unit, that we'd come to collect was parked further up the driveway. I had a look around it and noticed the battery cover was missing, as was one of the crossover leads on the batteries.

'I fetch a wire,' one of the guys said.

It'll take a little more than a piece of wire, I thought, but moments later he returned with the original battery lead, which to him must have been 'wire' in English. I pushed either end of the battery lead connectors onto the battery terminals but the next problem was whether the engine would turn over. If it did, it would save us a load of hassle recovering it.

I jumped in the left-hand-drive seat and slowly turned the ignition key. The lights on the dash panel lit up and the low-air warning buzzers sprang to life. Air solenoids started to click and the air suspension rose a little, caused by the air system receiving an electrical charge and opening the solenoids. The last turn of the key and, yes! Slowly at first but after a couple of seconds, the engine burst into life. A few gentle stamps on the accelerator pedal and the engine ticked over like a purring cat. I gave a thumbs-up to Stuart, who acknowledged my achievements with a sarcastic slow clap. The nurses and doctors looking on also gave a small cheer. Once again, I took a small bow as I sat behind the wheel.

I studied the controls for a while as the engine built up the air pressure to release the handbrake, and it was then that I noticed the gearbox was a tectronic semi-automatic set-up. OK, I thought, I've driven one of these before, so I should be all right. The low-air warning buzzer fizzled out, indicating there was enough air in the system, so I selected third gear and released the handbrake – we were off. I soon noticed the air-conditioning switch and turned it to the coldest setting on full blast with all available vents open – heaven!

The exit at the rear of the compound turned onto a T-junction that joined with the road passing the hospital's front entrance. I turned right at the junction and sounded the air horns to attract the attention of the Warrior crew and gave them a thumbs-up, which they returned. I moved off slowly to allow them to turn around and catch up. Whilst I waited, I wound down the driver's window; a layer of dust and sand on the glass was reflecting the sun's glare, causing a blind spot on my mirror. I'll just have to drive with it open and let the air conditioning work overtime, I thought. As I drove on, I had a play with the controls, just like a kid with a new toy.

The Warrior escort soon took up its position as lead vehicle, with Stuart taking the rear. I was OK driving on the road but as soon as we left the tarmac for the dirt track I had to take it easy. As we crossed the railway siding, the Warrior carried on at about 50 kph whilst I had no alternative but to slow down to about 20 kph in this road vehicle; even Stuart had to take it steady in the Foden. The Warrior eventually stopped at the junction leading back onto the severely potholed tarmac road. I caught up to within 50 metres of the Warrior when it turned right and headed towards the town centre. Stuart was dragging behind, so I opted to wait for a minute, allowing him to catch up. Because we'd shifted direction, the sun was now reflecting on the passenger-door window, which was also covered in a thin layer of dust. I pressed the window switch for the passenger side and the winder motor whirred as it wound down the glass so I could see in the mirror.

To my right, set back 100 metres, lay a 200-metre stretch of wasteland running alongside a two-metre-high breezeblock wall. Battered, flat-roofed single-storey buildings behind it dominated the landscape. Out of the corner of my right eye, I noticed a bunch of young kids, not much older than five or six years old, running down the wasteland beside the wall. The sound of shots being fired followed quickly, coming from behind the wall.

The kids were screaming and shouting, and at first it seemed as though they were playing some sort of game, but soon the burst of automatic fire changed that idea. It became apparent that the children were in fact running for their lives. I slowed down a little and flashed the Warrior with my headlights, desperately trying to get its attention, but my efforts were in vain. The Warrior turned into a left bend and went out of sight. There was no way the crew could have heard any of the automatic fire from inside a moving armoured vehicle.

More bursts of automatic followed, then a man in civvy clothing came into view. He crouched down, leaning on the long breezeblock wall we'd passed on our way to the hospital compound, and took careful aim with his AK rifle. He then continued to fire small bursts of automatic at the children. They scattered in all directions, trying to dodge the rounds as they ricocheted on the dusty ground or cracked above their heads.

No, no, no! This wasn't happening, I thought. I grabbed my rifle, jumped out of the cab and ran to the front near-side of the bumper for cover. I lay down in the prone position and without taking careful aim, I snapped a couple of rounds in his general direction, but he was still crouching against the wall edge. The crack of my rounds whizzing past his head made him look in my direction but he was soon distracted by the fleeing children, as if he was weighing up the situation – kill the kids first, then me.

Stuart jumped out of the Foden and took a position under the heavy front bumper and within seconds was ready to return fire. The kids were well scattered and about 100 metres ahead of the chogie. He opted to fire at the children first – obviously this was more important to him – and took aim once again, letting off a burst of three rounds. Instantly, a little girl fell to the ground like a rag doll. I couldn't believe my eyes. Did I just witness a little girl cut down by machine-gun fire?

'You bastard! You fucking bastard!' I shouted.

He turned to face me now, pointing his rifle towards my

position, but I didn't give him the chance to return fire; I was determined to drop him before he had the chance to drop me. I took aim and double-tapped a dozen rounds in quick succession in the hope he'd fall the same way the little girl had. At that precise moment, Stuart let off a few rounds from his position as did the Warrior with its chain gun. The crew must have heard the commotion and come thundering back. Chunks of masonry splintered in all directions as 5.56-mm and 7.62-mm rounds ripped through the target and into the wall behind. Within a second of our return fire, the enemy fell, or rather squelched, to the ground, and not entirely in one piece.

The commander of the Warrior poked his head out of the turret and beckoned me to get back in the truck and carry on driving; basically, to get the fuck out of there. I wanted to see if the little girl was alive but there was no chance of that; I suppose it was wishful thinking. I jumped back into the truck and wheel span the rear axle of the Actros, trying to achieve maximum power. Stuart did the same in the Foden, desperately trying to keep up. Within half a kilometre, the Warrior pulled over at the Y-junction and let us pass. By now, we were well out of the danger zone and on the main road, heading towards the dirt track leading to the GOSP.

When I reached the dirt track, I drove for a few hundred metres, then pulled over to allow Stuart to catch up – and to collect my thoughts. I lit a cigarette hoping it would help but it didn't. I couldn't get that little girl out of my mind. I couldn't help it; the emotions were too strong. I started to scream in anger and frustration. '*Bastard! Bastard! Bastard!*' I shouted, as I punched the steering wheel, then jumped out of the cab and kicked the fuck out of the moulded fibreglass bumper as well for good measure.

Stuart caught up and noticed what I was doing. He jumped out of the Foden and joined me in kicking the bumper. I looked at him and noticed his eyes were red raw; he too had been crying. Then, for some unknown reason, we started to laugh. Maybe it was the fact we looked like right idiots kicking the shit out of a tractor unit's bumper.

'C'mon, Kev, lets get back to the camp,' Stuart said, slightly out of breath.

'Yeah, I need a drink. Who do we know who has some alcohol?'

'No one. So you'll have to make do with a warm can of Coke.'

15

ON THROUGH THE NIGHT

Saturday, 29 March 1600hrs zulu No matter how hard I tried, I couldn't get that little girl out of my mind. Stuart did his best to keep my chin up but I had a feeling he was suffering just as much as me. He came up with an idea whilst we were waiting for a task and volunteered us both for sentry duty. This was a bit of a shock for Stag Thompson but he soon exploited Stuart's request and had us on rolling patrols around the camp area for a couple of hours. With half an hour to go before the end of our sentry duty, Second Lieutenant Connor gave us a task – that was the good news. The bad news was the recovery task was back in Az Zubayr, not a stone's throw from where the little girl had been killed.

Elements of Falcon squadron from 2 RTR, including a couple of Challenger 2s and various fire-support vehicles, such as Warrior AFV and Scimitars, stood in position defending the main road leading into Az Zubayr. Retaliation attacks from members of the Fedayeen militia and the Iraqi Army dressed in civilian clothes were expected, in particular hit-and-run tactics using mortars, RPGs and heavy-calibre machine-gun fire from the backs of chogie wagons. A Bedford TM 14-tonne truck had been sent to their location on an ammunition replenishment run, but it, of course, was overweight with shells, which, of course, burnt out the clutch. Stuart and I were tasked to recover the Bedford truck and take it back to the GOSP for repair.

I checked out the Foden and recovery kit whilst Stuart went to the CV for further details about the task, and more importantly to find out if we needed an armoured escort. We did, especially when undertaking a task at night. Ambush and sporadic attacks were common during dark hours, in particular those carried out by the local militia, because of their knowledge of the area.

Looking on the bright side – if there was one – the militia's military training and experience of soldiering was extremely poor. That isn't to say they couldn't pick up a rifle and point it at us – far from it; anyone who could point a rifle, trained or not, could and did kill coalition soldiers – what they lacked was the capability to plan any substantial military assault. Their elaborate imagination for some of their ambush attempts, though, had to be respected if we wanted to stay alive.

Stuart returned from the CV wearing a 'you're not going to believe this' smile. No armoured escort was available, so we had to make do with a bloody Land-Rover (again) with Lieutenant Pym and a craftie VM riding shotgun. The only comfort we had, albeit a slight one, was the three hand grenades given to us by one of the LI guys for added protection. The only concern I had with this was that neither of us had ever used one before. Predictably, Stuart couldn't hide the sheer delight in his eyes at the thought of throwing a few grenades around. For some reason, my intuition told me this job was going to turn into a cluster fuck.

The recovery kit checked and our rifles made ready, I turned over the engine whilst we waited for the Land-Rover. The sun had set and left only a slight hint of its light on the horizon. This meant we would have to travel tactically, and we didn't have a cat-in-hell's chance of grabbing any NVGs (night-vision goggles). Stuart was sitting silently in the passenger seat, punching the grid reference of our casualty vehicle into the GPS, when a rapid knocking noise came from his door. Stuart opened it and Lt Pym jumped up to show his face.

'Are you set?' he said, sounding excited but looking as if he was shitting himself. This was his first escort job and his first recovery task of the war. Apparently he had volunteered himself for the next available task so he could experience what it was like for us recovery mechanics. He was about to find out. Unfortunately for him, his first task was to be our escort, at night. I think he was hoping for a cushy daytime number.

'Yes, Sir. We're ready,' replied a concerned Stuart.

'Good. But bear in mind, I've just been told there's been a fire-fight at the location of the vehicle casualty. An attempt was made to take Falcon's position but it failed. They expect further attacks tonight. So stay vigilant. We move in five minutes.' He then gave us a half smile and made his way back to the CV.

'Why do I get the feeling we're not going to see this one through,' commented Stuart.

My thoughts exactly. Previous tasks had had their moments and yet we'd managed to pull them off without so much as a scratch, but this one just didn't feel right. Maybe it was because of the location, the fact it was a night job, or maybe it was because we'd had a particularly crap day. Whatever it was, we both thought something wasn't right about this one.

Lt Pym's driver pulled in front of us, stuck his arm out of the window and indicated with a thumbs-up that he was ready to move. With just our convoy light dimly illuminating the rear of our vehicles, we were off, ready to face T62s, T55s, mortars, RPGs and large-calibre machine guns – protected by our Land-Rover escort, in a recovery vehicle with a plastic cab and armed to the teeth with three hand grenades, four SA80s and a diminishing squaddie sense of humour.

We'd taken so many trips from the GOSP to Az Zubayr that we'd started to use familiar landmarks such as abandoned vehicles rather than the GPS for navigation. As long as the burnt-out T55s en route weren't removed, we knew exactly where we were. We wouldn't need the GPS until we reached the road leading into town. At night, however, the abandoned vehicles, military and civilian alike, became perfect sniper positions, especially for easy pickings, such as Land-Rovers and, more importantly, our Foden. We were concentrating so intensely, our minds would play tricks on us and make us believe we were seeing figures jumping around the vehicles. In reality, they were nothing more than shadows cast by the moonlight against bits of jagged metal splinters blown out of a tank's hull by a Challenger using the odd HE or DU shell.

Lt Pym was new to all this and his nerves certainly began to show. He crawled down the track at a mind-numbingly slow speed and every time a burnt-out vehicle came into view, he would slow down to a walking pace, seemingly pondering what to do next, but at the same time making us a perfect target.

I'd had enough of this. I jumped out of the cab and banged on the driver's door of the Land-Rover, making the young craftie jump out of his skin. 'Sir, do you think it would be best if we took the lead? After all, we know where we're going.' Boy, did I know what he was about to say.

'Good idea, Corporal Mervin. We'll follow you close behind.'

I jumped back into the Foden and took the lead, once again becoming the escort vehicle for an 'armoured' Land-Rover escort. Lt Pym kept his word and made sure his driver followed close behind; you could barely get a bus ticket between us. Stuart took the opportunity to keep dog-eye and stood guard through the cupola, wearing his three hand grenades and a mischievous smile.

Looking in my rear-view mirror, I watched the few street lamps rapidly around the GOSP and the floodlights of the PW holding area fading out of sight; we were now in total darkness, apart from the pale moonlight casting eerie shadows on the sand berms at the side of the track and on our T55 landmarks. My senses were once again firing on all cylinders. Every shadow gave the impression of movement and I couldn't help but give them a second glance, just in case.

We'd travelled about five kilometres and I thought, so far so good – until my instincts told me I should give a moving shadow a second glance. Straight ahead, I could see what looked like some sort of vehicle heading for us. But it was difficult to judge the distance in the soft moonlight, which only gave away a silhouette. I questioned myself – was it standing still or was it driving towards us? I wanted to think it was an abandoned T55 but that idea soon vanished when I caught a split-second moonlit glimpse of sand and dust being kicked up by the vehicle which indicated it was about 500 metres away. I had to make a decision, and quick – either we carried on and hoped it was friendly, or we stopped and took cover.

Stuart banged on the cab roof. 'Dead ahead, 500 metres, vehicle heading towards us.' He jumped back in his seat. 'I dunno about this one, Kev. We'd better jump out and take cover.'

Decision made. I came to a halt, switched off the engine, grabbed my webbing and rifle and ran to the Land-Rover. 'Sir, there's a vehicle approaching dead ahead. We don't know what it is and we're not taking any chances, so we're taking cover – now!'

He didn't question me. He and his driver jumped out of the Land-Rover, indicating to me that they were taking the berm on their left. Stuart and I took the berm on our right, diving over the top and running a few metres ahead of our vehicle to give us a clear arc of fire should we need it. Within seconds of positioning ourselves, we could hear the approaching vehicle, which was now 300 metres ahead. I came to the conclusion it was a B-vehicle rather than tracked. First, if it was tracked, it would have ignored the potholes and undulating surface and been right on top of us; and second, its engine didn't sound big enough to belong to a tracked vehicle. But the question of whether it was armoured or indeed friendly couldn't be answered until it was within ten metres of our position.

I grabbed the few seconds we had left and pulled two full magazines from my webbing and shoved them down the front of my CBA. If we were about to initiate a contact, I wanted to suppress as much firepower as possible and give them little chance of returning fire. Stuart did the same and also decided to position his three hand grenades in front of him. He was determined to use them. We were now ready for the worst. I only hoped Lt Pym and his driver had taken the same precautions.

Now there were just 200 metres to go before the approaching vehicle would realise something wasn't right, especially since Lt Pym's driver had left his engine running. At a guess, enemy or not, they would stop short of our vehicles and assess the situation. If they were friendly, they would realise the Foden and Land-Rover were part of the coalition and treat our vehicles like they were either abandoned or had been hit. In which case, they would search the immediate area for any enemy forces, booby traps or casualties. This would give us the chance to see, albeit by moonlight, if they were coalition soldiers.

Our vehicles, however, wouldn't be any assurance that we were friendly. Since the start of the conflict, coalition vehicles had been stolen from camps and used by the Iraqi Army and militia as decoys when executing counter-attacks and ambushes, and also as traps to ensnare unsuspecting recovery mechanics. If they were the enemy in an armoured, wheeled vehicle and had a big enough gun, they would most probably fire a few rounds into the Foden and Land-Rover in an attempt to eliminate any return fire. If it was a soft-skin vehicle, its occupants would no doubt leg it and take cover. That would be our cue to open fire and disallow the enemy any cover and hopefully drop the crew.

Stuart and I shuffled as low as we could into the top of the berm and took our aim at the approaching vehicle. Our target was now in sight roughly 50 metres ahead, and in the moonlight we could easily recognise its familiar silhouette – it was a Bedford TM. We both gave a sigh of relief but still had to make sure the crew was friendly, and hoped Lt Pym would have his soldiering head on and think the same.

Still, that was the least of our worries. We could now hear voices, Iraqi voices, about 100 metres behind our position, approaching across the wasteland from the outer perimeter of the GOSP. We couldn't see how many people there were, but guessed there were about three or four. They seemed to be unaware of what lay ahead of them and it wouldn't be long before they noticed Stuart and me.

Our situation had suddenly changed from being planned and under control to being a potential cluster fuck.

The Bedford TM, as predicted, stopped short of the Foden and its two-man crew quickly jumped out of their cab to suss out the situation, instantly showing us they were British soldiers. Our priority now was the approaching Iraqis, but we still had to let the Bedford crew know we were there, but how? I couldn't shout out and wait for their response; in doing so, I would have certainly given away our position to the Iraqis, who were now within 50 metres of us and sounded excited. They had either noticed Stuart and me, or could hear our vehicles' engines ticking over.

Stuart grabbed one of his hand grenades and nodded to me, letting me know what he was about to do and to be ready to dive back over the sand berm should the situation turn nasty. In the mean time, Lt Pym, unaware of the approaching Iraqis, inadvertently solved one of our problems and broke his cover to let the Bedford crew know where we were. This gave Stuart and me the few seconds we needed to sort out the Iraqis; and that is all we had. When we turned to face them, they were only ten metres away and still unaware of our presence. They seemed more interested in the vehicle engines ticking over. As they continued to walk towards us, they changed direction suddenly at the base of the sand berm and climbed it diagonally away from us. Even though it was dark, I couldn't believe they hadn't noticed us – we were less than three metres away, crouched down just below the top of the berm with our rifles pointing directly at them.

They reached the top of the berm then suddenly they stopped talking and stood motionless. They'd noticed Lt Pym and the others in front of the Foden. All four of the Iraqis were dressed in civilian clothes and appeared to be unarmed, which didn't mean anything, as they could have been militia or even Iraqi soldiers. On the other hand, they could have been deserters or just ordinary civilians. Whoever they were, Stuart and I weren't about to take any chances and continued to keep them covered.

One of the Bedford crew must have noticed the four figures standing on top of the berm and shouted at them to stand still. They immediately threw their hands in the air in surrender. The one nearest to Stuart began to shuffle his feet in an attempt to prepare himself to turn tail and leg it back down the sand berm. As he slowly turned to his left and looked down to check his footing, he was distracted by Stuart squatting close to his side and pointing his rifle at him. His face was a picture as his eyes widened and his jaw dropped; he had no idea we were right next to him and couldn't believe his escape was foiled.

'Coming down,' Stuart shouted, beckoning the four Iraqis to climb down the berm and head towards our vehicles. I stayed in my position to keep them covered just in case one of them miraculously conjured up a rifle from underneath his *dishdash*. I continued to protect the front of our position whilst the Bedford crew kept Stuart covered as he searched the Iraqis. The craftie protected the rear of the Land-Rover as Lt Pym radioed our CV and asked what we should do with the PWs. We didn't have long to wait, ten minutes or so, before a Land-Rover with four LI guys in the back turned up. The PWs were immediately escorted back to the PW holding area at the GOSP in the back of the canvas-covered Bedford TM, quickly followed by the LI guys. Lt Pym signalled to me to come down from the berm and be ready to move in two minutes. We then returned to our original task and carried on down the dirt track, remaining vigilant at all times.

We didn't meet any other oncoming vehicles, although

there were the burnt-out T55 landmarks, which thankfully didn't have any uninvited guests using them as sniper posts. It was a blessing, since it saved us from being blown to pieces by Stuart's hand grenades. More importantly, they hadn't been removed, which allowed us to navigate to the main road leading into Az Zubayr.

I stopped at the side of the dual carriageway as Stuart checked the map against the GPS. According to the grid reference, we had eight kilometres to go before we reached Falcon's position. I checked my rear-view mirror to make sure Lt Pym was right behind us, then continued down our route towards town. The dual carriageway was lit up in places by the odd street lamp, which seemed to defeat the object of driving tactically. Being illuminated whilst we moved, mind you, would still make us a harder target to hit than a vehicle using lights, as they provide a spot to aim at.

I was beginning to get used to driving on a public highway at night without lights; it actually gave me quite a buzz, so I decided to enjoy the experience, and there wasn't a policeman in the world who could book me for it. The thought of this soon put a smile on my face and I forgot about the war for a few seconds, reliving a fond teenage memory or two, but that's a different story.

Reality soon brought me back down to earth with a bump as a couple of jets screamed past at low level, dropping their ordnance on a target a few kilometres north. The explosions lit up the horizon and illuminated buildings before fading out and leaving a mushroom cloud of dense smoke. It was time to forget the fun and games and concentrate on the task.

Stuart checked the map. 'Five Ks to go; we should then be able to see Falcon's position, which should be on our right.'

'Just off the road, you mean?'

'Yeah, in some sort of compound. Probably a— *Look out!*'

Too late. I'd smashed through two chogie wagons blocking the road. I didn't see a thing until Stuart shouted out and by then there was no way I could stop. I must have hit them at about 70 kph. At the very last second, all I could see were pick-up trucks full of tomatoes parked diagonally across the road on a railway crossing. On impact, it sounded like an explosion as bits of pick-up truck and thousands of tomatoes hit the thick metal bumper of the Foden.

Stuart poked his head out of the window to see what was happening. A split second later, a report of small-arms fire came from behind. I checked my rear-view mirror and noticed the odd muzzle flash from three or four rifles. I put my foot down hard and checked the mirror again to make sure our Land-Rover was still following us; thankfully, it was, and it didn't appear to have any problems. Stuart picked up his rifle and returned a few rounds but couldn't really get an aim because of the movement of the Foden and the fact that the Land-Rover was only a few metres behind. He appeared to stop any more incoming, though.

'I don't believe it. We've just trashed one of those ambushes we were warned about!' Stuart shouted, as he changed his magazine. 'They must have expected us to stop.' He let out a chuckle. 'Thank fuck you didn't.'

Stuart was right; we'd been warned about such ambushes time and time again. Before receiving the warnings, being typical British squaddies, we'd have stopped to see if we could have been of any assistance, benefit of the doubt and all that. The Iraqi Army and especially the militia knew this and set up traps like this to prey on our good nature.

We approached a few more street lamps illuminating a 200-metre stretch of the carriageway, which was good –

and bad. Good because I could satisfy my urge to put my foot down, and bad because if I could see the road, the enemy could see me. I began to feel a little nervous and was pleased when we'd passed the lamps, once again reaching near-total darkness; however, my eyes needed a few minutes to readjust to their limited night vision.

'How we doing?' I asked, wondering if we were close to our vehicle casualty.

'Two Ks and we should be there,' Stuart replied.

I checked the mirrors again to make sure our Land-Rover was still with us. At first, I couldn't see it and felt a rush of panic run through my body, but then I caught a sudden glimpse of it when Lt Pym's driver veered towards the kerbside. For some reason, he'd increased the gap between us by about ten metres and I began to wonder if they'd been hit but I didn't want to risk stopping, not when we were so close to reaching Falcon's position.

'*Shit!*' I slammed on the brakes and came to a sudden halt. Leaning out of my window I shouted, 'What the fuck do you think you're doing?'

An extremely nervous young squaddie had jumped out in front of the Foden from his VCP, pointing his rifle directly at me.

'What's he think he's doing?' asked a surprised Stuart.

When the young squaddie heard me, he realised who we were and sighed with relief. 'Sorry, mate, you can never be too careful.'

'You don't think this truck was a bit of a giveaway, then?' I replied.

'I couldn't see who you were, until the last minute. We're expecting to be hit again tonight and I've been told to stop every vehicle and check all ID. I need to see yours, now.'

'You're kidding!'

'No, I'm not.'

'What's up with him?' asked Stuart.

'He wants to check our ID.'

'What? Is he fucking blind?'

To save any further argument, we produced our ID. He was, after all, only doing his job. The young squaddie then went on to check Lt Pym's ID and that of his driver. I began to wonder why he was on his own if further attacks were imminent but soon noticed he had a buddy with him sitting in his Land-Rover, just behind a wall of sandbags at the side of the road. He too looked a tad concerned, twitching at the slightest crack of small-arms fire and explosions, which sounded as if they were getting closer.

'Can we go now?' I asked sarcastically, when the young squaddie walked back to his pile of sandbags.

'Where you heading?' he asked.

'We've a job a few Ks down the road, at Falcon's position. They're part of 2 RTR.'

'Oh, the "tankies". Yeah, I know where they are, and it's less than a few Ks, mate. They're about half a K further down on this side of the road. If it was daylight, you'd see their position from here. Some sort of compound.'

We didn't waste any more time and left the VCP. As we moved off, the entire night sky was lighting up with sporadic explosions, followed by bursts of heavy machine-gun and small-arms fire a few kilometres ahead of us. We would have driven into it if it hadn't been for the young squaddie at the VCP. It wasn't uncommon to be given inaccurate grid references, even with GPS technology, and under any other circumstances it wouldn't really matter, but during a conflict, inaccuracy could drop you in a life-or-death situation, as we would have found out.

True to the lad's word, Falcon's position was just over half a kilometre down the road and you couldn't really miss it, even at night. A Challenger 2 and a Warrior AFV guarded the high-gated entrance, with half a dozen squaddies standing around them on sentry duty. Either side of the entrance had sandbagged gun positions armed with gimpies and LSWs, not unlike our gun positions back at the GOSP. The compound was set back from the road by about ten metres, with a three-metre-high concrete wall surrounding it.

I pulled off the dual carriageway onto the concrete drive leading to the main entrance and came to a halt. Immediately, we were surrounded by four of the six guards, all pointing their rifles at our cab. I knew what they wanted and took out my ID. Stuart did the same and showed it to one of the sentries on his side.

'We were told you were on your way,' the sentry said on my side.

I leant out of the window and pointed behind me. 'There's a Land-Rover with us with two occupants.'

He took a step back and glanced at the rear of the Foden, then nodded. 'Yeah, I see them. What do they want?'

'That's our armoured escort.'

'Your what?'

'It's a long story. Can we go in?'

He stepped back, still wearing his puzzled frown, and waved us through, with our Land-Rover tight behind. As soon as we'd cleared the ten-metre-wide entrance, the huge wrought-iron gates were closed, which gave us some sense of security. We then stopped about fifty metres further down, next to a building on my right, which appeared to be some kind of three-storey office block.

'Well, we made it,' commented Stuart. 'Now for the difficult bit.' He grabbed his rifle and jumped out of the cab to check on Lt Pym and find our vehicle casualty.

All I grabbed was the chance to rest and have a smoke. A few minutes passed and I began to feel a little nervous. Some battle was beginning to rage only a few kilometres away and I wanted to get the job done and out of there as soon as possible.

Stuart finally returned to the Foden. 'Our casualty is halfway down the courtyard, parked on the right-hand side.' He pointed in its general direction.

It was difficult to appreciate the size of the courtyard because of the near-total darkness but the soft ambient light shadowing the buildings surrounding it gave an impression it was about 100 metres square. Our vehicle casualty, as Stuart said, was halfway down the courtyard and to our right, and was parked next to a Challenger undergoing some minor repairs.

Stuart acted as a 'ground guide' and walked in front of me as I drove the Foden towards the Bedford TM casualty. I stopped short of the Bedford and turned around so I could reverse directly in front of it whilst Stuart gave it the once over. Sure enough, the details given to us were correct: it had a burnt-out clutch and couldn't be repaired on site. It had to be recovered and towed back to the workshop at the GOSP for repairs. Once lined up, I engaged the PTO (power take-off) and 'body live' switch so I could power the hydraulic system and prepare the vehicle for the task. Stuart removed what kit we needed from the side bins and we soon had the Bedford's front end attached to the recovery boom.

During the recovery task, we could hear a fierce fire-fight but hadn't noticed the sporadic explosions and machine-gun fire becoming more intense and getting closer to our location. It sounded as if the entire war had been transported to just outside the three-metre perimeter wall and both sides were knocking seven colours of shit out of one another on the dual carriageway. The situation was getting increasingly serious and we were preparing to leave and drive through the middle of it.

Stuart and I sat in the cab waiting for Lt Pym, who was standing next to his Land-Rover talking to some sergeant. The Challenger 2 next to the Foden suddenly burst into life and made its way out of the entrance, turned right and headed towards the fire-fight. Two Warriors then appeared from nowhere, quickly passing our Foden to join the Challenger. Where they came from, I don't know but I was pretty sure where they were going. Lt Pym signalled for Stuart and me to join him and the sergeant. We grabbed our rifles and quickly made our way over to them.

'You have a simple choice, lads. You either stay here until the situation further down the road has been sorted out, which could take all night, or you make your way back – now,' the sergeant said, emphasising the word 'now'.

Lt Pym looked at me, as if I should make the decision. In a way, it had already been made for us – we had to get back to the GOSP because the Bedford was desperately needed to supply the tanks and Warriors with ammunition. Although the British Army had thousands of vehicles mobilised, each one had a job to do. If a single vehicle was taken out of action, and many were, it meant extra work for the others. This in turn meant extra work for the crews. As it was, all vehicle types from all the battle groups of 1 Div were stretched to the limit, so if there was any chance of getting a vehicle repaired and back on the road, it would make life a little easier for all of us.

Making life easier by repairing a vehicle is one thing, but losing the life of your crew to recover it is another. In my book, a vehicle doesn't even come close to outweighing a human life. But we, or as it was, I, still had to make a decision. Although a fire-fight was well under way only one kilometre north of our location, I had to weigh up whether it was a direct threat to us. In the end, I decided it wasn't.

'Fuck it. We'll get back to the GOSP, as long as we leave straight away.'

The sergeant agreed, as did Stuart and Lt Pym, surprisingly. I expected him to overrule me but he didn't. I suppose he didn't fancy staying the night whilst a fire-fight carried on close by. None of us did – we were looking forward to getting back to the relative safety of the GOSP. In the mean time, we had to endure the unpredictable trip back.

As we moved out of the entrance with the Land-Rover in front of us this time, all hell broke loose to the right. A Challenger fired a few rounds at a target whilst a Warrior opened up with its 30-mm cannon and chain gun, lighting up the night with tracer and HE rounds. Whatever the target was, it must have been something substantial to attract such firepower. This was our cue to get the fuck out. Lt Pym's driver soon put his foot down and it was my turn to be close behind.

It wasn't long before we met our buddy at the VCP but this time he waved us straight through. Soon after, we came across the wreckage of the two chogie wagons I'd hit earlier. I'd certainly made a mess of them. Luckily, there wasn't anyone around, which was probably something to do with the heavy shit going on behind us, and we passed the wreckage without any problems.

Just a little further to go and we'd reach the dirt track for the GOSP, I thought to myself. Everything was going fine and not a single chogie, civilian or Iraqi deserter in sight. Finally, things were going right for a change, but still I held my rifle halfway out of the window in case of any unforeseen circumstances. Stuart took his position out of the cupola and protected his side and the front, including our escort, although it was difficult to see them at times because of the moon hiding behind the odd cloud.

We reached the dirt track without any dramas and the rest of the journey went without a hitch, apart from our eyes playing the odd trick on us. At one point, I thought I could see figures running across sand berms, and Stuart insisted he could see muzzle flashes coming from an abandoned Iraqi AFV. I think he was looking for an excuse to use his hand grenades.

We eventually reached the GOSP, which was eerily quiet. Not one vehicle could be heard apart from ours. The sentries at the VCP let us through and so did the sentries at the GOSP entrance. The Land-Rover pulled over to let us pass and drive to the workshop. We now had our own sentries to contend with at the workshop compound.

'Halt!' one of them shouted, then proceeded with half the password, eagerly awaiting our reply.

'Fuck off,' was Stuart's reply. 'You know who we are, you've seen us countless times. Anyway, we haven't a clue what the password is.'

That was true. The only time we ever knew a password was when we came across it by accident, either by talking to other squaddies or when we remembered to get it from the CV. And even then, it was due for a change because it only lasted for 12 hours, or, to put it another way, they changed as soon as we left to do a task.

The sentry eventually let us through, after arguing with Stuart about the reason why we had passwords, in which Stuart really took an interest. I drove into the workshop and reversed the Bedford into one of the holding bays. We then unhooked the casualty, packed away our kit and made our way back to the A1 packet. I boiled the BV for a brew before switching off the engine and Stuart reported to the

CV, where he met Lt Pym giving his debrief on the task. A few minutes later, Stuart returned with a big smile on his face.

'What's up?' I asked. He either had another task for us or a bit of gossip.

'I asked Lt Pym if he wanted to go on our next recovery job. He declined the offer because he said he has too much to do.'

16

THE STORY SO FAR
. . . 26 MARCH – 6 APRIL

Our night recovery task certainly helped us forget about the little girl, at least for a while. The Fedayeen militia and Iraqi Army were responsible for the execution of innocent women and children in Az Zubayr, and the sight we witnessed turned out to be one of these instances. Although the town was largely under British control, there was still a handful of militia hiding in the town, using automatic rifles and RPGs on British soldiers, as well as terrorising and murdering its inhabitants if they were found talking to soldiers belonging to the coalition forces.

The militia was running scared itself. When its members were caught, and it was only a question of when, dead or alive, their privileged lifestyle came to an end. This was the same for Ba'ath Party members still on Saddam's books. The diehards weren't yet willing to give up those fat cheques from their beloved leader and were still willing to destroy people's lives over money – the proverbial 'selling your soul to the devil'.

Whatever the militia's excuse, it couldn't bring back the

little girl's life it had disgustingly thrown away, nor the rest of the innocent lives it had extinguished. To capture the Fedayeen alive was an immoral act in itself, as far as we were concerned, because we were obliged to treat them with respect: give them medical treatment, food, water and shelter. The food was far better than that of our rat packs and some of it was even fresh. They had refrigerated water, clean clothes and blankets every day, also medical treatment at a moment's notice 24 hours a day. And what did we get in return from these bastards? Nothing but constant complaints and threats of lawsuits because they claimed they were being mistreated.

I listened to many of these parasites whilst Stuart and I helped to build the PW camp at the GOSP; complaints from the same bastards who had captured the small, innocent children of anti-Ba'ath Party followers or from anyone that dared say anything contradicting the regime. They would force children, some as young as three years old, to drink petrol and then shoot them with a tracer round. The burning phosphorous round would ignite the petrol and make it explode inside their stomachs. The parents, meanwhile, were forced to witness this unbelievable act of torture.

It was incredible to think that someone who killed innocent children one day, and was captured the next, could bring so much red tape into the works – only to have their complaints backed up by goody two-shoes tree-huggers back home; do-gooders who hadn't even been to Iraq but seemed to have all the answers.

By now, a week had passed since we had arrived at the GOSP. In the evenings, we were privileged to watch distant firework displays; artillery, rockets and air strikes still constantly pounded enemy positions on the outskirts of

Basrah and Az Zubayr. And we carried out the odd recovery job in and around Az Zubayr, thankfully without any real problems of ambush or sniper fire.

On one occasion, however, Stuart and I found ourselves in an area that hadn't been declared safe thanks to a cock-up on a grid reference we were given. It was a simple hollibone job: pick up a CVRT casualty stranded on the main road between the GOSP and Az Zubayr and bring it back to the workshops. No problem, we thought. On the way to the CVRT casualty, we followed the route given to us by the CV, which took us through hamlets and small villages we hadn't noticed before. BMP2s and BMP1s were left untouched, abandoned in dugouts on the side of dirt tracks. As we passed them, we would wave at the children playing on the wasteland surrounding the small farms and give a thumbs-up to the teenagers and young men who appeared to be nosing around the tanks. They would return the gesture, smiling as they did so.

When we returned to the GOSP and reported our sightings to the ASM, he very nearly had kittens. Stuart and I looked at each other, bemused at his reaction, and not understanding why. The ASM stormed off to the CV to 'have a word' with the lieutenant who had supplied us with the route. Apparently, the path we'd taken hadn't been declared safe and there'd not even been an attempt to do so; it was still just under surveillance. And as for the young men on the BMPs, they were probably militia (not necessarily Fedayeen) or Iraqi soldiers in civvy clothing who had been firing on unsuspecting British vehicles only the day before. They would hide in a BMP, or any other military vehicle, making it look as though it was abandoned. This gave them the perfect opportunity to take pot shots at or open fire on the unsuspecting tail-end Charlie with AKs, or even RPGs, and we'd just been waving at the bastards.

Danny, as per usual, had his ear constantly to the ground, listening for war stories. As soon as he cornered me, he reeled off the details with his semi-automatic tongue. There was a bright side to his stories; he did keep us abreast of what was happening elsewhere in the war. The newspapers we received were two weeks old by the time they reached our unit and transistor radios were hard to find. If we did find someone with a radio, we prayed it could pick up the BBC World Service because most radio and television transmitters had either been taken over or blown up by coalition forces. So, once again, I listened to Danny and added his stories to the information from the O'groups and briefings we'd had, thereby piecing together a comprehensive report of the war elsewhere in Iraq for my diary.

26 MARCH

US airborne soldiers land in northern Iraq. Other US forces defeat Iraqi positions near Al Najaf and Al Nasiriyah. SDG are involved in a battle with an Iraqi tank and infantry unit, and totally destroy their positions.

Iraqi paramilitary forces in the Basrah area are eliminated due to effective raids against their positions. Also, Iraqi tanks advancing out of Basrah towards British troops are ultimately defeated.

The Ba'ath Party headquarters in As Samawah is destroyed. Within the first week of the campaign, the Royal Engineers repair and replace sabotaged fresh water and oil pipelines in southern Iraq and provide access to a fresh water supply from Kuwait.

An assault on Az Zubayr, using infantry, Warriors and Challenger 2 tanks to clear the town of militia, is delayed until a horrific sandstorm has cleared. Bombardments continue on Basrah and the northern area of Az Zubayr.

27 MARCH

Militia and Iraqi troops carry out unsuccessful counter-attacks on US forces near Al Najaf. Minesweepers in the Umm Qasr channel discover two mines. Supply ships carrying humanitarian aid are stopped from docking at the port until the area is declared safe.

Attacks on the GOSP near Az Zubayr by militia firing machine-guns and mortars from pick-up trucks are eliminated by British troops defending their positions. Iraqi soldiers continue to surrender in their hundreds on a daily basis around Basrah and southern Iraq. Iraqi officers have been shooting conscripts in the back as they try to flee the fighting, even forcing them to fight at gunpoint.

28 MARCH

The headquarters of the Ba'ath Party are destroyed by coalition air strikes in nine locations around Iraq. The GOSP near Az Zubayr is finally declared safe and MSRs [main supply routes] from Az Zubayr to Basrah are vigorously defended by 7 Armoured Brigade after being made secure. US helicopters destroy Republican Guard positions of the Medina Division near Karbala.

A British soldier of the Blues and Royals, a lance corporal of the Household Cavalry Regiment, is killed and four others injured in an incident involving light-armoured vehicles of D Squadron.

WEEKEND WARRIOR

29 MARCH

Coalition forces continue to pound Baghdad with air strikes, targeting key installations including air defence and command centres. British forces push towards Basrah. 3 Commando secure positions at Abu Al Khasib after launching an attack on Iraqi forces.

30 MARCH

A Royal Marine commando of 9 Assault Squadron is killed in action on the Al Faw peninsula whilst saving others during an ambush by Iraqi forces. An officer of the Royal Marines, of 3 Commando Brigade, dies of natural causes. A soldier of 212 Signal Squadron, 1 (UK) Armoured Division HQ and Signal Regiment, based in Germany, is killed in a road traffic accident in Kuwait.

British and other coalition forces secure bridges across the Tigris and Euphrates rivers. Offensives are launched against Iraqi forces by coalition troops in and around Al Nasiriyah and As Samawah, isolating them from reinforcements. (V) Corps of the US Marines bombard the Republican Guard Medina Division. US soldiers find an ammunition dump of considerable size near Tallil.

31 MARCH

British and other coalition troops seize the Hadithah Dam on the Euphrates intact and defend their position from counter-attacks by Iraqi forces trying to sabotage the dam and flood the area. The US 173 Airborne Brigade complete their deployment in northern Iraq. Air strikes continue to pound Republican Guard positions around and in Baghdad.

US Marines (V) Corps carry on with their attacks

on Iraqi positions in Al Hillah and As Samawah, as well as Karbala. Attacks on Ba'ath Party headquarters continue with assistance from local civilians.

A British soldier of the Army School of Ammunition, RLC (Royal Logistic Corps), is killed near Basrah during an explosive-ordnance-disposal operation.

Iraqi forces are using microlight aircraft as 'spy planes'. Coalition troops are ordered to shoot them down if spotted.

1 APRIL

The Black Watch rescue two Kenyan civilians who have been taken prisoner by Iraqi forces in Az Zubayr. British forces destroy a convoy of Iraqi armoured vehicles north of Basrah.

A British soldier, a lance corporal of the Household Cavalry Regiment, is killed in an accident involving his CVRT. [Another soldier, a lieutenant also of the Household Cavalry Regiment, died on 22 April due to injuries sustained in the same incident.]

British forces attack and hold Iraqi positions at Basrah Airport and defend the area from any counter-attack. US troops rescue Jessica Lynch, the female soldier captured by Iraqi forces during the early part of the war. US Marines discover two Al Samoud II missiles at Al Hillah, which contravene UN resolutions.

British soldiers discover an ammunition dump containing artillery pieces and missiles near Basrah. They are destroyed by controlled explosions. US Marines fight back Republican Guard units of the

Baghdad Division at Al Kut. US Marines (V) Corps attack the Medina and Nebuchadnezzar Republican Guard divisions at Karbala. They also continue to defeat Iraqi positions of paramilitary forces at Al Najaf. Iraqi forces use the sacred Ali Mosque as cover and fire on US soldiers from these positions.

2 APRIL

The ICRC [International Committee of the Red Cross] send representatives to visit Iraqi PWs held by coalition forces in southern Iraq to ensure they are being treated in accordance with the Geneva Convention.

The Iraqi Air Force, although small, is still active and remains a threat, including any chemical air strikes. US Marines (V) Corps move closer to Baghdad, knocking back the Republican Guard Medina Division and securing positions around Baghdad. They also secure a bridge over the Euphrates River.

Attacks are maintained by 101 Air Assault Division on Iraqi forces at Al Najaf. At As Samawah, 15 Mechanised Division suffers tremendous air strikes and comes under attack from the 82 Airborne Division. Basrah continues to be pounded by British artillery and rockets whilst 7 Armoured Brigade Challenger 2 tanks destroy key Iraqi positions and armour.

3 APRIL

Coalition forces enter the Tharthar Palace 100 kilometres south of Baghdad. Iraqi forces shoot down a coalition FA-18C aircraft. A US UH-60 helicopter crashes in central Iraq.

British soldiers close in around Az Zubayr,

eliminating the Fedayeen militia threat, and discover a ballistic-missile battery. They also continue to destroy Iraqi positions around Basrah and advance at a fast rate. US 1 Marine Expeditionary Force continue to eliminate the Republican Guard Al Nida and Baghdad divisions at Al Kut and Baghdad.

US Marine (V) Corps carry out attacks and secure the southern routes into Baghdad and the international airport west of Baghdad. Many parts of Basrah are by now under British forces control.

4 APRIL

Coalition forces search buildings suspected of having been used as an NBC training school for Iraqi troops near Basrah. The retreating Iraqi Army around Basrah and in southern areas of Iraq has reportedly received injections against chemical agents, which confirms suspicions that there is a potential threat of chemical attacks.

US soldiers from the 3 Infantry Division reach southern Baghdad and continue with their attack towards the centre of the city. US forces increase security around Baghdad International Airport. British forces continue to expand the safe area around Az Zubayr and Basrah, pushing further out and destroying Iraqi forces or pockets of resistance from Fedayeen militia. The civilians of Basrah are pleased to see the British forces and welcome them to their city with open arms.

Plans are drawn up by 16 Air Assault to attack Iraqi positions at Adyar with support from 7 Armoured Brigade. Fedayeen militia attack VCPs on major routes around Az Zubayr.

5 APRIL

Az Zubayr is by now under British forces control. During searches of key installations, British soldiers discover a large amount of uninterred human remains in the grounds and within a police headquarters in the town. The bodies pre-date the current conflict and undergo an examination by forensic teams.

US forces continue their stranglehold on the south-western and south-eastern areas of Baghdad, pushing further towards the centre of the city. Further control is enforced at Karbala, As Samawah and Al Najaf. The British 3 Battalion, the Parachute Regiment gains control of the area around Az Zubayr and the GOSP, as the rest of 7 Armoured Brigade continue north towards Basrah.

6 APRIL

Three British soldiers of the RRF are killed in action during a battle with the remaining Iraqi forces in Basrah. Street clashes and FIBUA [fighting in built-up areas] continue in areas of Basrah as the British forces close in on the remaining positions of the Iraqi forces.

Two British tank battle-group formations from 2 RTR and the Scots Dragoon Guards link up in the centre of Basrah. 3 Battalion, the Parachute Regiment control areas of old Basrah which are inaccessible to British military vehicles.

17

THE ROAD TO BASRAH

The same old surroundings were taking their toll on us. We were well overdue a change of scenery, which soon came with a move to an area called Al Ashshar in central Basrah, code-named 'Smartie'. Exactly what and where this Smartie harbour area was, I didn't know at the time. I didn't really care, as long as it was anywhere but the GOSP.

The reports we'd been receiving over the previous few days had been a mixture of doom and jubilation: sadness at the loss of British and American soldiers' lives but excitement at the fact the coalition forces were gaining ground and capturing key objectives in such a small amount of time. We were winning this war and it wouldn't be long before it ended – well, that's what we thought then. In the mean time, we concentrated on our move to Basrah and supporting the rest of 7 Armoured.

Monday, 7 April 0400hrs zulu After an O'group, we checked and prepared our vehicles for the 150-kilometre drive to the centre of Basrah. We moved at 0530hrs zulu. For Stuart and me, however, there was a recovery task: to take 23 Royal Engineers CET (combat engineer tractor) to a field workshop hastily set up on the west bank of the Tigris, next to Bridge Four. First, we had to wait until A1 and A2 packets, along with the rest of the 2 RTR BG vehicles, had vacated the GOSP area. We could then sweep the MSR between Az Zubayr and Bridge Four for vehicle breakdowns. Although we had a CET on the hook, it was up to our Foden to recover any stranded vehicles making their merry way to the Smartie location and take the CET to the forward field workshop. In a nutshell, we were expecting to be rushed off our feet.

As we were hooking up the CET, first removing the damaged port-side track, we didn't notice the battle group moving out of the GOSP. A weird and uneasy silence fell upon us; a tumbleweed even blew past, just like in a scene from some old Western movie. We were now alone, open to ambush, Stuart cheerily reminded me.

Although we were aware of our vulnerability to sniper fire, our first concern was an American A10 'tank buster' circling ahead at low level. If the pilot decided we were the enemy and opened up using his DU 30-mm shells from its powerful multi-barrelled cannon, we were goners. But after a few low-level sweeps, I presumed he'd recognised we were friendly and decided to disappear. Foden recovery vehicles had already been attacked from the air because at high altitude the jib on top could look as though it was a mobile SAM or Scud-missile launcher.

The trip to the field workshop went surprisingly well, without any major dramas. The odd crack of small arms could be heard whizzing past our cab, as well as the occasional shell exploding in the distance, but nothing to write home about. And, of course, the local children were a problem with their 'Mister, Mister, water, water' tactics, but at least we didn't come across any other vehicle casualties.

The new workshop area was nothing more than dried-up swampland. Thank God it was a temporary set-up, otherwise the ground would have caused serious problems. The area was infested with flies, not unlike our very own bluebottles, the difference being these flies didn't go away when you attempted to whack them with a glove or whatever – they simply stood their ground. We couldn't wait to unhook the CET and get out of there.

With the CET dropped off, all we had to do was wait at the west side of the bridge for our packet to drive past and continue the journey to our Basrah location. We could then tag along at the tail end. As we waited, the amount of armoured traffic heading for Basrah increased. Challenger after Challenger, Warrior after Warrior, and troop carrier after troop carrier poured over the bridge towards the city. There were already hundreds of armoured fighting vehicles in the 'second city' from 7 Armoured Brigade, not to mention the hundreds of helicopters, fighters and ground-attack aircraft flying overhead and the thousands of infantry clearing the streets of the diehards from the Black Watch, RRF, Irish Guards, LI, the paras and the Duke of Wellington Regiment. We certainly meant business.

Stuart made a brew whilst we waited for our packet. We didn't say much, just left each other with our own private thoughts. I couldn't be sure but I guessed Stuart was thinking the same as me: wondering what the family was doing back home and if we would actually get through Basrah alive. So far, as far as being bumped was concerned, we'd got off pretty lightly; even the threat of chemical attack had subsided a little. Basrah, however, would be a totally different matter. We had been briefed about the maze of narrow streets and the real possibility of sniper fire and booby traps, and had also been told to expect to be ambushed at some point, especially soft-skin vehicles such as Land-Rovers, troop carriers and, of course, Foden recovery vehicles, simply because we were easy pickings.

'I think I can see our packet approaching,' Stuart shouted, nearly choking on a mouthful of tea. He pointed to his left, towards some military vehicles in convoy formation.

'Yeah, I think you're right. I recognise the Bedford without its front grille [a distinctive feature on a vehicle casualty we'd once repaired].'

I started the engine and moved closer to the side of the road, ready to join the rear of our approaching packet. The driver of the grille-less Bedford sounded his horn as he drove closer – he must have recognised us. I acknowledged him by giving the thumbs-up, then quickly fell in as the last vehicle, right behind Bobby's VM Bedford.

As we drove over the brow of the bridge, the outskirts of Basrah came into view. At first, I could see nothing more than smoke trails rising from burst oil pipes, which had been set alight by retreating Iraqi forces, and burning Iraqi military vehicles on the other side of the bridge. The smell of the Tigris soon began to torture my nostrils with a foul stench. Stuart began to pull a funny face as his nose caught a waft from the river.

After a few kilometres, the stench diminished, until we ran into another foul and disgusting odour, a smell that can only be described as rotting cabbage and stagnant water, which came from a huge municipal rubbish tip on either side of the potholed road. These rubbish tips were teeming with people, hundreds of them, all scavenging for anything of use in their pathetic lives.

Once again, children slowed the convoys down with their well-planned ambushes for food and water, remarkably with huge smiles. But these people were different to those I had encountered previously: not poor farmers scratching a living from the desert but the scroungers and beggars Saddam's regime wished to forget, the ones thrown into the gutter to rot. Many civilians back home who had seen these images on TV, would have come to the knee-jerk conclusion that it was us who caused such hardship, but we didn't have anything to do with it. These people had been suffering in this way for years, not months. Locals later told me they had been living on the rubbish tips for over 20 years.

As soon as we passed the rubbish tip, we came across buildings riddled with shell blasts and bullet holes. Bomb and shell craters were scattered either on or near the roadside, next to the odd pile of rubble where houses once stood. Iraqi tanks and armoured vehicles, still smouldering from shell strikes, also littered the roads. Women washed clothes in huge puddles of dirty, pungent water leaked from burst water mains sabotaged by the retreating Iraqi Army. Children filled plastic containers out of the same pond to use as drinking water. In one particular puddle, I saw children drinking the water whilst an ox stood in the middle taking a piss. This was real poverty.

The buildings started to increase in size as we reached the outskirts of Al Ashshar and moved closer to the centre of Basrah. Shacks and home-made buildings gave way to office blocks, shopping centres and hotels. The main road widened into different lanes, filtering into road junctions with traffic lights, islands and road signs. The streets were lined with streetlights but whether they worked or not was a different matter.

The city, although shot to pieces, appeared alive. People went about their business the best way they could, not unlike Londoners during the Blitz. Taxis were picking up fares, shops were open for business, even though they were battle-damaged, and markets were trading in home-grown produce, mainly tomatoes, fruit and meat. I expected to see chaos around the streets but there wasn't any. The sound of automatic fire in the background didn't even send the locals into a frenzied panic, diving for cover; they just looked around to make sure they were safe from stray rounds flying past and carried on walking.

This was so strange to witness and so different to how I would expect people back home to react in similar circumstances. Modern Britain and many other Western countries have unfortunately become self-centred, selfish and materialistic in their culture. The majority of the Western civilian public has been wrapped up in cotton wool for so long they've forgotten what the real world is like. Perversely, they're more interested in voyeuristic TV, so-called 'real-life' celebrity programmes or voting for manufactured pre-fabricated pop idols. The Iraqi civilians, however, had only one thought on their minds – survival; food, water, fuel and shelter most importantly. I'd learnt that the Iraqi people are true survivors and believe in what they do best – fending for themselves. I have nothing but great admiration for them.

The number of locals watching us drive through the streets increased as we got closer to the city centre. There seemed to be a different kind of onlooker. There were still the usual children shouting 'Mister, Mister' and the same old beggars but some of the crowd appeared healthier, well dressed and well groomed, with their close-shaven beards and crisp, clean dishdashes. At a guess, they could have been the business class that worked in the city but I couldn't help thinking that they had something sinister to hide.

It may just have been paranoia but the way they looked at us as we drove past seemed different to the usual crowds.

Rather than an idle glance, to me, they appeared interested to the point of taking mental notes, like how many vehicles there were and what type in each packet, how many soldiers were in a convoy and what armament they carried.

Evidence of fierce fire-fights could be seen whichever way we looked. Mortar splats in the middle of the streets, buildings peppered with small arms, even burnt-out, smouldering Iraqi armour with bits of crew scattered around them. Warriors and Challenger 2 tanks stood on sentry duty in what had been strategic Iraqi gun positions, whilst thousands of British soldiers patrolled the streets. This was the next immediate step of the conflict – to secure the area and maintain order.

Further shopping complexes and high-rise buildings were scarred with tank and artillery shell blasts and bullet holes. Soot rose up the walls from blown-out windows and doorways, some of which were still glowing from either shellfire or bombs from air strikes. Craters the size of houses were scattered around buildings, most likely places where guided bombs and missiles had missed their targets – or maybe they were targets?

The smell of the rubbish tip/shanty town we'd left behind at the edge of the city was replaced by a distinctive smell of shit. Animal, even human excrement lined the gutters; litter blocked the drains and sewers because it hadn't been collected since the start of the war, and continued to grow and grow; the rotting corpses of dead dogs and donkeys were left on the pavements, some having been hit by what looked like large-calibre shells. There was even the odd civilian lying in the gutter, either shot or blown up, their flesh rotting and festering. The 45-degree heat didn't help matters either, accelerating the deterioration. The rotting remains attracted rats, which attracted dogs, which attracted flies and health concerns, which could grow into epidemics – need I go on? I felt it was vital to win this war, and fast. Sanitation and clean water could then be restored, because the next battle was harder to win – the battle against disease.

Finally, we reached our destination, which was a bloody bus station. Our packet came to a halt outside the entrance whilst Captain Schaffer directed the convoy through. It wasn't unlike any other bus station back home, with a wide main entrance, bus lanes surrounded by a kerb with shelters equally spaced in the middle of the yard, and bus timetables with route cards riveted on the ends. Around the edge of the yard were sections of flat-roofed buildings containing various shops, such as a tobacconist and a café. And like home, they too had their shopfront shutters down and padlocked at the base. The entire yard was housed within a three-metre-high whitewashed brick wall.

Slowly, the entire packet drove through the entrance, manned either side by some of the LI guys. As soon as the vehicles were parked in their positions, sandbags were filled and distributed to vulnerable points around the yard to make walls for gun positions. On top of the flat-roofed buildings, sandbags were piled at key points towards the main entrance to make further gun positions and Cpl Stag Thompson soon made up a patrol roster, from which us recy mechs couldn't escape. Our Foden was parked at the front of the packet, down one side of a shopfront near the station entrance. This allowed us to drive straight out of the bus station without hindering other parked vehicles should we be called out on a task.

We'd reached our harbour area at the estimated time given at the O'group earlier that morning: 1300hrs zulu. Nicely settled in our new home, for a few days anyway, it was time for a brew and a spot of lunch – meatballs and pasta, again!

18

SAFE AS HOUSES

Whilst tucking into my delicious meal, I watched a couple of squaddies trying to smash lights around the bus station. They were nothing more than sodium street lamps dotted around its perimeter wall. The CV was straight across from our position, about 20 metres ahead, next to the left side of the entrance. Captain Schaffer watched them first try to take out the lights by throwing rocks at the protective Perspex cover around the sodium bulbs. All this achieved was for missiles to land near unsuspecting squaddies around the yard, which didn't go down very well with a few of them, who threw the rocks back at the culprits with twice the velocity and with a considerably better aim.

Their next idea was to shoot out the lamps with SA80s. The problem with this idea was the 5.56-mm round just made a nice neat hole through the Perspex cover and totally missed the sodium bulbs. Then Cpl Stag Thompson came to the rescue. He suggested that someone with a little knowledge of wiring could open the cover at the base of the lamp-posts and disconnect them. Thirty seconds later, Andy was knocking on our passenger door.

'All right, lads. The boss wants to know if you recy mechs have any electrical background. We're trying to disable the lights around the yard.'

I shrugged my shoulders, as if to say I haven't a bloody clue.

'Yeah, I do. I'll be right over,' replied Stuart.

I looked at him, frowning. 'You bloody liar! You know bog all about electrics.'

He smiled at me with a mischievous glint in his eye. 'I'll be back in a minute, this won't take long.'

'You'll end up killing yourself,' I warned, like a nagging mother.

'Watch and learn, son, watch and learn,' he replied, then giggled like a naughty schoolboy.

He grabbed his haversack and rifle and jumped out of the cab. A few seconds later, I could hear him scouring around in the bins at the rear of the truck. It sounded as if he was in the pioneer bin, which housed the digging tools, saws, axes and lump hammers. I had a weird feeling I knew what he was looking for. I looked in the rear-view mirror and, sure enough, he had the long-handled axe in his hand.

'You'll kill yourself!' I reminded him. Even Andy looked concerned and asked him if he was sure about what he was planning to do.

With a huge grin across his face, he walked over to Captain Schaffer and told him his brilliant idea. He reluctantly agreed and let Stuart carry on. Sure enough, he whacked the cover plates off and chopped, or rather hacked, at the wiring inside. A few bangs and sparks came from the lamp-posts as the three-phase current arced when the axe-head came into contact with the wiring but that was it – he'd solved the problem. Our area would now be in shadow against the streetlights outside the bus station, which is what the boss wanted.

Stuart walked back to the Foden with a smug grin on his face. 'Done the job, didn't it?' he boasted.

The sun had passed over the bus station. Thankfully, the shop on our right cast an inviting shadow over the Foden, which cooled down the breeze as it blew through our open windows and cupola. I folded down the back of my seat and stretched my legs over the top of the steering wheel for a well-deserved kip. Sooner or later, we were bound to be tasked for a job, so it was time to grab the chance to rest.

I had just settled when, *Boom!* A terrific explosion hit precariously close to our location, just on the other side of the perimeter wall. The shock wave rocked the Foden and bits of hot shrapnel and masonry rained down on us a few seconds later.

'What the fuck!' I shouted. I looked around in a pathetic attempt to suss out the situation. Another explosion soon followed, then another, all from the other side of the wall.

'I think it would be a good idea to replace the cupola, don't you?' Stuart said.

I turned to look at him and agree with his comment but he was halfway out of the cab. Getting the hint, I grabbed my kit and jumped out of the cab too. Stuart was already at the rear of the Foden, crouched down behind the heavy stiff legs which are used to anchor the recovery vehicle when the winch is in use. I quickly joined him whilst squaddies took cover behind the armoured CV, under Land-Rovers and behind the sandbag gun positions. Our next concern was the Bedford fuel tankers, which were the most vulnerable vehicles in the packet. If they were hit, we could have said goodbye to the bus station, ourselves and probably the entire Al Ashshar region.

'Can anyone see where this shit is coming from?' I asked

a bunch of LI guys behind me, who were taking cover in the shops' doorways.

'Fuck knows, mate,' one of them replied. 'At a guess, it's a mortar attack.'

I was inclined to agree; after all, he was an infantry soldier and would recognise the signature of the explosions.

Captain Schaffer shouted out orders to the LI guys taking cover at the main entrance. As he did so, another explosion rocked the bus station, only this time close to the main entrance. Thankfully, everyone had taken sufficient cover and no one was injured. As soon as the explosion had dispersed, the LI guys at the entrance returned fire with a few bursts from their gimpies and LSWs towards what they thought was the source of the attack. Across the road, there was an area of wasteland on which stood the odd flat-roofed building. One hundred metres to the left was a block of flats or offices, which had a clear bird's-eye view of the bus station yard and, more importantly, of us parked inside it. It was from this block of flats that the attack was coming. Once the source was established, the entire packet returned fire in that direction.

Stuart and I joined in the fireworks, emptying a couple of magazines into the building. Tracer rounds raced through windows and lumps of concrete pinged off the walls as round after round punched holes into the building. A few minutes later, a Challenger 2 raced towards the enemy position and pounded the building with a few HE rounds. A few seconds later, the area fell silent; the Challenger had cured the problem.

A mop-up squad from another unit was sent into the block of flats to conduct a search. They found evidence of a home-made mortar-type launcher and munitions, not unlike a 'pipe bomb' made out of a steel scaffold tube.

Crude but effective, and when trained on a target it can cause devastation within its killing zone. Luckily for us, the enemy on this occasion was a crap shot and the mortars had fallen short of their target. It didn't, however, leave much to the imagination regarding the kind of damage they could inflict. As for the guys who launched the attack, it was later discovered they weren't Iraqi soldiers but local militia, possibly Fedayeen.

Before the boss gave us the all clear, he sent out a few of the LI guys to go with the Challenger and make the area safe. Half an hour later, we were able to stand down and return to our vehicles to relax – as if! Adrenalin was pumping at such a rate of knots around our veins that we wanted to help clear the area. The boss eventually gave in to our constant nagging and let us assist with the patrols around the immediate area. So as not to have us roaming the streets and getting carried away, he had Stuart and me assist the sentries just outside the main entrance. We reloaded our magazines and, wearing our CBAs, Kevlar helmets and webbing, walked out of the relative safety of the bus station and into the streets of Basrah. The two sentries we were sent to assist were from the LI.

'All right, lads, come to help us on our patrol?' one of them said, as if he was full of the joys of spring, a corporal, named Paul; a huge lad in his late 20s and armed with a gimpie.

His mate, Simon, was a private; a young, fresh-faced lad who couldn't have been any older than 18 or 19. He seemed keen to destroy life but hadn't had the chance to live it yet. He didn't say much but I put that down to him being the baby of the patrol. He appeared obliged to obey Stuart and me, rather than his corporal, probably because we were the elders of the patrol. In fact, I wouldn't have been surprised if his memories of taking orders from his teachers at school were still as fresh as they were the day he left; having to take orders from the army as soon as he joined up hadn't given him the chance to make decisions for himself.

'Hang on a minute, I thought we were staying around this area, within sight of the bus station,' commented Stuart, although the glint in his eyes showed me he favoured the thought of venturing further afield.

'We were, but we're to help other patrols as the sandbag party remove sandbags from the Iraqi gun positions, to put the locals at ease,' answered Paul.

'A show of strength,' I quickly added. Paul nodded in agreement.

A few hundred metres further down the road there was a dual carriageway with a wide, sand central reservation with the occasional sandbagged S60 gun position, either intact or blown to pieces by shellfire. A CET followed the sandbag party using its shovel to transport the sandbags back to the bus station.

'There's a 500-metre-square section they have to clear within the next few hours. It's our job to guard them whilst they clear the area,' Paul explained.

We walked off towards the CET to meet the 20 or so sandbag party crew.

My first impression was it was a one-for-all type set-up but the whole operation was well coordinated and disciplined. I suppose it had to be because of the threat of sniper fire, booby traps and the like. There were five teams of four and each team had a guard watching their back. The other guard, another corporal from the attached light infantry unit, was already making a list of team members, including us guards.

With the teams ready, we walked alongside as they loaded the shovel of the CET with sandbags. Stuart's team, on the opposite side of the road and about 20 metres ahead of mine, led the front. The other teams concentrated on the adjoining side streets as the CET raced around to keep up. At first I felt uneasy about this, although vulnerable would be a better word. What the fuck am I doing? I thought to myself, as I reacted to every movement on the street. I treated every onlooker with suspicion, and with every chogie wagon that drove past I wondered if its passengers were about to open fire on us. My senses had never been so acute. One thing was for sure, sod this infantry lark, I'd stick to being a recy mech.

Our section of the street was soon cleared and made safe, so we made our way back to the bus station using the CET as cover, remaining in our team formations. The sandbag teams had now swapped rigger gloves for their SA80s and become guards themselves, watching each other's backs as we walked along the dual carriageway. We soon met the other teams from the adjoining backstreets and they in turn fell into formation, patrolling the dual carriageway, one team on one side of the road and one team on the other, staggered apart by about 20 metres. Everyone was watching every movement, listening and reacting to every sound, and after a few steps the last member of a team would do a 360 and check his rear.

We reached a roundabout and the bus station was now in sight, with only a few hundred metres to go. The all-round visual continued, not allowing any lapse in concentration just because we could see sanctuary ahead. At this point, I feared an attack of some kind. To my right, there was a breezeblock wall about two metres high and one hundred metres long lining the pavement, built around some wasteland. All we have to do is reach the end of this wall and we're almost home, I thought. But my worst fears came true. *Boom!*

A huge explosion came from the other side of the breezeblock wall. We ran to its base and took cover from falling shrapnel and debris. Civilians dived for cover in shop doorways and alleyways, and vehicles screeched to a halt as the occupants jumped out and ran for safety. Within seconds, the area was clear and eerily silent, until two Warriors thundered past heading for a gap in the wall to investigate the explosion. Paul was soon on his radio trying to find out what the fuck was happening. My fear factor was now racing towards the top of its scale. Was this an ambush? Did someone trigger a booby trap? At this stage, no one knew what had caused the explosion. We maintained an all-round defence just in case we were about to engage a contact. If anyone was about to attack, at least we could give them a bloody nose.

When the Warriors disappeared into the distance, the area fell silent once again, apart from Paul shouting into his radio trying to find out if it was safe for us to continue. At that moment, however, we had no choice but to stay in our current position, lining the wall like sitting ducks. My eyes widened, taking in every movement; only now, if it was at all possible, my senses were even more acute. I trained my rifle on every civilian as they appeared from their hiding places, treating them with suspicion. I was – yet again – shitting myself. Amidst all the excitement, I didn't hear Paul laughing but soon registered some of the other squaddies next to him joining in. Stuart crawled up to my position and pushed his way in between another guy and me.

'What's the joke?' he asked.

'Dunno, but I'm sure we're about to find out.'

Paul stood up and grabbed our attention. 'Listen in,' he shouted. 'It turned out to be a controlled explosion, made by the engineers blowing up Iraqi munitions gathered from the area. They were using the wasteland as a safe area to carry out these explosions. It appeared they forgot to inform other units, including us.'

This lack of communication between units was becoming a bit of a joke, to say the least. Soon afterwards, we had the all clear and made our way back to the bus station.

Although there was only less than 100 metres to go, we maintained our patrol discipline until we reached the main entrance, then, and only then, could we sigh with relief and relax, but only a little.

Stuart and I managed to get our heads down for a few hours, although it was difficult to sleep whilst our senses continued to overreact to the slightest sound. The rest of the packet exploited the lull and caught up with any admin, sleep and food whilst the LI guys were left to do their job and guard the bus station, and us. Within a few hours, however, nightfall meant all soldiers, including us recy mechs and VMs, were required for stag around key points in the bus station, thanks to Stag Andy.

Our few hours' kip came to an end with a deliberately soft knocking on my door. I opened my eyes to total darkness, which surprised me. I checked my watch then realised I had actually been sparked out for nearly six hours.

'Five minutes, Kev,' a voice whispered. It was one of the LI guys waking me for my stag – a one-and-a-half-hour stint at the gun position on top of the shop roof, left of the main entrance.

'Yep, all right, mate,' I muttered, still half asleep.

Stuart's stag was right after mine. He was to be woken half an hour later by the guy I was joining on the roof of the shop and would then join me. After one hour, I would wake the next guy on the list to join Stuart, who would wake the next on the list, and so on and so on, until the list started again at first light. The system appeared complicated but it worked. The idea was for no position to be left unmanned and each one to be kept at maximum strength at all times, using the resources available.

I checked my watch again, now that I was more awake. It was 2200hrs zulu. And like any squaddie on sentry duty, I began to work out in my head how long I would have after my stag to grab some kip before reveille. Easy enough to work out, I thought. Sentry duty was until 2330hrs zulu, reveille at 0300hrs zulu. Allowing half an hour of fucking about, three hours were left for kip. Could have been worse, I suppose. I quietly walked over to the left side of the shop and slung my rifle over my back to negotiate the makeshift climbing frame we'd made to reach the roof.

The rickety construction, made out of an old pine table and a steel-framed plastic chair precariously balanced on the top, would have been fine to climb without the added weight of a CBA, webbing and rifle. After a few grunts and groans, I managed to climb the three-metre obstacle and join the waiting sentry, who turned out to be Bobby. I made myself comfortable, sitting in the gutter, which was a good shoulder width and about 300-mm deep, surrounding the concrete roof. The walls of the building were roughly half a metre higher than the roof surface and offered cover against small-arms and machine-gun fire.

The sandbag walls of the gun position housed three flares for illuminating the area of an attack, a pair of NVGs, a stag list and comms to contact the CV should the need arise. The only weapons available were our own rifles but the lack of firepower wasn't a problem because the LI guys below were armed with LSWs and GPMGs, with a couple of 94-mm LAWs thrown in for good measure. Our roof-top position was only an early-warning OP (observation post) with a 200-degree arc of fire, covering the main street in front and the large roundabout to the south of our position.

Bobby gave me a progress report, which was literally nothing. The streets were empty of vehicles and people, which was expected because of the curfew. But not even a military vehicle could be seen, let alone heard. The only movement and sound came from wild dogs chasing each other as they defended their territory from rival packs. At that particular moment, Basrah was the quietest it had been for a long time.

Half an hour passed and Bobby left the rooftop for his waiting doss bag. I took over the radio and placed the strap over my head to secure the earpiece against my right ear. I was now on my own, if only for a while, before being joined by Stuart. I looked through the NVGs and swept the area, checking the dark shadows made by doorways and adjoining alleyways. To my right was a small narrow street, about fifty metres in length and roughly four metres wide with two-storey buildings, shops, I suppose, either side. It reminded me of an old Tudor street in London.

In the far distance, I heard the distinctive rumble of a Challenger 2, no doubt on patrol, but the sound of another vehicle caught my attention. It wasn't a track vehicle but definitely large, possibly a truck of some kind. Again, I didn't take much notice and carried on sweeping the area with the NVGs. The noise of the Challenger and the mystery vehicle were becoming louder but broken. The built-up area intermittently blocked out the noise as they approached our location. I could then hear the sound of muffled automatic fire. The odd burst at first but it soon became more and more intense.

Oh shit, I thought. I didn't like the sound of this. I concentrated my attention towards the roundabout and the noise of the vehicles, which sounded as if they were coming from the south of our location. If they were going to pass me, I would see them approach the roundabout first. I adjusted my position behind the sandbags so I could comfortably aim my rifle. The streetlights did a good job illuminating the roundabout and gave me a little time to suss out the oncoming vehicles. For a few seconds, I couldn't hear anything again, then the sound returned. The vehicles were now close, very close, but why couldn't I see them?

My attention was drawn towards the alleyway to my right. Of course, I thought, the road at the end of the alleyway. They must be heading towards the road that ran parallel with the back of the bus station. Sure enough, the vehicles passed the other end of the alleyway. The exit was narrow but I managed to catch a fleeting glimpse of a municipal refuse-collection truck with muzzle flashes of automatic fire coming out of the back. A few seconds later, a Challenger 2 rumbled past in hot pursuit of the truck. I couldn't believe what I was seeing; they were firing at the Challenger with automatic rifles. If they were lucky, they might have scratched the paintwork.

A report of a shell leaving the barrel of the Challenger, quickly followed by an explosion, soon filled the air, creating a fireball which rose above the north of our location. A few seconds later, bits of refuse truck came raining down on the bus station. The Challenger could then be heard doing a 180, as the tracks gouged its 60-tonne bulk into the tarmac and thundered back down the street. It was at times like this I wished I'd brought a camcorder. The sentries at the main entrance were busy talking into their radios, explaining what had happened to the switch-bitch on duty in the CV. No doubt the boss wanted to know what had happened after being rudely awoken by the commotion.

The explosion created a heightened sense of alert around the harbour area, with squaddies running for stand-to positions, but the excitement soon died down and they returned to their vehicles, leaving the LI guys and sentries to carry on with their stag duties – including me. I checked my watch, 2300hrs zulu, and I could make out the silhouette of Stuart walking across the bus station. Then, out of the blue, a public-address system sprang into life, chanting Muslim prayers over what seemed like thousands of loudspeakers, echoing through the narrow streets. I certainly didn't expect that. Back home at two o'clock in the morning, it was not uncommon for locals to be woken by the sound of chanting, but it was usually drunks!

I could hear Stuart puffing and panting as he climbed onto the roof. He settled in the gutter and I gave him the details of my stag. Half an hour later, it was my turn to grab a few hours' kip, which proved to be difficult with our Iraqi 'Tom Jones' blasting through the streets.

19

HOW THE OTHER HALF LIVE

It wasn't long before 0300hrs zulu came around, and with it a knock on my door from Stag Andy. He handed me a piece of scrap paper with a grid reference scribbled on it – oh joy, a job!

Stuart remained in the cab snoring his head off whilst I visited the CV for further information about the vehicle casualty. It was a US Marine HumVee utility vehicle with a puncture that required our air compressor to blow up its spare tyre – simple enough. The HumVee, along with its crew, was one of many attached to 2 RTR BG to assist with target recognition. The grid reference of our HumVee casualty was in the grounds of a Ba'ath Party government headquarters on the other side of the Al Ashshar region of the city, about four kilometres north of our location. Our REME LAD HQ, along with 2 RTR BG, used the building as a FOP (forward operations post).

As a result of the continuing threat of retaliation attacks and snipers, the 'armoured escort' rule was still in place, so Stuart and I had to wait for an escort to be organised. In the mean time, we grabbed the chance to check our recovery kit and give our weapons a 'pull-through'. We even managed to grab some breakfast, which, of course, was meatballs and pasta (surprise, surprise).

Finally, our armoured escort, a CVRT Scimitar, arrived at the main entrance. We made our weapons ready and I started the Foden's engine, moving towards the waiting CVRT. Yet again, we left the relative safety of our well-protected harbour area to venture into the uncertain streets of Basrah. The CVRT didn't hang about, a typical characteristic of tracked-vehicle drivers. All they knew was flat out or stop, there was no in-between. On this occasion, however, driving flat out was very much appreciated. The last thing we wanted was to drive at a slow, crawling pace and have some overambitious 'would be' Fedayeen teenager, overdosed on testosterone, taking pot shots at us.

Turning left out of the main entrance, we headed north to the roundabout, about 100 metres from the bus station. Turning left again, I noticed the burnt-out wreckage of the bright-orange refuse-collection truck from the previous night's activities. Amazingly, the only part of the truck left untouched was the rubbish compactor fitted to the rear of the vehicle. The tank round must have passed through the open compactor and exploded on contact with the front of the hopper, leaving very little of the occupants who had been firing at the Challenger. The only human remains visible were the odd arm or leg mangled around twisted bits of hopper and cab.

The hustle and bustle of the morning city traffic soon congested the roads and the knackered traffic lights didn't help matters. Orange and white taxis, chogie wagons and trucks were all trying to find their way through the jams. Unlike traffic jams back home, though, here the locals had a sense of decorum about them. They seemed to understand the concept of good manners and gave way to traffic rather than try and selfishly push themselves through. Military vehicles, mind you, didn't hang about for anyone. It was a case of get out of the way or be squashed by a 27-tonne truck; not surprisingly, the locals generally pulled over.

But just like home, there's always one which refuses to move out of the way, even for an armoured vehicle close on its tail – literally. A donkey and cart plodded along the busy road as if nothing else mattered, totally oblivious to the tailback it was causing. No one could get past because of burnt-out vehicles and parked cars on the side of the road, and the cart driver wasn't going to budge an inch, not unlike caravan owners. Our only option, short of running over the cart, was to wait for a few hundred metres until the road to widened and we could safely pass. After what seemed an eternity, we reached the wider section of the road and the CVRT managed to pass the cart. Before I drove past, Stuart and I had conjured up a little surprise for this potential 'caravan owners' club' member.

'Right, now!' I shouted, as I leant out of the window and lined up the donkey with my front wheel. Stuart hit the red switch on the dashboard and gave the cart driver a blast from the air horns. We giggled like naughty schoolkids but as I looked in the rear-view mirror, hoping to see the donkey bolt with fright, it was just carrying on as if we weren't there.

'Bollocks! It didn't work,' I said, disappointed.

'Give him the exhaust-brake treatment,' Stuart suggested.

Not downhearted, I came to a halt so the donkey could carry on ahead and gain about 20 metres. I then raced alongside it and leant out of the window. '*Now!*'

Stuart pulled on the exhaust-brake switch as I slammed on the anchors, sounding off a deep, loud grunt from the engine and engulfing the donkey and driver in a cloud of thick, white smoke – not even a twitch. This donkey must have seen everything; nothing would startle it.

'Er, Kev, where's the CVRT?'

I pulled myself back in the cab and looked straight ahead. 'Shit! We've lost it.'

Stuart checked the map against the grid reference, in the hope of finding out where the fuck we were.

'C'mon, Stuart, where are we?'

He frantically scanned the map in desperation. We were more concerned about getting a bollocking for losing the CVRT than being under threat of ambush or sniper fire. 'Hang on, I think I know where we are,' he replied.

I continued driving on the same road, hoping we would eyeball the CVRT, and as luck would have it, I spotted it a few hundred metres ahead, stuck in a traffic jam.

'Thank fuck for that,' I said, sighing with relief.

The drivers of the CVRT were trying to turn right over a narrow single-carriageway bridge. Unfortunately for them, oncoming traffic was doing the same. As we approached the bridge, a stench similar to rotting vegetation, like the smell of a stagnant pond mixed with the already bad odour of shit filled the air. The smell, which we were slowly getting used to, was coming from the canal that ran into the adjoining River Tigris. As we drove nearer, the smell became more intense and increasingly acrid.

The road veered alongside the canal's steep four-metre concrete embankment before it reached the bridge, and it was here that I noticed the water in the canal was purple. I thought British canals were bad but this took the biscuit. What was making the canal's water turn purple, I didn't know or care; all I wanted to do was get clear of it. Whatever it was, it was beginning to sting my eyes and nostrils.

The traffic approaching from the opposite side of the bridge quickly backed up as the CVRT driver grew increasingly impatient and forced the traffic out of the way, making enough room for us to pass, and the canal soon disappeared into the distance, along with the stench. A few minutes later, we were driving alongside the River Tigris. Palm trees lined the wide and surprisingly lush green lawns on the embankment, virtually level with the river. On the river's edge were half a dozen bronze statues featuring important members of the regime, including yet another of Saddam in the centre, his right arm outstretched, as if he was welcoming visitors to the city.

Opposite the embankment and to our left stood a block of very grand-looking buildings, nestled majestically alongside the river, a total contrast to the area of the city in which we were camped. These were the mega-expensive apartments or holiday homes used by top-ranking regime members. This was the part of the city visitors and world politicians once saw, giving them a false impression that all Iraqi citizens lived in such wealthy surroundings. It certainly fooled some of the paint your arse blue, howl at the moon brigade, a few MPs and certain naive ex-Cabinet ministers. Next to them were hotels and Ba'ath Party government buildings, all surrounded by high walls and heavy iron security gates. Not that these were built to act as deterrents; under the old regime, locals were shot for just walking next to these buildings, let alone trying to get into one uninvited.

The CVRT stopped outside one of these buildings and we were greeted by a couple of sentries at the main entrance. Two huge swing gates made out of decorative wrought iron and painted black and gold, with a Ba'ath

Party emblem welded onto a brass plate in the middle of the gate, secured the main entrance. Across the ground was a spiked pole running along a gully, which could be electronically raised to protrude above the surface should a vehicle attempt an unauthorised entrance – or exit, as the case may be.

The spike mechanism had been sabotaged to stop foreign troops entering the grounds. This stopped it from being lowered and left the sharp tips protruding, as the US Marines had discovered when they drove over them in their HumVees. I did wonder why sandbags weren't used, but apparently they had been. It seemed they were only effective for the odd two or three vehicles before they split, allowing the spikes to poke through the sandbags again. These particular vehicles had arrived at night and were under fire at the time, so I don't think they were too concerned about getting a puncture.

Luckily, only one B-vehicle had sustained a puncture and that was the HumVee we were visiting. The CVRT passed the sentries at the gate and drove straight over the spikes. Because of the weight of the Foden and its bulky tyres, an extra half a dozen sandbags were thrown down for good measure and we soon caught up with the CVRT. The entire complex consisted of two three-storey buildings built out of sandstone, one facing the entrance to the complex and the other directly behind, separated by a paved driveway. Both buildings were surrounded by lush gardens. At the side of the road which encircled the front building there were three-metre-high decorative black-iron street lamps spaced around the circuit. I was amazed none of them had been knocked over. The lawns, however, were slightly damaged by parked Warriors and CVRTs, some of which must have done the odd handbrake turn judging by the freshly ploughed grass.

The entire complex couldn't have been any more than 200 metres square and with a handful of Warriors, half a dozen CVRTs and four HumVees parked in the gardens, there wasn't a lot of room to manoeuvre a Foden recovery vehicle. Luckily, our vehicle casualty was parked just off the concrete circuit between the second building and the three-metre-high north-side perimeter wall. All I had to do was drive past the HumVee a little then reverse down the side of it.

Stuart jumped out of the cab and stood in front of the Foden, directing me with hand signals as I reversed. After a few tight manoeuvres, I managed to pull up alongside the casualty where two of the occupants were sitting in the vehicle drinking Coke – what else! I pulled on the handbrake, put on my CBA and Kevlar helmet, picked up my rifle and haversack, and joined Stuart as he was introducing us to the crew. Stuart then started to suss out the HumVee. Sure enough, the offside rear (for a left-hand drive) tyre was definitely flat. In fact, it was ripped to pieces.

'Hi, buddy!' came a voice from behind. It was one of the HumVee's crew, L/Cpl Chris Hawthorn, a tall, blond lad about 30 years old.

'Take more than a bit of wind to blow this up. Do you have a spare?' I asked.

'A spare? You must be joking,' answered Chris. 'If we did, where would we put it?' He pointed to the lack of space on the back of the HumVee. It was jam-packed-full of kit. Even the roof and sides of the vehicle had bergens and webbing strapped to them. 'One of our guys has gone to ask our sergeant for permission to change it for a new one.'

'Permission?' Stuart asked, frowning and looking confused. 'Why do you need permission?'

'Of course we do. We can't just change it. The old one has to be inspected.'

Stuart and I looked at each other, slightly bemused by Chris's reply. We couldn't get our heads around the asking-permission thing. The Americans, it seemed, played this war game differently to us Brits. Stuart and I knew that if it was a Land-Rover and it didn't have a spare, the crew would have either begged, borrowed or stolen one to get it back on the road. In fact, it would most likely have been stolen, because asking for permission or to borrow something isn't in the British squaddie handbook of charm and deportment!

'How long will he be?' Stuart asked.

'Shouldn't be too long, about ten minutes or so.'

Stuart's eyes beamed wide open. I knew what he was thinking – we had ten minutes of snooping time. 'We'll be back in a bit, mate. Just going to have a look around.' He'd already thought of a cover story in case we were collared. 'We can say we're looking for the boss. One of them is bound to be here somewhere.'

I slowly shook my head and smiled. 'That is the most feeble excuse you've ever come up with but I suppose it might work.'

We headed for the front building, which was more lavish than the one behind it. The first obstacle was the sprawl of communication cables strewn across the ground, coming from various CVs. We then had to step over Warrior crews sunbathing and catching up on much-needed sleep. We reached a back-door entrance leading into a lobby and our eyes took a few minutes to adjust to the dimly lit room. As soon as we were used to it, the lobby showed off the full splendour of its architecture.

Underneath the spaghetti of cables and the radios which filled the desks, the floor was lavishly tiled in marble, which continued a little way up the adjoining walls, meeting solid oak and decorative plaster panelling. Wall-mounted lights with gold-plated swirls for brackets were dotted around the room. The ceiling had plaster mouldings surrounding panelled oil paintings with gold-leaf edging joining a huge chandelier hanging from a gold chain in the centre, most likely made from cut-glass lead crystal.

Although the room looked pretty bare, we could certainly get a feel for how the other half lived. Power was restored and the lights in the lobby were switched on, and more importantly so was the air conditioning, which offered a welcome cool atmosphere compared with the 40-degree heat outside.

'I can now understand why HQ wanted to use this building, Stuart. Stuart?' Too late, he was off.

At a guess, he'd gone down the corridor that faced us as we entered the lobby. I gingerly walked past a bunch of officers talking to each other and down the corridor, peering into each of the rooms on either side. The first two rooms I looked into, again lavishly decorated, were full of military stores, ammunition and rat packs.

Stuart appeared from further up the corridor holding what looked like a rolled-up flag wrapped around a piece of wood.

'Let's get the fuck out of 'ere,' he whispered out of the corner of his mouth.

I didn't ask why; I didn't need to. I knew exactly what he'd done. We quickly vacated the premises and headed for the Foden.

'Hi guys, what have you there?' Chris asked.

'Nothing, just some old rags to wipe our hands with,' I said, as Stuart climbed in the cab to hide our booty (two Iraqi flags).

'Just some rag?' Stuart mumbled in my ear as he joined me around the HumVee.

'It was the first thing that came into my head,' I whispered.

Stuart quickly changed the subject. 'Any news on your spare tyre?'

'Yeah, it's on its way,' replied his mate, another lance corporal. I think he said his name was Carl.

'We might as well remove the flat, Stuart. Where's your wheel brace, mate?' I asked.

'We don't have one,' replied Carl.

I don't believe this, I thought. I fetched our toolbox from the pioneer bin, hoping we had the right size of ring spanner. Luckily, we did.

'I'll fetch a bottle jack,' Stuart said.

I looked at Carl. 'I don't suppose you . . .'

'No, we don't.'

'And I thought you Yanks had everything,' I commented.

'That's only a myth,' replied Chris. 'You'll be surprised how much kit we've borrowed off you guys.'

'Yeah, I know. A toolbox, a jack and a fucking Foden recovery vehicle for starters,' Stuart added sarcastically, as he struggled back with the heavy jack.

Chris didn't appear to find Stuart's comment funny but I don't think Stuart intended it to be. I started to undo the wheel nuts whilst Stuart placed the bottle jack underneath the offside rear suspension leg.

'Bollocks!' he shouted. 'We'll need some skidding. The jack is just burying itself in the dirt. I'll fetch the six-by-three.'

The six-by-three is a piece of timber, six by three inches by about one metre in length, used for various tasks, including supporting jacks in soft ground. I finished loosening the wheel nuts and waited for Stuart with the skidding.

'Fancy a Coke?' asked Chris.

'You bet. Cheers, mate.' Chris passed me a can of lukewarm Coke, which I didn't mind. I savoured each gulp as it tingled the back of my throat. 'This is heaven,' I said, as I took a breather between gulps.

'I'll leave this one for Stuart,' Chris added, and placed a can on the rear of the HumVee. I took a few more gulps from mine and placed my can next to Stuart's.

'Have you had many American vehicles to recover?' asked Chris.

'No, not really. In fact, you're the—' *Crack! Crack!* 'What the fuck? That's incoming!'

'*Contact!*' Someone shouted.

Chris looked around to see where it was coming from. *Crack! Crack! Crack!* Another snap of small arms whizzed past our heads.

'Get the fuck down,' I shouted.

He didn't hang about and took cover behind me, lying underneath the nearside sill of the HumVee chassis. I then heard a thud, quickly followed by a muffled scream, coming from the opposite side of the Foden.

'Shit! That was Stuart. He's hit. Can you see him?' I asked Chris. But he just shook his head. 'I'm gonna find him. That scream sounded as if it was Stuart.'

'No, Kev, stay down.'

Too late. I grabbed my rifle, climbed to a crouching position and darted for the front bumper of the Foden.

Crack! Crack! Crack!

Oh, shit! They were for me, I thought. The dirt kicked up around my legs as the rounds punched into the ground only a few metres away. I was now pinned down and couldn't move any further. I had no choice but to stay beside the driver's-side wheel.

'Stuart!' I shouted, but no reply. 'Stuart!'

Crack! Crack! Two more rounds ripped into the ground next to me. I was now virtually becoming part of the wheel rim as I tried my hardest to make myself a smaller target. I attempted a quick recce around the top of the surrounding buildings for any clue of a report but I couldn't see anything that gave away an enemy position. No muzzle flashes, smoke, nothing. I thought about taking a risk in between bouts of incoming and dashing to Stuart's aid but something in my head said no fucking way. And thank God it did. A burst of automatic hit our position just as I was going to make a run for it, pinging off the front end of a Warrior parked behind me.

'*Stuart!* For fuck's sake, answer me,' I shouted.

'Yeah, yeah. I'm OK. I'm not hit. I just . . .' He interrupted himself with a groan.

'What! What's happened?'

'I'm only winded.'

I sighed with relief. His groans were caused by him doing his Superman act as he dived off the top decking of the Foden and crash-landed next to the front nearside wheel. Slowly leaning towards the front of the wheel on my side, I looked to Stuart's side of the Foden. I could just make out he was lying across the length of the nearside wheel facing the front with his rifle covering his arc of fire. I caught his attention and gave him the thumbs-up. He responded by doing the same, indicating he was OK.

Another few rounds hit the ground, quickly followed by further bursts of automatic, which definitely gave us the impression there was more than one weapon firing at us.

'See anything?' a voice shouted from behind me.

'Nothing, Sir,' someone replied.

Everyone from the immediate area dispersed and was soon taking cover either inside one of the buildings or on the sides of armoured vehicles around the compound. The turrets of the Warriors frantically searched for reports of the incoming, eager to quash the threat with their chain guns and 30-mm cannon fire. Stuart and I continued to cover the rear of the compound where the back of some office blocks or flats overlooked our position.

A blue wooden door boxed in a brick housing was situated on top of its roof, which must have been some kind of fire escape. It was about ten metres above and fifty metres ahead. This was the suspected area of the incoming and now the target. To my immediate right, Chris and Carl were crouched down next to the offside rear of the HumVee.

'For fuck's sake, someone return fire!' a voice shouted.

Half a dozen rifles behind me returned a few double taps in the general direction of the blue wooden door. Bursts of automatic from behind the fire escape quickly responded to our greeting. Until then, no one knew the exact position of the enemy but they had compromised their position and were about to face a deafening barrage of firepower. Within seconds, it seemed everyone let rip into the fire escape. Stuart and I concentrated a few double taps towards the wooden door, quickly followed by Chris and Carl with their M60 machine gun and M16 rifles. There must have been a mixture of 20 SA80, LSW, GPMG, M60 and M16 rifles, all firing at the same time at the one target. The noise was incredible.

A figure from behind the fire escape momentarily pointed his AK from around the left-side corner and let off a quick burst of blind automatic fire into the air, confirming our target. The rounds cracked high above our heads and didn't make us take cover. Instead, we continued to pump as many rounds at the target and drop it as soon as possible.

The Warriors within the compound decided to join the

fire-fight and helped to totally obliterate the fire escape. Moments later, the brick surround, let alone the door, was shot to pieces and collapsed in a heap of rubble. Two figures dropped to the ground – no more snipers. A group of LI guys went to investigate the snipers' position and soon returned shaking their heads. Obviously nothing else could be found, apart from two chewed up Fedayeen militia bodies.

With the excitement over, we picked ourselves up and continued with our business. I noticed a few bullet holes in the tailgate of the HumVee but astonishingly the Coke cans were still in one piece. I finished mine before continuing the recovery task, just as Sgt Steve Pacey turned up with the spare tyre. He was a well-tanned Californian type, in his mid-30s, who could have easily been perceived as a typical US Marine. The spare wheel he was carrying, however, also had a bloody puncture.

'There's only one thing for it. You guys will have to take it to our workshop back at Shaibah,' Steve said.

Stuart disappeared into the HQ building to explain the situation and find out if we could take it to Shaibah. Meanwhile, I struggled to think how I would be able to recover this US-built vehicle with my British-built Foden – and we're all supposed to be members of Nato?

Ten minutes later, Stuart emerged from the HQ building. 'We're to take it to Shaibah, which is where Al are heading anyway. In the mean time, we're to return to the bus station.'

'I'll come with you,' added Steve, overhearing our conversation.

We hooked up the HumVee by the only means possible with our British recovery kit – the rear suspension – which meant we had to secure the steering using a strap on the steering wheel. At that particular moment, the entire squadron of Warriors decided they wanted to move out at the same time, which, of course, resulted in a traffic jam as we all headed for the same exit. After about 15 minutes of shoving parked vehicles out of the way, we managed to find our 'armoured escort' and made our way back to the bus station. I parked the Foden, complete with the HumVee on the hook, in our usual position, whilst Steve continued to talk about the stories he'd heard from other American units in the war.

Within half an hour of returning, A1 packet was ready to move to Shaibah, at the ECP 4 location of 2 Battalion REME workshops. The route back to Shaibah took us through a different area of Basrah. It was just as bad as the others, reaffirming to me the desperate conditions these people had endured under Saddam's regime. Row after row of flat-roofed single-storey buildings lined the battered streets, while locals waved at us as we drove by, pleased to be free from the fear the regime placed upon them. There was still the lingering smell of shit wafting through the air, bomb craters in the roads and shelled buildings but the Iraqi people, yet again, wore huge smiles, which made us smile. Until we saw the blown-up bodies of children lying in the gutters.

There had been many reported cases of children as young as five years old being forced at gunpoint by Fedayeen militia to gather S60 shells, grenades and 7.62-mm small arms abandoned by fleeing Iraqi forces. They would then pile the extremely unstable munitions on the side of the road, using crude devices to detonate them. Unfortunately, these incredibly dangerous booby traps would explode prematurely and blow the children to pieces, which was why the militia didn't want the job. They were designed to kill British and US soldiers but we knew not to go anywhere near them. Unsuspecting and curious children, however, didn't, resulting in predictable and terrible consequences.

Steve had the same sentiments as us, as far as Saddam Hussein and his followers were concerned. He also couldn't give a toss about WMD or nuclear-weapons programmes, which seemed to have sent the 'wrapped in cotton wool' world into a frenzy. He too wanted the Iraqi people to be able to live a normal, fear-free life, without oppression and torture. In fact, the way he spoke, it was as if he was talking on behalf of all the American forces in the conflict, as well as us Brits. At least the coalition was singing from the same hymn sheet. It was a case of fuck the WMD fanatics and fuck the tree-huggers back home, we were in Iraq to liberate!

After hours of swapping stories and arguing about who had the best armed forces in the world (of course, we do), we reached Steve's workshop at Shaibah Airfield. The time was nearly 1300hrs zulu. Stuart and I quickly unhooked the HumVee and packed away the kit, said our goodbyes and joined our packet towards the end of the airfield, behind the control tower. We passed many units camped on either side of the runway, all waiting for the next move. All that remained was to chill out for a few days before the next push.

20

THE STORY SO FAR
. . . 7–13 APRIL

Our chill-out meant plenty of stag and GDs (general duties). I couldn't wait for our next job, which didn't appear until the day we moved out of Shaibah. From 9 to 13 April, nothing really exciting happened – for us, anyway. I wrote a few more blueys home and updated my diary, including details, not only from my local source of information, but from Steve as well, with his American perspective.

7 APRIL

British forces maintain control over large areas of Basrah, although pockets of resistance from the Fedayeen militia still remain. Backed up by 3 Commando, 7 Armoured and 16 Air Assault respond with overwhelming firepower.

3 Battalion, the Parachute Regiment continue to patrol areas deemed difficult for armoured vehicles. The Ba'ath Party headquarters is destroyed at Karbala. US 82 Airborne Division carry out humanitarian-aid work around the As Samawah region. The 101 Air Assault Division maintain the offensive against Iraqi positions at Al Najaf. Saddam's lush palaces in Baghdad are stormed by US troops.

Suspected Republican Guard headquarters are taken by 3 Division. Iraqi armoured vehicles are destroyed by US troops north of the capital. 1 Marine Corps keep a stranglehold on the east of Baghdad.

8 APRIL

Rasheed Airport is taken by US Marines when they push towards the south-east of Baghdad. A USAF [United States Air Force] A10 'tank buster' crashes near Baghdad International Airport. The pilot ejects and is found unharmed.

Pockets of resistance are pounded by 7 Armoured and 16 Air Assault around Basrah. Elements of 7 Armoured assist US forces at Al Nasiriyah. British forces topple a statue of Saddam in Basrah, much to the delight of the locals.

US troops find themselves under attack near Karbala.

9 APRIL

An American Air Force F-15E strike-attack aircraft is reported missing over Baghdad. The Spanish ship Galicia *arrives at Umm Qasr seaport with a field hospital and humanitarian aid.*

US forces have control over all routes into Baghdad but pockets of resistance continue to be mopped up by the 101 Air Assault Division. Warehouses of tinned food and medical supplies in Baghdad are captured from the Medina Division of the Republican Guard.

2 RTR BG head north to assist 16 Air Assault and US troops at Al Amarah. In the west of Iraq, Al Rutbah is cleared and made safe by coalition forces.

US troops topple a statue of Saddam in the centre of Baghdad.

10 APRIL

The Australian and British navies complete mine-sweeping in the Umm Qasr waterways. They soon turn their attention further north towards the waterways of the Tigris and Basrah.

US troops capture the Abu Ghraib complex and find it to be empty of its occupants. Security is increased at Baghdad International Airport and the university is cleared of Iraqi forces. Coalition and Kurdish forces occupy Kirkuk, including the second-largest GOSP in Iraq.

Saddam Hussein is thought to have been hiding in the grounds of one of his palaces in Tikrit.

11 APRIL

A ceasefire agreement is under negotiation between coalition forces and the Iraqi 5 Corps near Mosul. Humanitarian aid arrives at the port of Umm Qasr from the Red Crescent and the United Arab Emirates.

Elements of US forces and 1 (UK) Armoured Division continue to secure Basrah and surrounding areas, including Al Amarah. Australian forces start Operation Baghdad Assist, delivering humanitarian aid and much-needed medical supplies to Baghdad and the surrounding districts.

12 APRIL

Fifteen Iraqi Air Force strike-attack aircraft are captured at Al Asad Airfield.

The presidential scientific advisor, Amir Hamudi Hasan al-Sadi, surrenders to US forces in Baghdad. Coalition operations are completed in Al Qa'im in western Iraq.

An RAAF (Royal Australian Air Force) C-130 transporter aircraft flies in medical supplies to Baghdad International Airport. Iraqi police are back on the streets of Basrah under the watchful eye of RMPs of the British Army.

13 APRIL

US Marines enter Tikrit, Saddam Hussein's home town, and secure the Presidential Palace. Clashes between Saddam supporters and US Marines erupt on the outskirts of Tikrit.

Water and electricity supplies are under repair with local and US military engineers working around the clock to restore power in Baghdad. Abu Abbas, a terrorist, is arrested by US troops in southern Baghdad. USAF continue with air patrols over Baghdad, adding security to the area.

Looting of medical supplies and food continues in Baghdad, Basrah, Tikrit and other major towns and cities around Iraq. Seven US PWs are rescued by US Marines.

Mosul is returned to relative calm after local militia are quashed by US forces.

British forces report that locals have held kangaroo courts in and around Basrah. Locals had taken the law into their own hands and were taking revenge by capturing local militia, Iraqi soldiers and Saddam supporters, in particular known Ba'ath Party members, and executing them, either by public stoning, setting them alight or simply shooting them.

The Iraqi people are now confident the regime is crushed and finally trust that the coalition is going to stay until the end.

21

COME AND HAVE A GO IF YOU THINK YOU'RE HARD ENOUGH!

Monday, 14 April 0400hrs zulu Yet another O'group before we set off for our next location, a Republican Guard barracks in Al Amarah, grid 017–173. This was to show the locals we wouldn't let them down, and to say to the Iraqi Army and Republican Guard, come and have a go if you think you're hard enough! We hoped to rub their noses in it by taking over one of their barracks. Once we were told where we were heading, we couldn't wait to get there.

Our O'group gave us brief details about the area, which was potentially hostile to say the least, with probable booby traps and mines planted around and within the camp area. It was also reported that snipers were a threat and pockets of Iraqi soldiers dressed in civilian clothing were ambushing military vehicles. What concerned us, however, was the thought of the local infestation of mosquitoes and the threat of D&V (diarrhoea and vomiting) caused by the flies.

Every time we moved to a different location someone had to break down, either just before or just after we moved off. Stuart and I decided to take on additional responsibility and ensured all vehicles were serviced to a reasonable standard, given the circumstances, like making sure they had the right levels of coolant and lubricants, the correct tyre pressure, that grease points were actually greased and air filters were blown through and cleaned – basic preventative maintenance. We even gave instruction on the use of differential locks and how to use the gearbox correctly when driving off-road. And this was to regular soldiers!

Our convoy was half the size it usually was because the rest of A1 packet had left 20 minutes earlier to establish our harbour area at the next location. All we had was Bobby's Bedford fitter's truck, the second Bedford with SSgt Charlie Buckle and a couple of crafties towing the 'mashy' trailer. Leading the convoy was a Land-Rover, with Lt Connor navigating. My Foden took the rear – as usual.

Half an hour into the journey and all seemed OK as we travelled across country from Shaibah Airfield, passing the perimeter fence of the BIA (Basrah International Airport). Within a few kilometres, we'd be on Route 6 which would pass through Basrah once again and take us all the way to Al Amarah. So why had we come to a grinding halt? I lit a cigarette and waited in the cab, refusing to get involved in whatever the problem was ahead. Curiosity got the better of Stuart, however, and he decided to find out what was going on. The entire packet had congregated around the bonnet of Lieutenant Connor's Land-Rover, and he stood in the middle of the crowd. I soon realised what the problem was – we were lost.

A map was spread across the bonnet and everyone was arguing about what our best option was for rejoining the route. It wasn't long before I could hear raised voices, Charlie's in particular. He was a tall guy, in his early 40s, with a typical VM attitude, and didn't suffer fools gladly. He was the type to say, fuck ceremony and get the job done. His temper, usually under control, could suddenly erupt when he became frustrated, especially when young officers were in charge and they got us lost. I had a feeling it was going to be one of those days.

Five minutes later, a decision had been made and the crowd dispersed. Stuart returned to the Foden with a smug grin on his face as he climbed into the cab.

'What's up with you?' I asked.

'Charlie isn't all that impressed with our navigator, so he suggested we lead the way, as we seem to be the most intelligent out of the packet.'

I couldn't believe it. Charlie risking his reputation on a couple of 'civvy soldiers', as he called us, to navigate all the way to Al Amarah. Fair enough.

'At the T-junction, turn right, then bear left onto the main drag. That will take us over Bridge Two and into Basrah,' instructed Stuart.

'So how come LT didn't know that?' I asked.

'Officer training, maybe?'

I moved to the front of the packet and led the way to Bridge Two. As we came within 200 metres of the bridge, we came across a vehicle casualty that had broken down on Route 6. Like a bad penny, it was the same Bedford and trailer we'd towed across the border from Kuwait. I pulled over, next to the driver's window, which was surrounded by kids of all ages, shouting their usual plea for water and food. Thankfully, a couple of Warriors were parked a few metres away, acting as a mobile roadblock and guarding the entrance to the bridge. A further two Warriors were on the other side of the dual carriageway guarding the exit.

Charlie and the rest of the packet stopped at the side of the road to see if they could do anything to get the Bedford moving.

''Ello again!' I shouted, leaning out of the driver's window and facing the same crew – Stupid Boy and Mike.

Mike just shook his head as he sat in the passenger seat, trying his best to ignore the children. 'You're not going to believe this, Kev, but Mark's done it again.'

My face dropped. 'Not the . . .'

'Yep. The clutch.'

'There's only one option. A straight-bar pull like last time,' added Stuart.

Charlie was none the wiser and left the decision about what to do entirely in our hands. Four minutes later, we were ready to move, with a thumbs-up from Stupid Boy to indicate he was ready. I climbed back into our cab and we moved off, followed by the rest of the packet.

The bridges over the Shatt al-Arab waterway had been at the centre of fierce fighting. They were the gateway into the city of Basrah and therefore it had been important for us to take them intact. Five bridges in total spanned the Tigris and Shatt al-Arab waterway in Basrah. Bridge Two and Bridge Four saw the worst of the fighting. In particular Bridge Four, because it provided the main route into the city. Ferocious fighting on all five bridges continued for just over two weeks, from 21 March to 6 April, with the enemy using everything they had to prevent the advancing British forces. And because Bridge Four was the main route in and out of Basrah, thousands of civilians were caught up in the battle as they desperately tried to cross it to escape the fighting. The Iraqi forces took advantage of the civilians and used them as shields when they knew they were about to lose the bridge. This tactic did slow down the advancing battle groups of the British forces, mainly the RRF, from taking the bridge, as they had to wait until the Iraqi forces fled towards Basrah or surrendered.

Our return drive through Basrah revealed yet further horrors of war. The usual sights of bomb craters and battle-damaged buildings lined the streets, whilst children played in the dirty water, but this time there appeared to be a feeling of hope and a sense that the war was very nearly at an end. The reports we'd had over the past few days indicated the regime had been all but toppled and that humanitarian aid was flooding over the border into Iraq unhindered.

The riots in the city over the previous week were not as bad as reported back home. Out of sheer frustration, the locals had looted shops, which had nothing in them anyway. And as for the hospitals, the locals grabbed as many medicines as they could for their own families. Back home, the reports on news channels made these rioters look like louts on a day trip, stealing from hospitals and damaging any healthcare facilities they had. That couldn't have been further from the truth. Unless an Iraqi was a Ba'ath Party member, and in the minority, he or she didn't get any healthcare at all. Falling sick and having the money to pay for treatment wouldn't even guarantee healthcare. If you weren't a registered Ba'ath Party member, then tough.

The arrival of humanitarian aid and water tankers made the locals feel that something was happening. Convoy after convoy of civvy water tankers and ISO containers poured into the city. Many locals were already filling their plastic containers from tankers parked on the side of the road. It was definitely a sight for sore eyes.

As we left Basrah behind, the weather changed for the better as far as us Brits were concerned: the sky was swollen with thick black and dark-grey clouds, and it actually started to rain, dramatically cooling the air. This part of the country was obviously geographically cooler than the south and the barren desert sand started to give way to vegetation. There were paddy fields filled with rice and vines of ripe tomatoes – we even passed an orchard. A true Garden of Eden, which was very apt considering the country we were in.

Stuart soon exploited the cooler weather by grabbing a pair of army-issue socks and placing two cans of Coke in each. Using green string, he tied the socks onto his exterior mirror frame. The rain soaked the socks and the cool air rushing past them cooled down the cans to a comfortable drinking temperature. Half an hour later, Stuart handed me a can from his external cooler. The contents never touched the sides. The feeling of cold Coke rushing down the back of my throat was sheer heaven. The empty sock was soon filled with two more cans ready for our stint in the next location. As anticipated, however, the rain didn't last long, only 20 minutes at the most, but at least the temperature was cooler and we now had a few cold cans to drink.

The long, monotonous stretch of tarmac reached a few buildings on the side of the road, with the odd general store amongst them. I noticed a Warrior on our side of the road, roughly 100 metres ahead, parked behind a CVRT Scimitar. The commander of the Warrior waved his arms at us and pointed to the CVRT.

'We'd better stop and check it out,' I said. I pulled over, next to the Warrior, and leant out of the driver's-door window. 'What's up?'

The Warrior commander pointed to the CVRT. 'The driver can't get it in gear.'

'Not another CVRT gearbox,' muttered Stuart.

I nodded to the commander. 'We've already got a casualty but we have a couple of VMs with us.' I pointed towards the fitter's truck behind us.

'Nice one. Do you think they could do anything? It's a bit dodgy around here. We've already had someone shoot at us out of the back of a passing chogie pick-up truck.'

Stuart's ears pricked up at this point and all of a sudden he became interested in the situation. Charlie was already heading towards the Warrior. The commander explained the situation to him and after a few minutes' chinwagging, Charlie took charge and beckoned his fitter crew over.

'Kev,' Charlie shouted, 'can you and Stuart keep your eyes peeled whilst we look at this CVRT? The LI guys in your casualty vehicle can assist you.'

I jumped out of the cab and headed towards Mike and Stupid Boy to explain what was happening and they took positions at the rear of the packet whilst I took the nearside, overlooking the front of the Foden. Stuart took a position at the rear of the Foden, crouching down and leaning his back against the offside tyre.

A crowd of about a dozen or so had begun to congregate around us; the grown-ups were curious about what we were doing and the kids were waiting for freebies. Some of the men, however, didn't look like the usual onlookers. We'd developed a sixth sense about these situations and something didn't feel quite right. One of them, about 30 years old, with his neat, close-cut beard and crisp, clean white dishdash, walked towards my position and stared right into my eyes whilst I was crouched down. I quickly stood up and positioned my rifle into my right shoulder, pointing it towards the ground but ready to raise it just in case I had to drop him with a few rounds. The whole scenario seemed to happen in slow motion as he walked towards me. For some reason, I didn't trust this guy one bit.

'Go on, do something stupid, give me a fucking reason,' I muttered through gritted teeth. As he walked by me, he changed his glare and looked away, towards his left. Shit, he'd lost his bottle, I thought. I was convinced he was about to do something.

'Maybe next time,' I said, as he passed me.

He snapped his head around and looked at me as if he could understand what I said but carried on walking. I blew a drop of sweat from the tip of my nose as I kept an eye on him, still walking slowly down the entire length of the packet. I was tempted to drop him there and then but thought better of it.

Twenty minutes passed and the repair to the Scimitar was well under way. Spanners and wrenches were being thrown all over the place, along with a few choice words from Charlie. I was sniggering as Charlie laid into one of his VMs when I was distracted by a little boy, no more than six years old, tugging at my desert-cam trousers. I looked down at a scruffy, bare-footed Iraqi child with dusty hair and a dirty face, wearing a grubby dark-blue pullover and grey trousers covered in holes. Pulling my attention away from his clothes was a worried, if not frightened, look on his face. His wide brown eyes glazing over with tears told me something wasn't right with him.

'Mister!' he said.

'What's up, mate?' I cheerfully replied, and crouched down to his level to look less intimidating.

'Mister!' he said again, and pointed across the road towards what looked like an old barn in the middle of wasteland, about 200 metres away. I stood up to get a better view and came to the conclusion that was where he lived. The boy continued to tug at my trousers but with a little more force, as if he wanted me to follow him.

'Stuart! Over 'ere a minute,' I shouted.

He walked over with a puzzled look on his face, looking at the kid. 'What's up?'

The boy continued to tug at my trousers and tried to drag me across the road. This boy definitely wanted me to follow him.

'Can you see what this kid is doing? He wants me to follow him.'

Stuart looked at him and smiled. The boy then let go of my leg and clamped himself onto Stuart's, trying to drag him towards the shack across the road. 'We'd better see what he wants, it's obvious he's spooked about something,' he said.

I agreed. 'I'll tell Charlie what we're doing.' I left Stuart with the boy, who was now beginning to cry.

Charlie also agreed but wanted Mike and Stupid Boy to go instead, just in case of any mishap that would leave the packet without a recovery crew – bless him. I walked over to Mike and explained the situation. By the time we both walked back to Stuart, he was trying his hardest to calm the little boy down.

'Is this the boy?' asked Mike.

'Yeah, we think he wants us to go to that building over there.' Stuart pointed towards the shack.

'We'll check it out, but make sure the boy doesn't follow.' Mike was pretty stern about that. There was a strong possibility of APMs (anti-personnel mines) and booby traps. 'We'll shout if we need you.' He made ready his rifle and gave a nod to Stupid Boy standing next to him, then they made their way across the road. As they walked off, the little boy started to scream and tried to pull himself free from Stuart's grip.

'This kid is spooked to fuck,' Stuart said, and passed him to me. ''Ere, Kev, it's your turn.' He then made a sharp exit towards the rear of the packet.

'Oh, cheers, mate!' I knelt down to try and calm the boy but he was having none of it. I looked up to see how far the other two had gone, and they were about 50 metres away from the shack. 'Fuck's sake, hurry up,' I muttered. I looked at Stuart who was trying his hardest not to laugh. He turned away, diverting his attention towards the rear of the packet and looked down the road with his back to me. I knew he was laughing, though, because his body was jerking to the rhythm of his concealed amusement.

Mike slowed down his pace as he approached the shack, and raised his hand, indicating that Stupid Boy should stop a few metres behind him. He then signalled to Charlie for two squaddies to come forward.

'Kev, Stuart! Go and see what he wants,' Charlie shouted.

We both grabbed our webbing and as I secured mine around my waist, Stuart was already halfway across the road heading towards Mike. I caught up with him and we both crouched down next to Mike, ready for his instructions.

'Right, listen to what I say, this is important. I want you and Stuart to stay here and cover us as we search the building. When I give the word, approach the house with caution and meet Mark and me at the rear of the building.'

Stuart and I nodded our heads, acknowledging his instructions. He and Stupid Boy then walked the last few metres to the front of the shack. Stuart and I positioned ourselves in a shell crater, lying in the prone position roughly two metres apart, covering Mike's approach. Bullet holes were now clearly visible in the front wall of the shack.

I glanced at Stuart, crouched down to my left. 'All right, mate?' I asked.

'Yeah,' he replied, poised and ready to open fire. He was enjoying all of this. 'See those bullet holes in the wall?' He pointed to what I had already noticed.

I just nodded my head and made myself comfortable, training my rifle towards the open window of the shack. Something had gone off here and I wasn't only thinking of a fire-fight. I had a feeling the building was hiding something.

The other two had now disappeared out of sight, which meant they were either inside or to the rear of the building.

'All clear!' Mike cried out. 'Stuart, Kev, on me!' We jumped up and slowly walked towards the shack, first checking every footstep for booby traps or landmines.

Stuart reached the doorway first. 'What the fuck has happened in here?'

As I entered the building and stood on the front door, which was covered in bullet holes and looking a little the worse for wear, I could understand why he asked the question. Two militiamen were lying to our right, just inside the doorway. Judging by the mess they were in, they were hit pretty hard. Next to their AK assault rifles lay a couple of half-used 7.62-mm ammunition boxes, half a dozen belted rounds and a few rat-pack tins of mush. This only indicated the shack was used as a more permanent fixture, increasing my suspicions it was hiding something.

The building itself was a crude breezeblock construction and nothing more than a single-storey 4x8-metre shack. Two beds made out of wooden pallets were tucked into the top left corner with dirty single mattresses thrown on the top. A somewhat battle-damaged pine table leant to one side underneath the single window at the front of the building, which was now covered in holes and splinters. Remarkably, a couple of shelves fixed halfway up the left-hand-side wall, just above the beds, had survived the onslaught. The odd bowl and plate, however, which may have been sitting on them weren't so lucky. They were smashed to pieces on the rough sandstone slab floor. A few other bits of personal items were scattered around the floor with the odd shred of clothing but that was it. No water supply or drains; no electricity or gas supply – nothing.

We made our way towards the rear of the building and walked out of the back entrance into a small yard. Two more bodies lay next to their AK rifles towards the right-hand-side wall; again, next to opened ammunition boxes.

'Kev, over 'ere!' Stuart shouted. He was standing towards the end of the 10x10-metre garden lined with tomato plants with a small ditch as a perimeter. I carefully walked towards him, trying my hardest to dodge anything that resembled a booby trap, and noticed he was standing over a shallow pit in the dry sun-baked sand. The pit turned out to be a shallow grave, which was occupied.

'Why do I get the feeling these bodies are related to that little boy,' Stuart said. I couldn't reply to his comment because I couldn't believe what I was looking at. Lying inside the shallow grave were most probably the boy's mum and dad, and a little girl of about eight years old, who may have been his sister. My stomach started to churn. Three civilians shot in the head, and for what reason?

I felt a familiar tug on my trousers – it was the little boy. I looked down at this incredibly brave young man as he stared into the pit, looking totally confused as to why all this had happened. I put my left arm around his tiny shoulders in a feeble attempt to comfort him. The war was beginning to piss me right off. It simply wasn't fair; but then war wasn't supposed to be. I now knew what the reality of war was all about – the end of reason, the end of compassion, the meaningless end of innocent lives – and I hated it!

'Stuart, Kev! C'mon, we're going to get the fuck out of here,' shouted Mike, from the back door of the shack.

I turned round to acknowledge him. 'Yeah, OK, Mike.'

'What about the kid?' asked Stuart.

'I haven't a clue. I suppose he'll have to stay with one of the locals.'

The little boy looked up at me and started to jabber on about something but I couldn't understand him.

'What's he saying?' asked Stuart.

'How the fuck do I know?'

He began his trick of tugging at my trousers and tried to drag me towards the road, where we were heading anyway. As far as the boy was concerned, we weren't moving quickly enough. When we reached the vehicles, the crowds had increased and looked as though they were wondering what we were doing. A scruffy-looking man in his 30s, dressed in a brown, tight shirt and red trousers, walked up to me and took my hand, shaking it vigorously.

'Thank you, Sir, thank you,' he said, and repeated it over and over again.

'Who the fuck's this?' asked Stuart, pointing at the stranger.

The little boy suddenly lost his grip on me and grabbed the bloke's leg instead. He picked up the boy and gave him a big hug. Stuart and I looked on, slightly confused at the boy's actions. It was obvious he knew the man but what relation was this man to the boy?

'I'm his father, you saved his life. Thank you, thank you.' Again, speaking good English.

'If you're his father, who are the bodies behind that building?' Stuart asked, pointing towards the shack. That was a question I too wanted answered.

'The woman is my wife and the girl is my daughter. The man is my wife's father.'

'So, what happened?' I asked.

He explained what happened. In a way, I wasn't shocked but it was still a terrible story to hear. The militia had shot them (which was my guess anyway) but the reason for their execution was beyond reason. They wanted the shack as a gun position to take out coalition vehicles. The owner of the building, the boy's grandfather, refused them entry, which was a big mistake. The militia shot the boy's sister to try and make the grandfather change his mind but it made him ever more stubborn. He was determined not to let them have it. Because of his stubbornness, he was forced to dig the shallow pit and place the little girl in it. Its size, however, must have raised suspicions – they wanted it big enough to hold a further two adults. Sure enough, the granddad and the little girl's mother were forced to kneel in front of the pit, and were shot in the back of the head, falling into their own graves.

I asked the boy's father when this happened and why the militia didn't kill him or the boy. He quickly replied it had happened two days ago. The boy's father was in Al Amarah at the time, selling tomatoes in the market, and didn't know anything until he arrived back the following day. He and the boy had since been staying with relatives. The boy was in the building when the militia stormed the shack but had managed to escape and raise the alarm with some British infantry unit passing by. They subsequently destroyed the gun position but were ordered to carry on to their next objective and leave searching the shack. So, they didn't know anything about the graves.

His story may have sounded unbelievable but under the circumstances I had no reason not to believe him. I did ask how he knew how his family was killed. He quickly answered that some of the locals had heard gunshots when the militia took the family to the garden. They knew then what had happened but were powerless to do anything about it. If they had tried to help, they too would have suddenly disappeared, only to be discovered in a ditch – dead. The little boy knew what had happened to his mother, sister and granddad, and I thought he deserved a medal for bravery. After all, it was him who'd brought the enemy's OP to our attention.

The boy's father passed what I would call his prayer beads to me, which were nothing but a string of black plastic beads. He wanted me to keep them as a thank you for getting rid of Saddam. He then just walked away with the little boy waving to us over his father's shoulder. It wasn't until later I realised that to be given such a gift was an honour. Although worth next to nothing, to me the beads were priceless. We waved back not even having learnt their names, wishing them all the best for the future. But what future did they have? It was better than what they'd had before, I suppose, but now it was without his wife, daughter and father-in-law. That's one hell of a sacrifice for the sake of freedom. This was why the liberation had to succeed: to make sure the innocent lives that had been lost weren't in vain.

I hadn't noticed that the VMs had since finished the repair to the CVRT. Stuart and I jumped back in the Foden and started the journey to Al Amarah. Four hours later, and without any further vehicle casualties or excitement, we reached our destination. I turned right into the main entrance and pulled over so Sir could re-establish his position as navigator and fall in at the front of the packet. It saved him from answering any embarrassing questions as to why he was navigating from the rear.

A huge double archway greeted us as we left Route 6 and drove onto a long driveway. On either side of the entrance was a 'show of strength', with two Iraqi military vehicles standing on fancy plinths surrounded by white painted chains: a T62 tank to the left and a BMP1 armoured personnel carrier to the right. The main entrance was a long, straight dual carriageway of about two kilometres which ended at a roundabout. There, we turned right, then immediately left through a gated three-metre-high breezeblock perimeter wall with rolls of barbed wire spread over the top of it. The layout of the camp was not unlike any other military complex, with barrack blocks, a gym and various hangars spread around the area. There was even an open-air swimming pool, which we left well alone as it looked a little the worse for wear. It was half full of stagnant water, making it the perfect breeding ground for mosquitoes.

We were greeted at the gate by 16 Air Assault, who gave us directions towards the area in which our packet was camped. It was nothing more than a piece of waste ground towards the area's southern edge. The perimeter wall, which was to the left of our camp, stood between us and a road leading through the barracks. To the other side of the road were huge hangars made out of corrugated-iron sheeting, also looking a tad the worse for wear. Locals were stripping them of the corrugated sheets and were even using oxyacetylene cutting torches to dismantle the iron-girder framework.

I parked the Foden behind Bobby's wagon so he could diagnose the Bedford casualty. Sure enough, it did require a clutch, and he could replace it on site, which saved me taking it elsewhere. I unhooked the vehicle and parked well behind it so Bobby and Tony could work around it. With our job done, it was time to grab something to eat and chill out until the next job arrived. I checked my watch – a few minutes until 1000hrs zulu. Lunchtime.

An O'group was called soon after. NBC state-zero dress-one, which meant no need for NBC noddy suits but, as usual, our haversack with respirator had to be carried at all times. Within the first few hours of arriving, 2 RTR and 16 Air Assault had found 18 ammo dumps, so the threat of booby traps and mines was reiterated. Barrels of an 'unknown nature' had also been found and were under investigation.

The good news was 19 Brigade were taking over from 2 RTR BG by the second week of July, and elements of the battle group would be out of theatre by 7 May. The TA and reserve attachments would have first refusal to fly out, and seats were already being booked for the first flights home. One of three ships, which were already on their way to Kuwait, had been booked to take back armoured vehicles, stores and soldiers. Other than that, it was a case of keep vigilant and chill out.

Around the camp area the dress state was also relaxed a little, as far as body armour was concerned, so we dropped the CBAs and Kevlar helmets for fresh T-shirts and floppy hats or berets, though haversacks and weapons still had to be carried at all times. And, as usual, whilst everyone else either sunbathed or caught up on writing a few blueys home, us recy mechs still had to recover vehicles. Our next task, however, gave us a feeling of pride.

Phil and his crew had been sent out with his CRARRV to recover a T62 tank which was to be restored and laid on a plinth at 2 RTR's unit in Germany as a monument to a sergeant from the regiment who had been tragically killed in action earlier in the conflict. But Phil returned empty-handed and with a look of defeat on his face. 'Fucking tank. It was perfect, just what we wanted, but there was no way of recovering it,' he said, with some disappointment.

Stuart and I looked at each other, nodding simultaneously and wearing smug grins.

'Do you mind if we have a go?' asked Stuart.

Phil looked surprised. 'You've only a Foden. What makes you think you'll have better luck?'

'Still, it's worth a try,' I replied.

Phil paused for a second before answering. 'I suppose it will keep you two out of mischief for a few hours.'

He gave us the grid reference, which turned out to be a few kilometres towards the boundary of the barracks, but still within the relaxed area. We drove towards what looked like a T55 and T62 graveyard: remains of power packs and gearboxes littered the area, along with burnt-out and bombed warehouses around the edge of a huge yard area. Towards the end of the yard was the T62 Phil had struggled to recover. We could see the tracks the CRARRV had gouged in the sand alongside it.

I parked next to the T62 and jumped out of the cab to join Stuart, who was already checking the immediate area for booby traps. About half a dozen children playing nearby soon arrived on the scene, curious as to what we were going to do. And, of course, to see if they'd get any freebies. Thankfully, they stood a safe distance away and didn't bother us like children had done before. Maybe because one of the older kids, who looked as if he was in his late teens, was in control of the youngsters.

Although Phil had checked the tank for booby traps, and no doubt the children had been playing in and around it, Stuart and I still carried out our search for any exploding devices. It was all too easy to miss one. Nothing was found, so we climbed aboard the tank and scratched our heads, wondering how we were going to recover this 30-tonne lump of metal. Now we'd committed ourselves, there was no way we were leaving it behind, and there was no way we were going to ask for help from the regulars.

The first problem was the turret; it was facing starboard (right), with the barrel at 90 degrees to the hull. Second, the portside (left) track was locked, and third, the decking was damaged. The engine had also been sabotaged, so there was no power to turn the turret, but we'd expected that. The first job was to free the track so we could move the bloody thing; it would be a waste of time to try and move the barrel around and change the decking otherwise. Stuart climbed into the driver's hatch and played around with the brakes. Within a few minutes, he had managed to free the locked track. I climbed into the turret and wound it around by hand using the small metal wheel. All we had to do now was search for some decent decking, of which there was plenty to choose from sprawled around the area.

With the decking replaced, we now had to think how we were going to pull the tank using our Nato recovery kit on this old Warsaw Pact tank. Our only option was to tow it using our reevable chains, crossed and tightened, then to hook them onto the recovery hooks on the front of the tank, praying they wouldn't jump off. Using only first gear to keep a continuous strain on the chains ensured that wouldn't happen.

The ground was reasonably level, so there weren't any foreseeable problems. Stuart jumped in the driver's hatch to try his hardest to steer the tank and apply the brakes if necessary. All hooked up, we were ready for the off. I took the strain and started to move, slowly. There were a few sharp turns to negotiate but, after about two hours and a few dodgy moments negotiating the odd bend, we eventually reached Phil's CRARRV, much to his surprise.

'Where do you want it?' I shouted, leaning out of the window wearing a smug 'cat got the cream' grin.

'How the fuck . . .'

'TA trained, mate, TA trained.'

I stopped in front of the flat-roofed building next to Phil's CRARRV. Immediately, a crowd of squaddies eager to take a closer look gathered around us. Stuart and I unhooked the tank and stowed away the kit.

'You jammy bastards!' Phil said, still in shock and slightly embarrassed.

'All right here, is it?' I asked.

'Yeah, a low-loader will take it from here. But how did you do it?' he kept asking.

Stuart took him to one side and explained what we did. Of course, the excuses soon followed from Andy and Danny as to why they couldn't get it. Danny even had the cheek to call us 'cowboys' and said he would have belly lifted it instead, using the tanker strops.

'But you failed, Danny, and we didn't,' I reminded him.

The excitement of recovering the T62 would be the last during our brief stay in Al Amarah. The only other tasks we had were having to lift the odd APU (auxiliary power unit) out of Warriors and using our compressor to blow out the dust from air filters. It wasn't long before boredom set in around the entire camp – so the RSM of 2 RTR stepped in and gave us the usual shit about safety and informed us of our new curriculum for the next few days. This included first aid, NBC training (as if we needed it), CFTs (combat fitness tests – which consisted of a quick jog around the camp) and the APWT (annual personal weapons test – for which a makeshift range was set up south of the camp). This gave us mercenary-thinking TA lads the chance to complete our annual tests and qualify for our tax-free bounty for the year's camp. Each TA soldier has to attend a certain number of training weekends and complete a two-week course or camp each year, and also pass annual soldiering tests to qualify. Regular soldiers also have to take the same tests but don't receive the tax-free bounty. To make sure we received ours, we grabbed the chance to take part in the regular-army tests our battle group laid out for us.

Many of the soldiers from various units on the camp couldn't compete in the activities due to D&V. On the first day, three soldiers from our REME LAD were either throwing up or constantly sitting on makeshift bogs dug out of the sand. By the second day, a further twelve had gone down with it. Several had to be casevac'd out to a field hospital in Kuwait. The remainder had to be isolated for three days whilst the illness took its course. Within a week, a total of 27 had suffered. A rapid response to this epidemic soon followed, and health-and-safety standards tightened around the camp.

The clement weather had changed and warmed up a tad too, just to add to the problem. So it was goodbye to our 'British' weather and welcome back to the dry desert heat. Only this time, the sun was hotter than ever, with temperatures averaging over 45 degrees. Because of the heat, an order was given to any soldier on GDs (excluding sentry duty) not to work between 1100hrs and 1500hrs local, the hottest part of the day.

Sunday, 20 April 1800hrs zulu We'd been in the camp for nearly seven days and finally we were to move out the following morning. There had been an O'group the previous night during which we were updated on situations. Reveille at 0300hrs zulu; A2 packet will move out at 0900hrs zulu; A1 packet will move out at 1000hrs zulu; all kit to be packed away by last light; location: Shaibah Airfield (again) for six days of rehabilitation, which meant our reintroduction to normality, whatever that meant. We were also told the war was over. Apparently the war had ended (unofficially) on 16 April.

Returning to the Foden, I was welcomed by three morale parcels, along with a bundle of blueys, which had been left in the driver's-side footwell. Receiving parcels, especially letters, lifted our spirits to such an extent – well, it's hard to explain what we actually felt. We may have been shot at, bombed, mortared and shelled, which did tend to piss us off a bit, but as soon as we received some mail, it was all forgotten about.

I threw my rifle and haversack on the bunk and settled down to read my blueys first, before ripping open my parcels like an excited kid at Christmas. Stuart sat in his seat with a miserable look on his face because he hadn't received any. At first I felt sorry for him, but thought, no, I don't; he'd received countless parcels and blueys long before I'd had any, so it was his turn to feel pissed off.

Out of the six blueys, four were from Helen. Two of these were dated 22 March and had been sent to the SDG, which, of course, was where she thought I was. The other two had the correct BFPO address and were more recent, well, two weeks old, which was recent for army post. The last two were from Mother. They contained the usual shit: '. . . everyone is fine but worried about you . . . we keep watching the news . . .' and things like that.

Now it was time for the morale parcels. Stuart soon perked up when I revealed the contents of the first one: biscuits and chewy fruit sweets, along with the usual toothpaste and deodorant. The other two boxes contained much the same but were still very much appreciated. I did, however, receive a nice surprise in the form of a copy of the *Sunday Sport*, which went down extremely well with the troops. In fact, I immediately had a great idea on how to raise a few dollars. I rented out the newspaper/jazz mag for $1 a time, providing it was returned in 'good condition'. The first day I made $20, which was enough to buy a carton of cigarettes and get a haircut, for which some robbing bastard charged me $5.

22

THE STORY SO FAR
... 14–21 APRIL

At the end of our seven-day stint at Al Amarah, I grabbed
a few minutes to update my diary for the last time.

14 APRIL

*Pockets of resistance, like that of the Medina
Division of the Republican Guard at Tikrit, occupy
US forces, but on the whole there are only limited
skirmishes. US forces step up efforts in Baghdad to
restore order. Talks begin to restore an Iraqi
government.*

*Coalition forces step up security around Arbil,
Mosul and Kirkuk for the arrival of further
humanitarian aid. The arrival of water tankers was
a welcome addition to the much-needed supplies,
whilst the battered local water infrastructure
undergoes repairs. Operations continue in Baghdad
and Tikrit where hidden arms caches are discovered.*

15 APRIL

As Samawah welcomes its newly appointed local police force as they conduct patrols with US forces around the area. Baghdad also starts to introduce a police force.

US Navy, along with the Australian and British Royal navies, continue patrols and mine clearance around the port of Az Zubayr at Basrah. 16 Air Assault investigate suspect chemicals found in Al Amarah. The Iraqi 12 Armoured Brigade surrender at Ar Ramadi near Baghdad.

16 APRIL

US 1 Marine Corps continue operations to secure areas around Baghdad. US forces also continue to increase their stronghold in and around Tikrit. British forces secure Al Qurnah. They also maintain efforts to restore power and the water infrastructure in Basrah and Az Zubayr.

Humanitarian aid is now running effectively through Iraq, despite efforts of resistance from the militia. Suspect missiles are discovered by British forces at Al Amarah along with 140 ammunition dumps.

17 APRIL

US forces capture Barzan Ibrahim Hasan, Saddam's half-brother. The US 4 Infantry start operations north of Baghdad, later making contact with Iraqi armour at Al Taji. Kurdish forces capture Samir Abd al-Aziz al-Najim, a Ba'ath Party official, near Mosul and hand him over to US forces. Khala Khadr Al-Salahat, a member of the Abu Nidal terrorist organisation, surrenders to US forces in Baghdad.

18 APRIL

The Deputy Prime Minister of Economics and Finance, Hikmat Mizban Ibrahim al-Azzawi, is captured by coalition forces. A route is cleared and secured between Al Taji and Samarra by US 4 Infantry Division.

Medical teams continue their efforts rehabilitating hospitals across Iraq. Six power stations are now up and running in Baghdad as power is restored. British forces complete repairs to the railway lines between Basrah and Umm Qasr. Shipments of humanitarian aid and medical supplies can now be increased and run more efficiently from the port to the city.

A total of 420 ammunition dumps have now been found in Al Amarah, along with SAMs, short-range missiles, RPGs and small-arms cartridges. Also missiles, mines and other munitions, some of which were apparently supplied after the 1991 Gulf War. Investigations also continue into barrels which have been found which appear to show traces of WMD. Tests continue.

19 APRIL

British forces complete urgent repairs to a desalination water-purification plant near Basrah which was sabotaged by retreating Iraqi forces. Tankers can now increase deliveries of much-needed drinking water to the city.

Coalition forces detain Abd al-Khaliq Abd al-Gafar, Minister for Higher Education and Scientific Research. British forces report suicide bombers operating around the Al Amarah area.

The MEK [a sympathetic Iranian group], backed

307

by Iraqi forces and the militia, have reportedly been entering over the Iraq–Iran border. Elements of the British 7 Armoured Division are sent to investigate.

Approximately 1,200 people protest in Al Amarah, complaining that aid and water aren't getting through quickly enough. British forces are attempting to step up humanitarian operations around the area.

20 APRIL

Australian forces conclude that Operation Baghdad Assist is a success. Medical supplies safely make their way to hospitals in Al Nasiriyah. In the same town, US forces complete repairs to water pumping stations, water purification plants and pipelines. The Central Euphrates regional commander, Muhammad Hazmaq al Zubaydi, is detained by coalition forces.

21 APRIL

A visit to the hospitals and power plants of Baghdad is arranged for the head of the Office for Reconstruction and Humanitarian Aid, General Garner, and his British deputy, Major General Cross.

An estimated $600 million is discovered hidden behind a false wall in a government building in Baghdad. The Royal Australian and British Royal navies continue to sweep the Shatt al-Arab waterway in southern Iraq and reopen major shipping channels.

Ba'ath Party commander, Mohammed Hazma al-Zubeidi, and the Deputy Chief of Tribal Affairs, Jamal Mustafa Abdullah Sultan al-Tikriti, are arrested by coalition forces. Elements of 1 (UK)

Division and US forces make plans to reduce their numbers in Iraq.

Captured weapons are now being handed back to the newly formed Iraqi Army. British forces, however, report that former Iraqi soldiers and even children are trying to sell the weapons, which are quickly becoming black-market commodities, back to the coalition forces.

23

ANYTHING TO SAY
TO THE PRESS?

In my experience, war correspondents are a necessary evil. By which I mean you can't live with them, you can't live without them. Of course, like all trades, there are good and bad professionals. To me, war correspondents report what they see in a battle, but it's the soldiers that actually experience it.

When I look back at some of the stories these so-called professional journalists wrote in newspapers and talked about on news bulletins, it makes me rage with anger. They simply didn't explain to people back home what was happening on the ground – and how could they? After all, their movements were restricted, which left them only one option: to make an unqualified guess at the conclusion to their story. It should also not be forgotten that their words were those of excited non-combatants with little understanding of the conflict, reflecting a civilian's fears and confusion, rather than those of a soldier who was actually involved in the fighting and could keep a relatively level head. I was under the impression the media had to wave the neutral flag and give an impartial view; but no, that rarely happened – especially in my opinion in the case of the BBC. Instead, they carefully and cleverly added their own subtle digs, twisting the facts to suit their political standpoint, and attempted to persuade the civvy viewers back home that they were reporting exactly what was happening. In a nutshell, they wanted people back home to believe the soldiers were invaders rather than liberators. If these same journalists and correspondents had been around in the summer of 1944, would they have thought the British and allied forces on D-Day were liberators or invaders? I know what I think.

During my tour, I had the chance to meet some of the top brass of global journalism, one of whom (I won't reveal her name, to save embarrassment) I supplied with hot water from my BV so she could wash her hair behind her Land-Rover early one morning surrounded by 'don't give a shit' squaddies having a strip wash – bless her! Surprisingly, she didn't ask me any delving questions but then again RPGs and automatic fire had cracked above our heads only the night before and I think she was still getting over it. And it is here that one of my big problems with war correspondents lies – experience, or lack of it. Basically, the lady in question shit herself. I'm not saying I didn't – I suppose we were both battlefield virgins – but the big difference was I'd had the best training in the world from the best army in the world in order to cope with war. She hadn't. What kept me alive was my training, rifle, kit (believe it or not) and, of course, luck. What kept her alive was nothing more than good fortune. In a war, you can't just rely on that, as many of her colleagues soon found to their peril. She saw the end of the war and returned home, thanks to the constant supply of squaddie bodyguards and mountains of armour and firepower that accompanied her wherever she went. But even with such protection, her safety could not be guaranteed. In my opinion, the media should not have been allowed anywhere near the theatre of battle – no way. They risked their own lives and, more importantly, they risked the lives of their squaddie bodyguards.

It has to be remembered that during Op Telic and Op Iraqi Freedom, war correspondents were given unprecedented access to battle groups and units within them. This was the first time ever in the history of war reportage that such generous parameters were granted to the media in the hope it would allow people back home to gain an insight into what was really happening – fat chance! Some believe the journalists had a simple job to do – to report the conflict as it unfolded. If only that was the reality. I saw a side to some of them I never knew existed – one tainted by greed. Many didn't care how they were going to get their story, or who they upset or hurt when they had it; all they cared about was themselves and that 'exclusive' to escalate their career prospects. And these exclusives often included false or incorrect information. But that didn't matter because they were right and that was that. You only have to think back to the false accusations that appeared in the *Daily Mirror* in May 2004 concerning British troops' ill-treatment of Iraqi PWs. Remember those fabricated pictures? Yet again, proving my point that the media were determined to air their political views, rather than take a neutral position.

The support group of 1 (UK) Armoured Division provided the 140 officially registered correspondents (many, of course, weren't) and media organisations with first-rate information. This was all supplied by the TA (the Territorial Army media operations group) through the FPIC (field press information centre). The FPIC accommodated correspondents from organisations such as the BBC, ITN and Sky, not to mention making information available to other foreign journalists. To ensure they received up-to-date details, the FPIC offered journalists the chance to move forward with their assigned battle-group units through the DSG (division support group), using EPVs (enhanced protection vehicles).

Most journalists relished the protection but some didn't. It came with extra clauses, if only for their own safety. Restrictions within certain areas and theatres of battle, for example, didn't go down very well with the arrogant 'do you know who I am?' journalists, many of whom were, in fact, British. The DSG tried their utmost to allow them access to individual soldiers, bringing them to the journalists rather than reporters finding them themselves. Of course, the odd few ignored this rule and went ahead, doing their own thing anyway, trying to find an unsuspecting squaddie to pounce on.

It was constantly being drummed into the minds of the journalists that they must obey the rules, if only for the sake of their bodyguards. It wasn't long before the freedom of speech card came out from the 'don't give a shit' brigade of war correspondents who cared only for themselves. I'm pretty sure one of the ideas behind the liberation of Iraq was to allow the Iraqi people freedom of speech, which they had been living without. And here were a bunch of arseholes demanding they had the right to do what they pleased – during a war! In a way, this was ironic. My knee-jerk reaction to such selfish behaviour was, here's a rifle, now fight for freedom rather than exploit something you've never lived without. They took for granted that they 'have the right'. Although this may work in a Western society, it certainly didn't work in Iraq, especially whilst the fighting was in full swing.

Choosing to ignore the rules and basically biting the hand that fed them, off the journalists went, out into the unknown. But what they found was nothing but the cold shoulder from British and coalition soldiers. After all, we had our job to do and we also knew which journalists obeyed the rules. They seemed to forget we – the armed forces – were the ones who had invited them into the country in the first place, thus, to a certain extent, knew which ones we could trust. Of course, we couldn't let them disappear with their tails between their legs, so we gave them stories in the tradition of true British squaddie humour – hey, Scoop! Want a story? We've had reports that Saddam Hussein has just been seen escaping through the streets of Basrah on the back of a donkey, dressed in drag!

Really? When was this? Do you have any other details? Who spotted him? Yep, many of them were gullible all right!

At the time, we giggled at the thought of our stories reaching the headlines because some journalist had beamed their so-called front-line story to millions of television viewers.

I don't think our story of Saddam dressed in drag reached home, nor the one about Iraqi forces using scorpions as spies by tying mini-cameras on their backs and sending them into our camps. There were literally thousands of stories like these, told every day to hundreds of journalists. In a way, it gave us the chance to relieve some of the tension and our fears about the war, and also to get our own back on certain news channels who seemed to be supporting Saddam and his regime – they know who they are!

Thankfully, some journalists were genuine and had a tremendous passion to report what they saw, rather than what they thought they saw. Too many were eager to please their bosses and feed them with bullshit, who in turn were eager to please their readers with promises of exclusives, no matter what the cost.

24

BACK TO BLIGHTY

Monday, 21 April 0300hrs zulu The morning after we had heard the news, Stuart and I were up with the lark. We couldn't sleep anyway, what with the thought of going home soon. There was still doubt lingering in the back of our minds, though. This was the British Army, remember, renowned for changing dates and times, so we calmed down and thought along the lines of 'we'll believe it when we see it'. Between 0300hrs and 1000hrs zulu, there was nothing to do except hurry up and wait.

The area was full of frenzy and panic and mayhem. Squaddies ran around like headless chickens, trying to meet deadlines before they moved off. The tasks should have been completed the night before but there's always a last-minute job the SNCOs (senior non-commissioned officers) want done. But within an hour, the area had calmed down and everyone had returned to their vehicles, waiting for the off. Half an hour later, the first packets moved off, quickly followed by our A2 packet.

Although the war was technically over, there was still a threat of retaliation from militia and stubborn Iraqi forces refusing to surrender, so CBAs and Kevlar helmets had to be worn at all times. Yeah, right! As soon as we were clear of the barracks and on the main dual carriageway, it was T-shirt time. I didn't see much of the trip back to Shaibah because I fell asleep for most of the journey and didn't wake up until we were near the southern region of Basrah and its usual pitiful sights. A few hours later, we were turning into the airfield at Shaibah. I was amazed we hadn't had a single recovery job.

Our camp area was towards the south of the airstrip, close to the taxiway. Stuart followed the rear of our packet, parking behind A2. All that was left was to chill out with nothing to do until morning. I checked my watch: 1515hrs zulu – time for a brew. I made the tea whilst Stuart put up a side shelter, attaching it to the nearside rear of the Foden. He even made a shower cubicle from 'urban cam' scrim. Our shower, which we were about to test, was nothing more than a one-gallon metal oil can we'd found at the GOSP location in Az Zubayr.

As we sat all cleaned up and relaxed in our deck chairs, soaking up the evening sun, Lt Pym suddenly came running over. 'There's a Pizza Hut and a Burger King!' he shouted excitedly. 'I'm sending down a couple of crafties with an order; what do ya fancy? Bearing in mind it's a four-hour wait for a pizza but only about a one-hour wait for a burger, and you can only get a Whopper meal.'

No one seemed to care about the wait. After all, it was a chance to taste real food. We placed our orders for a Whopper meal for a mere $5 and eagerly awaited the Land-Rover's return. A few of the REME LAD joined Stuart and me under our shelter and the topic of conversation soon turned to the flight home. We even told each other some of our private thoughts about what we were going to do as soon as we landed home. The airfield had 8,000 squaddies on it and it was a safe bet each one of us was doing the same. The first thing I planned to do was to have a plate of fried eggs and chips. But I still had a niggling doubt that the dates home would suddenly change.

We'd placed our food order at 1700hrs zulu, and time was ticking by; the wait was becoming unbearable. The crafties finally arrived with our orders two hours later and, as soon as the meals arrived, we ripped the bags open to reveal the best meal in the world. I savoured every bite. The Coke with real ice was a treat in itself.

Three and a half minutes later, we all started to get the odd twinge in our stomachs. We'd been eating rat packs for so long we'd forgotten what real food tasted like. We'd also forgotten that we'd lost loads of weight, which meant our stomachs had shrunk, and we'd just punished them with a burger and chips, washed down with half a litre of ice-cold Coke. The ASM had warned us but knew his words were falling on deaf ears.

Whilst we suffered a mild attack of indigestion, it was time to call it a night. It made a change to retire for the evening without having to keep one eye and one ear open. Even so, it didn't seem natural to relax too much. I folded down the driver's seat and placed my doss bag over it. I made myself comfortable and clasped my hands behind my head, watching a dust storm brew up in the distance. Although it didn't look as fierce as others we'd seen in the past, it electrified the air, releasing what can only be described as pink lightning; I'd never seen such a phenomenon. The cool air blowing through the open windows of the cab soon sent Stuart and me to sleep.

The following morning, some mad bastard screamed past in his 432 APC (armoured personnel carrier). He was quickly followed by another, then another. I looked out of the windscreen and could see a convoy of tank transporters bringing back the armoured vehicles from Al Amarah, including Warriors, Challenger 2s and CRARRVs.

'What the fuck is happening?' I muttered.

Stuart poked his head down through the cupola; he must have slept on the roof. 'I see the heavy shit has arrived. They've turned up to have their armour removed and be de-bombed, ready for 19 Brigade's arrival.'

'The war's definitely over, then,' I replied.

There was no way I was going to get back to sleep with the racket of armoured vehicles racing past, so I turned over the engine and switched on the BV to make a brew. As I made the tea, I could hear Stuart talking to someone; it was Bobby.

'Fancy a brew?'

'No thanks, Kev, I'm too busy. Have you handed in your rounds yet? If not, you'd better do it soon. The RSM is collecting it all in, including explosives, grenades, LAWs, the lot. And, by the way, we're on local time now.'

I checked my watch, which said 0500hrs zulu. Local time was 0800hrs. But it didn't matter what time zone we were using because we had slept through reveille, which was at 0300hrs zulu.

'Fucking zulu, now fucking local. And is that British Summer Time or fucking GMT?' Stuart muttered from the roof of the cab, struggling to change the time on his wristwatch.

'We'd better return our rounds,' I said, searching the cab for loose rounds or mini-flares and emptying the magazines into my Kevlar helmet. I then made my way to the RSM who was sitting on a concrete slab 50 metres to the right of the Foden.

'Throw your rounds in this box, son, and give the sergeant your flares,' he said, without even looking up at me.

I poured my rounds into the already full ammunition box as the sergeant and RSM boxed up the discarded flares and grenades.

'You're TA, aren't ya?' the RSM asked in his south London accent, and this time he looked straight at me.

'Yes, Sir,' I replied.

'What did you think of your first war?'

First war? Did he know something I didn't? I didn't really know how to answer that question. 'It was an education, Sir.' Not much of an answer, but what was I supposed to say?

He smiled and even thanked me for the work I'd done. He then told me to fuck off, which I did without question. I returned to the Foden, only to be greeted by one of the LI guys in his Bedford fuel tanker.

'Need any fuel, mate?'

I checked the gauge, which registered half full. 'I suppose I'd better fill up,' I replied.

'The war may be over, but not for you recy mechs, eh, mate,' he said.

I managed to just about raise half a smile at his comment but he had a point. I climbed onto the top decking and removed the hose from the tank filler neck by loosening the Jubilee clip around the hose, prising it over the lip of the filler neck using a screwdriver. Although this wasn't the done thing when refuelling, it was certainly quicker. Refuelling the tank from the top of the filler tube, or swan neck, caused a rush of air to escape up the tube, giving a blow-back and covering you in diesel. Refuelling directly into the tank prevented this.

The LI guy handed me the nozzle and I placed it in the tank, squeezing the lever beneath the handle of the nozzle. We chatted for a few minutes about anything and nothing, but it was long enough to overfill the tank. The auto switch-off on the handle was broken and diesel kept on flowing out of the nozzle.

'Shit!' I shouted, as I released the handle on the nozzle. ''Ere, mate, you'd better take this.' I handed back the nozzle as diesel overflowed down the side of the tank and onto the decking.

The LI guy stowed his hose away and drove off to refuel any other vehicles. In the mean time, I struggled with the filler tube. I attempted to replace the hose over the lip of the filler neck but it just wouldn't stretch that extra millimetre. I was left with only one option: I had to lean back holding the hose with both hands and try to force it over the lip using my weight as leverage. When I pulled, my weight was enough for the hose to give way and fall back into place over the lip. But at the same time, the sudden jolt caused me to lose my footing and slip on the diesel-soaked decking. I ended up hanging by my right thumb, which was now caught behind the swan neck. A split second later, my thumb gave way and I ended up in a pile on the ground.

'*Jesus motherin' fuck!*' I shouted, or something to that effect, as I jumped around holding my thumb. I risked a sneaky look and pulled my thumb away from my grasp, only to reveal it was sticking up at some strange angle. I panicked at the sight of my weird-angled thumb and gave it a whack – a feeble attempt to knock it back into shape – which only caused a further stab of excruciating pain. I struggled to climb back in the cab of the Foden and lay back in the driver's seat. I was beginning to feel the blood drain from my head and soon felt faint and nauseous because of the pain. Why is Stuart taking so long, I thought to myself. He was too busy talking to the RSM.

I couldn't believe what I'd done. I'd been machine-gunned, shelled, mortared, targeted by Scud missiles, ambushed and shot at by snipers, yet managed to get through the conflict without so much as a scratch. Soon after hostilities cease, I end up breaking my bloody thumb by slipping off the back of the Foden.

Stuart returned, only to find me moaning in the cab. 'What the fuck have you done?'

'Don't ask, just don't ask. You won't believe it, anyway.'

'I'll get a medic,' he said, jumping out of the cab, and was off before I could stop him.

The last thing I wanted was the whole camp to know, so I slowly climbed out of the cab one-handed and went to look for a medic myself. I walked towards the A2 packet where I found Lt Pym.

'Sir!' I shouted, holding my thumb tight against my chest. 'Get me a fuckin' medic, this is killing me.'

Lt Pym's face was a picture. If I hadn't been in so much pain, I'd have been laughing.

'What's happened?' he shrieked.

'Fell off the Foden,' I replied, in between bouts of throbbing pain.

'C'mon, we'll find you a medic.'

Thank God for that, I thought, and walked onto the space where his Land-Rover had once stood.

'Shit, I forgot! I've loaned out my Land-Rover. Never mind, we'll walk, it's only a few hundred metres to the aid station.'

'*Walk!*'

'It's only a few hundred metres, it won't take long.'

A few hundred metres and plenty of cursing later, I reached the aid station. Lt Pym left me to it and returned to the LAD whilst I went through the first assessment. The diagnosis was that my thumb was either broken or dislocated. Either way, I had to have it X-rayed at the field hospital, which was situated at the bottom of the airfield.

It was still about a kilometre away but thankfully I was given a lift in a Land-Rover ambulance driven by an overkeen medic using me as an excuse to use his blues and twos. Five minutes later, I was checking in at the hospital reception.

The entire hospital was made up of large green field tents with plastic grated sheets covering the ground. The reception was made up of three smaller 12x12 tents in a line. Benches lined either side, with the reception desk towards the entrance.

I handed over my MEDCARD and gave them my service number, then took a seat with the other casualties waiting to be seen by the MO (medical officer). The driver who had brought me down left me to it and returned to the aid station. I was now at the mercy of the medical corps.

Half an hour later, a female captain nurse approached me. 'Lance Corporal Mervin?'

'Yes, Ma'am.'

'Follow me, please, I'll soon have you sorted out.' We walked through the suffocating heat of the reception and into an air-conditioned assessment room.

'Take a seat, I'll be back in a minute.'

Thank God she offered me a seat, otherwise I'd have collapsed, first with the pain and second at the sight of all the medical shit lying around. I'd never been overkeen on hospitals or 'medical tools', the mere sight of them sent my head spinning, although having injections had never bothered me, providing I never looked at the needle. I lay down on the trolley bed and carefully relaxed my aching thumb on my chest. The cool air blowing from the large air-conditioning ducts above my head soon took my mind off the surroundings and I was beginning to doze off.

'Right, Lance Corporal Mervin,' a voice shouted.

Bollocks! I thought, I was enjoying my snooze. I opened my eyes to find some major standing to my left. I quickly sat up to greet him and forgot about my thumb. '*Jesus, fuck!* Oops, sorry, Sir,' I said, apologising for my outburst.

'That's quite all right, we've heard worse. Now then, whilst you're in pain, it would be a shame to waste the opportunity.'

'What do you mean, Sir?' I had to ask.

'This!' he replied, grabbing my thumb and manipulating it. 'Now, does that hurt?'

'*Fuck's sake!* Too right it fucking hurts!' I didn't apologise for that particular outburst.

'Yep! Definitely not dislocated, but it could be a scafoid fracture. Would you like to have a prod around?' he asked the captain nurse.

Oh please, no. Take his word for it, please, I thought. The captain looked at my pathetic face and must have seen the pain in my eyes.

'No need for that, Sir. I think he's been manhandled enough.' She smiled and gave me a wink.

Oh, thank you, thank you, I thought.

'Have it X-rayed and I'll have a look at the pictures; we'll then take it from there,' the major ordered. I sighed with relief as he walked off to see his next victim.

'You'll be waiting for a while, at least a couple of hours, so you might as well grab some sleep,' the captain said, in her soft voice.

'Fair enough, Ma'am,' I replied. I made myself comfortable and was soon in the land of nod; well, as much as I could be with an aching, throbbing thumb.

Two hours or not, it felt as if I'd had my eyes closed for only two minutes. I was rushed to the X-ray tent for a few snaps, then back on the bed waiting for 'Doctor Jekyll' to have a look. He diagnosed a fracture of the scafoid, a bone at the base of the thumb. The problem with this kind of fracture is that it doesn't show up on X-rays until it starts to heal, and it can take a couple of weeks before any healing is evident. So a 'back slab' cast was placed on my wrist to support the thumb. I then received the biggest shock – that it would take at least six weeks to heal and I was to stay overnight in a ward for observation. I was escorted to Ward Four and given a bed for the night. I had no change of clothes, no wash and shaving kit, and the worst nightmare of all was I had only three cigarettes left.

'Can I go back to my unit and fetch a wash bag and a change of clothes?' I asked the corporal nurse at the ward desk. I was really only looking for an excuse to fetch a few more packets of smokes.

'Fat chance of that, mate. You can't go anywhere now. We'll sort out a Red Cross wash kit but that's all we can do for you.' She handed me a plastic bag containing a single throwaway razor, a bar of soap, a toothbrush and a small tube of toothpaste. I placed my goodie bag on a trolley at the foot of my bed and introduced myself to the other patients in the ward.

Opposite my bed was a staff sergeant, who had been knocked over by a Challenger 2. On his right was another sergeant. He had his right leg in plaster, but I never found out why. To his left, a corporal from the RRF had his left arm plastered up to his elbow. He'd been shot three times by his mate (he assured me it was an accident). To my left was a young 'trog' (RLC driver). He'd fallen off the top of his truck (at least I wasn't the only one). And to my right was a young Marine of the USMC. His left foot had been bitten by a camel spider and gone septic, swelling up like a football.

A couple of beds further down was a small Iraqi boy

about three years old, with his head covered in bandages. His elder brother, who was in his early teens, closely guarded him. I was later told the young boy had been caught in some crossfire between two local tribes fighting over territory and was hit by a 7.62-mm round at the base of his skull, which passed clean through his head. This small boy's presence was a powerful reminder of the innocent civilian casualties caught up in the conflict. The horrible term 'collateral damage' was applied to these types of casualties.

After my brief introduction to the inmates, I took off my boots and settled down on the bed. It was quite a novelty to lie down on a bed with clean sheets and a fluffy pillow. Half an hour later, lunch was served, which surprised me because I didn't realise how quickly the morning had passed – it was 1300hrs local. I ate the noodles, which were a nice change from meatballs and pasta, and settled down on my bed to read a donated Stephen King novel.

The following morning I was woken by screams of agony coming from the young Iraqi child. His injuries had been so severe his chances of survival were doubted at first, but thankfully it looked like he'd pull through. In the mean time, he had the pain of recovery to contend with. The bandages around his head were constantly soaked in blood, even though his wounds were dressed every day. None of us liked the idea of this child being in so much pain. It sounds stupid, but we wanted to suffer his pain for him. He simply didn't deserve it.

We'd all try and cheer him up by acting the fool at the foot of his bed: pulling faces, pretending to hurt each other like the three stooges or telling silly jokes, although he couldn't understand us. We even made balloons out of surgical gloves and drew silly faces on them with felt-tip pens and tied them above his bed. Occasionally he'd smile, which was priceless to see, and not just for us stupid squaddies and nurses, but also his parents, who visited him daily, and especially his elder brother, who never left his side, day and night.

We couldn't help but feel guilty for the boy's injuries, because in a way it was our fault he was shot. We felt we had to do something, so we had a whip-round in our ward and managed to collect $53 for the family, which was the equivalent of six months' wages in Iraq. At first, the boy's father wouldn't accept it, which was fair enough; pride, I suppose. We explained he must take it for the boy, and so he accepted it.

By 1600hrs local, I was getting concerned about when I'd be released. I'd run out of cigarettes and could only stretch one small bar of soap so far. The other inmates had twice seen the doctors and surgeons doing their rounds, but they'd totally ignored me. One of the other inmates then offered me a cigarette, so we made our way to the smoking area outside, whilst the nurse went to find out what was happening with me.

Our smoking area was at the rear of the ward, about 50 metres to its left. A few pallets were piled on top of one another to make a crude bench and a couple of steel bins were placed next to them for any rubbish or cigarette butts. As we smoked, other doctors and surgeons joined us. Not just army, but also navy and air force medical personnel working in the 'tri-service' field hospital, which is how the British armed services now operate.

The hospital also ensured it never distinguished between friend and foe, treating us all the same. Each Iraqi PW, however, was escorted by a nurse and two armed soldiers whilst they used the toilets or walked – or hobbled on crutches, as the case may be – around outside for a little exercise. There were also a few enemy soldiers in the hospital who'd had limbs amputated, having either faced British soldiers in the heat of battle or stepped on their own mines. One thing was for sure, I didn't feel sorry for them.

When we returned to our ward, the duty corporal nurse gave me some bad news; I was to stay for at least two more days. I couldn't believe it. But I had no choice and certainly no means of fetching some extra kit, not unless I risked walking back to A1 packet without telling anyone, which amounted to being AWOL. I just had to put up with the situation and make the best of it. The first thing I noticed was that the satcom telephones never seemed to have any queues. I had four phone cards, unused, so I telephoned Helen that evening and explained what had happened, putting her mind at rest. I think in a way she was pleased I was in hospital and away from any danger.

It was now the third day of my 'sentence' and I was establishing myself in the ward. I was even allowed to join the escape committee. Stupid idea, I know, but we had to think of things to do, otherwise we'd have gone mad with boredom. We even arranged EFI runs and took it in turns to fetch supplies from the shop, which was beyond the perimeter of the hospital and therefore out of bounds to inmates. If we were caught, we weren't exactly shot at dawn, but we did have to hand over some of our supplies to the nurses.

Thanks to the EFI runs, I now had a wash and shave kit, shower gel and deodorant, and some cigarettes. Some of the inmates in our ward, such as the young US Marine and the sergeant, had been given early release, but as one victim left, another soon filled the vacant bed. In particular, a nice young lady with long, blonde hair, about 20 years old. Through no fault of her own, she had us around her little finger; she wanted for nothing. She'd been stung by a scorpion on her left hand, which had raised her temperature and caused her hand to swell up, but she recovered within a few days.

One day, I returned from the smokers' corner and noticed I had some visitors waiting for me from A1 packet: Phil, a guy called Q Green, Smudge (a VM reservist) and Stuart. They'd also brought all my kit, which confused me a little initially.

'You missed the Doc, Kev,' Phil said.

'You're going home, you lucky bastard,' added Stuart.

Q Green reiterated the fact. 'We spoke to the doctor whilst you were having a smoke and he said you would be useless to us because of your injury, so you're going home tomorrow. Leaving at 0830hrs by helicopter for Kuwait, then a plane home.'

'We booked in your bergen and webbing at the reception; they'll store it in an ISO container until you're discharged,' added Phil.

'So this is goodbye, then. Not the way I planned it, but . . .' I didn't know what else to say. I shook their hands and wished them all the best. 'Say goodbye to the lads for me, won't you,' I said to Phil.

'Trust you to go home a week early,' commented Stuart.

'Well, hopefully I'll see you again on some TA training weekend. And as for the rest of you . . .' Again, I didn't know what to say.

Our farewells said, they walked out of the ward and disappeared down the corridor. I just stood watching them leave; I couldn't believe what was happening. I sat on the side of the bed, gobsmacked.

'You lucky bastard, Kev,' a voice came from my left. It was Trog.

'I can't believe it either, Trog. I thought I'd end up doing

GDs or something. I never expected to be sent home.'

Trog sighed. 'But what use would you be? You can't write anything down cos you're right-handed; you couldn't be a switch-bitch or even wipe the CO's arse. And could you put on your respirator within nine seconds?'

He was right; I'd be useless to everyone, including myself. And if there was an unexpected chemical attack, I'd have no way of carrying out the IA drill and donning my respirator, which was one of the doctor's main concerns.

Early the following morning, I was woken by a commotion from a few beds down – it was the little boy. Excruciating screams pierced our eardrums as the boy thrashed around in agony. A couple of nurses tried their best to calm him down whilst a doctor attended to his head wound, but it was no good. He suddenly stopped thrashing about and fell still and silent – he was dead.

A few hours later, a medic arrived to take a gaggle of us to a waiting helicopter that would helivac us to an RAF casevac station at Kuwait City Airport. I said my goodbyes and thanked the staff for looking after me. There were sad faces all around. They weren't for me, of course; it was obvious who they were for.

One unnerving helicopter ride later, I was sitting in a tent at the back of the airport with other casualties, waiting for the plane to take us home. An RAF VC10 aeroplane converted to take battle casualties was ready to take us to the RAF base at Akrotiri in Cyprus. When we landed, we were split into two groups. One lot were waiting to board a plane which would take them to their units in Germany, while the rest of us got on a waiting Boeing 727 medivac conversion to take us to Birmingham International Airport.

As we disembarked the VC10 and walked down the portable steps, we played a horrid prank on one of the casualties. In true sadistic squaddie-humour style, we took the piss out of each other's injuries, and in particular a soldier with both eyes bandaged; he couldn't see a bloody thing. We guided him down the steps and once on the tarmac we let go of his arms, directing him back towards the runway. The poor bastard continued to walk, nervously at first, but then he quickened his step once he gained confidence and realised the ground was flat. He must have walked about 50 metres before he realised it was a prank because of all the giggling he could hear behind him.

Saturday, 26 April 0600hrs BST Five hours after taking off from Cyprus, I was back in England, greeted by a cold early-morning mist. And all I was wearing was my light desert DPM trousers and a T-shirt. We were ushered to a hangar towards the end of the airport, which was chosen to keep us away from any prying civilian eyes, including those of journalists. Inside the hangar, a colonel greeted us and fed us instructions whilst our luggage was searched by the snowdrops for 'war trophies'. The colonel had also arranged for taxis to take us home, paid for by the army – or the taxpayer, depending on how you look at it. Some of the casualties were travelling as far as Devon and even Geordieland in the North-east.

There were also telephones and fax machines for us to use, should we have wanted to tell anyone of our arrival home. We all declined the offer, wanting to surprise our wives and girlfriends. The colonel even offered us a no-strings-attached loan of £25 to help us with any unexpected purchases during our journey home. This gesture wasn't declined. After a bit of form-filling and promising to report to my unit on Monday morning, I was soon in a taxi heading down the M6 motorway.

By 0800hrs, I was ringing the front doorbell. When my

wife answered the door, I didn't know who was more surprised. After the welcome tears and hugs, I was lying down on the sofa with my now four-year-old daughter watching *Playhouse Disney* on my widescreen television. Helen cooked the egg and chips, which I'd been dreaming of for months, but I couldn't manage to eat it all.

I couldn't get it out of my head that the war was over for me, and I was actually at home. For a split second, I felt as if I hadn't been away. I looked in the mirror hanging in the hallway, however, and found myself looking at a stranger: a scruffy, dirty-looking tramp with stubble. What the fuck am I doing here? I thought to myself. I shouldn't be here. I must have stared at the mirror for a good few minutes before my daughter tugged on my left leg. She immediately brought back memories of the little boy back in the small village near Al Amarah, and his dead family, whom we found in the shallow graves.

Many other memories of the conflict have since suddenly rushed to the forefront of my mind, triggered off by some otherwise innocent sight, smell or gesture. These memories, I have been told, will continue for many years to come.

'You're not leaving me again, are you, Daddy?' Rachel asked.

I looked down at her and smiled at this beautiful girl, with long blonde hair and wide, bright-blue innocent eyes, living in her safe and secure country, none the wiser as to what Daddy had been doing. Straight away, I had a another flashback, of the little girl I gave the bar of rat-pack chocolate to when we crossed the border into Safwan.

I changed my mind; I did belong here. 'C'mon darling, let's watch *Bear in the Big Blue House*. I think it's just started.'

Epilogue
MY THOUGHTS

The conflict had been over for ten days (unofficially) when I returned home on 26 April 2003, although sporadic fighting has continued between Saddam's diehards and the coalition forces. The war didn't officially end until 1 May, but even during the height of the fighting, the majority of us said the troubles wouldn't end with the Iraqi surrender. We knew we would win the war, there was no doubt about that, but there were concerns about the resulting power struggle between the Arab tribes. Thankfully, the generals and other coalition leaders knew this, even though the media didn't portray this at the time. But what passed many lips, especially those of the British soldiers, was the idea that Iraq now faced its own 'Northern Ireland'.

As soon as we heard the news that the Iraqi forces had surrendered, we knew the hard work to keep any peace would start immediately. Iraq is full of conflicting tribes and clerics, crying out for the chance to fight for what they call their right to rule over others, in the name of religion. This is where the British soldiers can play their trump card and win the hearts and minds of the locals, which is what they have been doing since 20 March 2003, thereby gaining the confidence of the soldiers on the ground, so the locals and coalition forces can work together and get rid of these arseholes. Unfortunately, some of these tribal leaders, clerics and foreign insurgents don't agree with the majority of the Iraqi people and would love the chance to be the second Saddam Hussein. Two years after the fall of his regime, these tribal leaders and insurgents still thwart the liberation, with suicide bombers and mortars a daily risk to life. I wonder if some of them would still want to rule Iraq if it didn't have any oil.

It will take many years, if not decades, for Iraq to stabilise and become a secure nation. You only have to read the history books and to see how many problems Germany faced for many years after the First and Second world wars, as did Eastern Bloc nations like Bosnia, Serbia and Croatia, to name but a few. In comparison, who could have imagined in the 1970s that in 30 years' time a group of former IRA members would be talking peace with the UK government? Or at the height of the Cold War that in 1991 Communism would collapse and Russia would hold democratic elections?

The idea of a western-style democratic Iraq, however, will never happen. Arabic nations have a totally different outlook on life compared to many in the West. Democracy and freedom will only work if the Iraqi people are left alone to use it in their own way. On Sunday, 30 January 2005, they finally had the chance to put these ideals into practice. And it will certainly be remembered as one of the most important dates in modern times for Iraq.

Nearly two years after the liberation, Iraq held its first democratic election in fifty years for its fourteen million eligible voters. Over 60 per cent of the electorate voted at the 5,000 available polling stations, putting the total amount of UK voters in the 1997 election to shame. The elections, however, were marred by violence and intimidation. Even on election day, car bombs, gunfire, suicide bombers and other IEDs (improvised explosive devices) were used by insurgents, mainly by the followers of the Sunni militant leader Abu Musab Al Zarqawi, to kill and maim anyone who risked voting for democracy.

So, what happens next? Does this mean the coalition can finally go home? After all, their work is done. Well, not quite. It will be many years before the country is deemed stable, so the peace-keeping will continue. The new government, using its democratic foundation, can now concentrate on rebuilding its economy, enforcing law and order, debate new issues and remove any lingering trace of Saddam's regime. As for the Iraqi people, the memory of over 35 years of oppression, fear and torture will be harder to remove.

During Operation Telic and Operation Iraqi Freedom, the coalition forces made great progress towards rebuilding Iraq. During this preliminary reconstruction, it has to be remembered that many emergency repairs were carried out during continual bombardments with enemy shells, mortars and missiles, not to mention machine-gun and sniper fire. And yet the coalition forces, along with TA soldiers, carried on regardless. Our achievements during and soon after the conflict included the following:

- Hospitals were repaired, restocked and reopened and healthcare was made available to *all* Iraqis, rather than the chosen few. Before the conflict, healthcare was only available to those in the Ba'ath Party and regime members, equating to only 35 per cent of the population.
- Half a million children were immunised against disease.

MY THOUGHTS

- Clean drinking water was available for the first time to many people, thanks to repairs to existing water supplies and the laying of fresh pipes.

- Sewerage pipes and water mains were replaced or repaired in towns and cities around the country, along with those in desalination plants and pump houses.

- Battle-damaged schools were repaired and reopened after clearing them of ammunition dumps and unstable booby traps. Attendance was set to rise above levels recorded before the conflict and girls who were not related to the old regime members were now allowed to attend school for the first time. Schools and college libraries could now have textbooks that no longer mentioned Saddam Hussein.

- Power cables and pylons were being replaced along the entire length of the country and power stations were now generating twice the volume of electrical output as before the conflict. Telephone and communication lines were reconnected and new ones laid.

- Umm Qasr seaport and its waterways were cleared of anti-ship mines to allow humanitarian aid, medical supplies and food to be unloaded from ships.

- Oil refineries were cleared of mines and booby traps, and sabotaged pipelines were replaced and repaired, so millions of barrels of crude oil could be exported around the world.

- Democratic elections were being organised and city councils and their members were preparing to replace the old regime leaders.

- Streets in towns and cities were being patrolled by 50,000 policemen and 100,000 civil defence personnel, who had undergone a training programme devised by British and American forces. Also, a further 80,000 Iraqi soldiers, previously part of Saddam's organisation, were retrained and patrolled the streets alongside coalition forces.

It has to be said, the coalition forces, working under such extreme conditions, achieved remarkable results, and they were much appreciated by the Iraqi people. And because of this appreciation, it is imperative that the rebuilding continues.

Two years on and Iraq continues to rebuild itself, thanks to the skills of the coalition forces and the determination of the Iraqi people. But, yet again, these achievements go unnoticed because they don't make good news. Instead, death and destruction appears to top media coverage, as if willing the liberation to fail. But those of us who were there, and those who continue to serve in Iraq, know differently.

During my flight home I was surrounded by soldiers with many different injuries. Some had bits of limbs missing whilst others had broken bones and wore scars where bullets had been removed, and yet we still managed to raise a smile and have a laugh. We took the piss out of each other – especially me with my broken thumb. We were in high spirits because we knew we had done well and achieved some great things.

Then I landed at Birmingham Airport and my mood suddenly changed. For some reason, I felt I wasn't welcome in my own country. During the months that followed my return to the UK, I found it increasingly difficult to settle into civvy life.

I was welcomed home with insults and my boss terminated my employment contract. He was legally within his rights to do so, there being a 13-week probationary law that allows employers to sack any employees without having to give any reason within this time period. My boss's attitude prior to my call-out had seemed positive, even though he was more interested in his holiday, and I had assumed everything would be OK for me to return to work. Boy, was I wrong on that one. I hadn't a leg to stand on. I asked the army to see if they could help but their hands were tied. I even asked my local MP to see if the Government could help, but no – they turned their back on me. I felt as if they wanted to wash their hands of my predicament.

Because of bad press, biased media reports and anti-war politicians jumping on the bandwagon, if only to gain the publicity vote, some people turned against me. In my home town, I was called a murderer and someone even spat at me as I walked along the high street. I began to feel paranoid.

A few months soon became one year and within that time I still hadn't found full-time employment. Although I'd applied for many jobs for which I was qualified, it was becoming obvious to me that companies didn't want a TA soldier on their books. In fact, two potential employers admitted they didn't want to employ me purely because I was a TA soldier and they were afraid I would be called out again. I found it virtually impossible to find work and convinced myself it was because I had been in Iraq.

In the end, I had no alternative but to use my HGV Class 1 licence, which ironically I'd gained through the TA as part of my recovery-mechanic training. But then I faced the same problem as before. Not even haulage companies wanted a TA soldier on their payroll, which confused me a little because there was a shortfall of Class 1 drivers in the country. The only work I could find was part-time driving for an agency, because it didn't care where I'd been or what I'd done, as long as I had a valid HGV1 licence.

Unfortunately, the story doesn't end there. Soon after I started working, for a number of reasons, I had no alternative but to leave the TA. First, driving for a living tends to mess up your social life, so, of course, it started to mess up my TA life. And, second, I was earning a third of my previous salary and simply couldn't afford the time off to continue with the Territorials. My situation, however, was by no means unique. I'm aware of a further five reservists who faced the same predicament when they returned home; and it's quite possible there are a great deal more.

Many of those who didn't call me a murderer or spit at me asked me stupid yet predictable questions: what was it like?, did you shit yourself?, and the most pathetic question to ask a soldier fresh from a conflict, did you kill anyone? But there were also some thought-provoking questions from a sympathetic few, one of which was, do you think it was worth it? Of course, my answer is yes, it was worth it, and for many reasons. First, because the Iraqi people certainly needed liberating, that goes without saying. Second, it had to be worth it because many coalition soldiers paid the ultimate price for that simple word we take for granted – freedom. If you disagree with that and think they died for nothing, then argue with the families who lost their husbands, fathers, sons and brothers in the conflict. Anyone who says they died for nothing should think again.

Another interesting question I was repeatedly asked was, would you do it again? Yes. For me, I was fighting for the next generation. Children can now grow up in a country that is no longer controlled by an evil dictator. They can now say what they want without the risk of being dragged off the streets, never to be seen again. They no longer need to live under the threat of torture because they may have been heard saying something against the regime, or fear family members disappearing because they refuse to support Saddam Hussein.

So why did certain British MPs, in particular the likes of Clare Short and George Galloway, spread their traitorous poison against the liberation? And why did such MPs back in August 1990 shout from the rooftops urging the government to do something to free Kuwait from the clutches of an evil dictator?

Seventeen months after the 2003 conflict, why did UN Secretary General Kofi Annan suddenly change his mind and decide that the liberation was in fact illegal? I would like Annan, Clare Short and George Galloway to go to Iraq and stand in the middle of Basrah and shout out, 'I disagree with the liberation of your country and I disagree with the toppling of Saddam and his regime', since they clearly do. They would soon realise they had made a big mistake to have fooled the British public into thinking they knew what went on during the conflict. However, as much as it pains me, they are entitled to their opinion. Thankfully, since 20 March 2003, so are the Iraqi people.

Appendix

MEN AND MUSCLE: BRITISH AND IRAQI HARDWARE USED ON OP TELIC

Approximately 45,000 personnel served on Op Telic, of which 26,000 worked with 1 (UK) Armoured Division and 16 Air Assault Brigade.

In just a few weeks, 1 (UK) Armoured Division was transported from Emden in Germany to Kuwait. This amounted to 1,029 armoured vehicles, including 120 Challenger 2 MBTs, 150 Warrior armoured personnel carriers, 36 AS90 self-propelled guns, 2,926 B-vehicles, 18 light guns and 215 engineer vehicles, including tracked, armoured and B-vehicles.

A total of 23 trains were used to transport the equipment to the port of Emden and 19 ships set sail with their cargo of military armour, vehicles and equipment destined for Kuwait. Whilst the ships sailed, the majority of troop movement to the region soon followed. RAF and civilian aircraft flew from Hanover, where around 900 soldiers were deployed per day.

In Marchwood, Southampton, further movements of military vehicles and equipment were under way. A total of 4,350 vehicles were loaded onto ships including light B-vehicles and Land-Rovers, light ARVs (armoured reconnaissance vehicles) and APCs, 2,400 trailers, 1,700 ISO containers, 4,800 items of 'heavy' kit, including helicopters and bridges, 3,000 tonnes of ammunition and 55,000 tonnes of other equipment and stores. A total of 6 trains and over 3,000 freight movements by road were used to load the 40 ships required to sail to Kuwait.

This enormous task involved many personnel. At Marchwood, this involved 17 Port and Maritime Regiment RLC (V) and the 165 Port Regiment RLC (V) and consumed nearly 20,000 man-hours for the 40-day operation. Soon after, the RLC regiments, both TA units, were deployed in the Gulf where their services were required once again. In Emden, the task of moving large amounts of equipment was by no means an easy undertaking either. Personnel used included 6 Supply Regiment RLC, 24 Regiment RLC, 69 Movement and Control Squadron and the 170 Pioneer Squadron.

With its heavy armour and motorised firepower in the field, plus support forces, including reconnaissance, engineering, medical and military police, 1 (UK) Armoured Division ensured the breach into Iraq. Securing points of entry for other coalition and airborne forces, 16 Air Assault Brigade defended key locations such as ports and oilfields/plants. Elements of 1 (UK) Armoured Division included:

7 Armoured Brigade
2 Royal Tank Regiment
1 Battalion, the Black Watch
The Queen's Dragoon Guards
Royal Scots Dragoon Guards
3 Regiment, Royal Horse Artillery
1 Battalion, Royal Regiment of Fusiliers
32 Armoured Engineer Regiment
28 Engineer Regiment
Headquarters and Signal Regiment
2 Battalion, Royal Electrical & Mechanical Engineers
33 Explosive Ordnance Disposal Regiment
Royal Logistic Corps (16 Air Assault Brigade)
7 Parachute Regiment, Royal Horse Artillery
1 Battalion, the Parachute Regiment
3 Battalion, the Parachute Regiment
1 Battalion, the Royal Irish Regiment

Household Cavalry Regiment
7 Air Assault Battalion
23 Engineer Regiment
3 Regiment Army Air Corps
Royal Electrical & Mechanical Engineers
13 Air Assault Support Regiment
16 Close Support Medical Regiment
Royal Logistic Corps (102 Logistics Brigade)

Headquarters
2 Signal Regiment
36 Engineer Regiment
33 Field Hospital
34 Field Hospital
202 Field Hospital
4 General Support Medical Regiment
3 Battalion, Royal Electrical & Mechanical Engineers
6 Supply Regiment, Royal Logistic Corps
17 Port & Maritime, Royal Logistic Corps
23 Pioneer Regiment, Royal Logistic Corps
24 Regiment, Royal Logistic Corps
5 Regiment, Royal Military Police

RAF
Sentry AEW1, command and control aircraft
Tornado GR4, bomber/reconnaissance
Tornado F3, air-defence aircraft
Jaguar GR3, attack/reconnaissance
Harrier GR7, attack aircraft
VC10, refuel tanker aircraft
Tristar, refuel tanker aircraft
Nimrod Maritime, reconnaissance/patrol
Chinook helicopters
Puma helicopters
Plus 7,000 personnel, 27 support helicopters and 100 fixed-wing
aircraft

APPENDIX

Navy
HMS *Ark Royal* (aircraft carrier)
HMS *Liverpool* (type-42 destroyer)
HMS *Edinburgh* (type-42 destroyer)
HMS *York* (type-42 destroyer)
HMS *Marlborough* (type-23 frigate)
HMS *Richmond* (type-23 frigate)
HMS *Grimsby* (mine-hunter)
HMS *Ledbury* (mine-hunter)
HMS *Brocklesby* (mine-hunter)
HMS *Blyth* (mine-hunter)
HMS *Ocean* (helicopter carrier)
HMS *Chatham* (United Nations)
RFA *Argus* (hospital ship)
RFA *Sir Tristram* (auxiliary)
RFA *Sir Galahad* (auxiliary)
RFA *Sir Percivale* (auxiliary)
RFA *Fort Victoria* (auxiliary)
RFA *Fort Rosalie* (auxiliary)
RFA *Fort Austin* (auxiliary)
RFA *Orangeleaf* (auxiliary)
HMS *Turbulent* (submarine)

Amphibious
HQ 3 Commando Brigade
40 Commando, Royal Marines
42 Commando, Royal Marines

Tank and artillery rounds used – Op Telic
120 Challenger 2 MBTs deployed
1.9 tonnes DU shells used
540 HE shells
36 AS90 self-propelled guns deployed (9,000 assorted rounds used)
105-mm light guns (amount deployed not available) (11,000 assorted rounds used)
2,000 bomblet shells

WEEKEND WARRIOR

Northern Corps: surrounded northern Baghdad and Tikrit with about 10,000 to 15,000 troops. The divisions included the Adnan Mechanised Division, the Medina Armoured Division, with its feared reputation, and the Nebuchadnezzar Infantry Division. Armour was mainly of Russian origin, consisting of the type T72 tank, BMP1 and BMP2 armoured fighting vehicles, BMD1, BTR60BT armoured personnel carriers, anti-tank missiles, the 122-mm 2S1/2S3 self-propelled gun and other artillery pieces.

Southern Corps: surrounded southern Baghdad with about 10,000 to 15,000 troops. The divisions included Baghdad Infantry Division, Hammurabi Armoured Division and the Al Nida Armoured Division. Armour was the type T72 tank, self-propelled guns and artillery, BMP, AFV and anti-tank missiles similar to those used by the Northern Corps.

Regular Iraqi Army: surrounded the north of Baghdad and Tikrit with a strength of about 15,000 troops in each division, including Mechanised Division, Nebuchadnezzar Infantry Division, Medina Armoured Division and the Adnan. Armour included T72 tanks, self-propelled guns and artillery, BMP, AFV and anti-tank missiles of the Republican Guard Divisions.

1 Corps: surrounded Kirkuk supporting the Republican Guard with about 10,000 troops per division, including 2 Infantry Division, 8 Infantry Division, 38 Infantry Division and 5 Mechanised Division. Armour consisted of the ageing type T54 tank and the more modern but still outdated type T62 tank. The other armoured vehicles of the mechanised battalions were the same as the Republican Guard. The Iraqi forces also had the use of about 60 helicopters, which included the Russian-built Mi-25 Hind and the Western SA 316–319 Alouette III, and the SA 342 Gazelle attack helicopters.

2 Corps: surrounded the area north-east of Baghdad to the border with Iran with about 10,000 troops per division, including 15 Infantry Division, 34 Infantry Division and 3 Armoured Division. Armour, similar to 1 Corps, included type T54 and T55 battle tanks and the use of attack helicopters.

3 Corps: surrounded southern Iraq with about 10,000 troops per division, including 15 Infantry Division, 51 Mechanised Division and 6 Armoured Division. Armour, similar to the 1 and 2 Corps, included the ageing type T54, T55 and T62 battle tanks, armoured personnel carriers and the use of attack helicopters. 3 Corps defended Basrah and the Euphrates River, leading towards the Kuwaiti border.

4 Corps: surrounded north-east Baghdad supporting 3 Corps around Basrah and the Kuwaiti border with about 10,000 troops per division, including 14 Infantry Division, 18 Infantry Division and 10 Armoured Division. Armour consisted of type T54, T55 and T62 tanks, armoured personnel carriers and the use of attack helicopters.

5 Corps: surrounded Mosul and northern Iraq with about 10,000 troops per division, including 4 Infantry Division, 7 Infantry Division, 16 Infantry Division and 1 Mechanised Division. Armour included the type T54, T55 and T62 tanks, armoured personnel carriers and the use of attack helicopters.

Iraqi Popular Army: the Iraqi military had a People's or Popular Army, with a total of 19 units and an estimated 50,000–100,000 soldiers to call upon. The civilian 'part-time' army had only a few weeks' military training. Their effectiveness was not measured in military capabilities but in their skill at mixing with locals, dressed in civilian clothing, to carry out terrorist-like tactics against Iraqis opposed to Saddam and the coalition forces.

Special Republican Guard: Iraq's ground forces were only about a third of the size of what they were before the 1991 Gulf War and sanctions had destroyed their combat readiness. The

Special Republican Guard consisted of an estimated 400,000 troops and 400,000 security forces.

Republican Guard (Baghdad): estimated at 15,000 troops including 4 infantry brigades, an armoured unit and an air-defence unit. The brigade was the only military unit allowed inside Baghdad, where its members were from Saddam Hussein's al-Bu Nasir tribe (his own birth tribe). Republican Guard 1 Brigade provided security whilst 2 Brigade protected Saddam's presidential palaces and the northern province of the city. The Republican Guard of the 3 and 4 Brigades defended the southern provinces. The armoured units had two tank regiments, consisting of the Russian-built type T72 tank.

Iraq's most modern weapons were reserved for Saddam's most Elite Republican Guard divisions, with 80,000 soldiers divided into two corps. Although the commander-in-chief was Saddam himself, his youngest son, Qusay Hussein, fronted the divisions, with Ibrahim Ahmad abd al-Sattar Mohammad al-Tikriti as the general.

Unit 999: based in Salman Barracks, south-east of Baghdad. Unit 999 included 6 battalions, totalling around 1,500 to 2,000 troops, specialised in relations with neighbouring countries. 1 Battalion specialised in Iran (Persia), 2 Battalion specialised in the southern borders (Saudi Arabia), 3 Battalion specialised in Israel (Palestine), 4 Battalion specialised in Turkey, 5 Battalion specialised in mining waterways and other maritime operations (Marine). The 6 Battalion specialised in the dissident Kurds in the north and the dissident Shiite tribes in the south of Iraq.

Security Services: surrounding Baghdad, totalling 5,000 personnel, maintained and secured Saddam's control within the Iraqi armed forces. Certain personnel were also involved in watching top military officers for any signs of a *coup d'état* and for instigators of any civilian uprisings against the regime, monitoring tribal leaders and officials.

APPENDIX

Weaponry
Scud missile and launcher
Al Hussein ballistic missile
Al Samoud ballistic missile
Roland surface-to-air missile
Strela 1 surface-to-air missile
Strela 2M surface-to-air missile
Strela 3 surface-to-air missile
FAW 200 cruise missile
Anti-tank missile

Chieftain tank (taken from Kuwait in 1990)
Type T72 tank complete with 125-mm main gun, infra-red sights
    and 12.7-mm machine gun
Type T62 tank complete with 115-mm main gun and 12.7-mm
    machine gun
Type T55 tank c/w 100-mm gun
Type T54 tank c/w 100-mm gun
BMP1 AFV (tracked) c/w 73-mm cannon
BMP2 AFV (tracked) c/w 30-mm stabilised cannon
BMD1 c/w 73-mm cannon and 7.62-mm machine gun APC
BTR60BT c/w 14.5-mm machine gun and amphibious APC
BTR60BU command vehicle c/w close-line and telescopic
    antennas
BDRM1 and BDRM2 NBC protection and amphibious AFV
    c/w 14.5-mm machine gun
BDRM85 armoured 85 Spandrel missile-launch system c/w X5
    missiles
BDRM SA9 armoured SA9 missile-launch system c/w X4 missiles
BRRMU command vehicle c/w antenna pods
BDRM RH armoured NBC reconnaissance vehicle fitted with
    detectors
NSU234 armoured air-defence vehicle (tracked) c/w X4 20-mm
    canon and gun dish
2S1 armoured self-propelled gun (tracked) c/w 122-mm NBC
    munitions-capable gun
2S3 armoured self-propelled gun (tracked) c/w 155-mm NBC
    munitions-capable gun

347

Russian- and Chinese-built infantry soldier light support
weapons

Mirage F1 jet fighter
MiG-29 jet fighter
MiG-21 jet fighter
SU-25 AN-26 transport/troop-carrier aircraft
AN-12 transport/troop-carrier aircraft
MiG-25 Hind transport/troop-carrier helicopter
SA316/319 Alouette III helicopter
SA342 Gazelle attack helicopter

Zhuk patrol ship

Iraqi Chemical and Biological Agents
Known agents which had been stockpiled and even used by the
Iraqi forces against the Iranian Army and Iraqi civilians included:
anthrax, botulinum toxin, CS gas, cyclosarin, gas gangrene, ricin,
rotavirus, sarin, sulphur (mustard) gas, tabun, trichothecenes,
VX, wheat smut.

GLOSSARY

2 RTR: 2 Royal Tank Regiment
AFV: armoured fighting vehicle
A'mechs: armoured mechanics
APC: armoured personnel carrier
APU: auxiliary power unit
APWT: annual personal weapons test
AS90: artillery self-propelled 1990
ASM: adjutant sergeant major
BAOR: British Army of the Rhine
BATCO: British Army tactical communication
BATS: biological agent treatment set
bergen: a soldier's backpack
BFPO: British Forces Post Office
BG: battle group
blue on blue: friendly fire
a bluey: a letter
BMP: armoured fighting vehicle, Russian-built
BV: boiling vessel
CBA: combat body armour
CET: combat engineer tractor
CFT: combat fitness test
Cfn: craftsman
CHAVRE: Chieftain armoured vehicle Royal Engineers

chogies: nickname used for Iraqi militia
civvy: civilian
CO: commanding officer
CP: command post
Cpl: corporal
Cpt: captain
CRARRV: Challenger armoured recovery and repair vehicle
CS: close support division
CS95: combat soldier uniform 1995
CSR: chemical safety rule
cuvvies: coveralls or overalls
CV: command vehicle
CVR(T): combat vehicle reconnaissance/recovery (tracked)
CVT: combat vehicle (tracked)
dishdash: full-length garment worn by men in Iraq
DKP: fuller's earth
doss bag: sleeping bag
DPM: disruptive pattern markings
DSG: division support group
DU: depleted uranium
D&V: diarrhoea and vomiting
ECP: equipment collection point
EFI: Expeditionary Forces Institute
EPVs: enhanced protection vehicles
FAA: forward assembly area
Fedayeen: Saddam's militia
FOP: forward operations post
FPIC: field press information centre
Gas! Gas! Gas!: verbal NBC alarm
GDs: general duties
gimpie: *see* GPMG
GOSP: gas oil separation plant
GPMG: general purpose machine gun, also known as a gimpie
GPS: global positioning system
GS: general support
HE: high explosives
IA: immediate action
IPE: individual personal equipment

GLOSSARY

ISO: International Organisation for Standardisation
K *or* klick: kilometre
LAD: light aid detachment
lance jack: lance corporal
LAW: light anti-tank weapon
L/Cpl: lance corporal
LI: light infantry
LSW: light support weapon
MBT: main battle tank
MoD 90: Ministry of Defence 1990s (identification card)
mogies: media operations group
MRE: meal ready-to-eat
MSR: main supply route
NAAFI: Navy Army Air Force Institute
NAPS: nerve agent pre-treatment system
NBC: nuclear, biological, chemical
noddy suit: NBC suit
NVGs: night-vision goggles
OC: officer commanding
O'group: order grouping
OP: observation post
PSAO: permanent staff army officer
PT: physical training
PTI: physical training instructor
QMS: quartermaster sergeant
RA: Royal Artillery
RAAF: Royal Australian Air Force
rat pack: ration pack
RE: Royal Engineers
recce: reconnaissance
recy mech: recovery mechanic
REME: Royal Electrical & Mechanical Engineers
RHA: Royal Horse Artillery
RLC: Royal Logistic Corps
RM: Royal Marines
RMP: Royal Military Police
RPG: rocket-propelled grenade
RRF: Royal Regiment of Fusiliers

RSM: regimental sergeant major
RTA: road traffic accident
RTMC: Reserves Training and Mobilisation Centre
SA80: small arms of the '80s
SAM: surface-to-air missile
SDG: Scots Dragoon Guards
Sgt: sergeant
SNCO: senior non-commissioned officer
snowdrop: RAF police
split-arse: female
SSgt: staff sergeant
stag: guard duty
STAB: sad Territorial Army bastard
SUSAT: sight unit small-arms Trilux
USMC: United States Marine Corps
VCP: vehicle checkpoint
VM: vehicle mechanic
WO1/2: warrant officer (1st and 2nd class)
zulu: Greenwich Mean Time